IMAGES
of America

MORAVIANS *in* NORTH CAROLINA

ON THE COVER: Dr. Henry Theodore Bahnson (standing right) grew *Victoria amazonica* water lilies in his pond, which was located behind his home on Church Street in Salem. The giant lily pads gave pleasure to everyone who saw or sat on them. Sylvester E. Hough captured this image c. 1890. (Collection of Old Salem Museums & Gardens.)

IMAGES
of America

MORAVIANS *in* NORTH CAROLINA

Jennifer Bean Bower
Old Salem Museums & Gardens

ARCADIA
PUBLISHING

ISBN 978-0-7385-4329-1

Published by Arcadia Publishing
Charleston, South Carolina

Printed in the United States of America

Library of Congress Catalog Card Number: 2006926980

For all general information contact Arcadia Publishing at:
Telephone 843-853-2070
Fax 843-853-0044
E-mail sales@arcadiapublishing.com
For customer service and orders:
Toll-Free 1-888-313-2665

Visit us on the Internet at www.arcadiapublishing.com

This book is dedicated to those who have and continue to preserve their family photographs for future generations and historians.

Contents

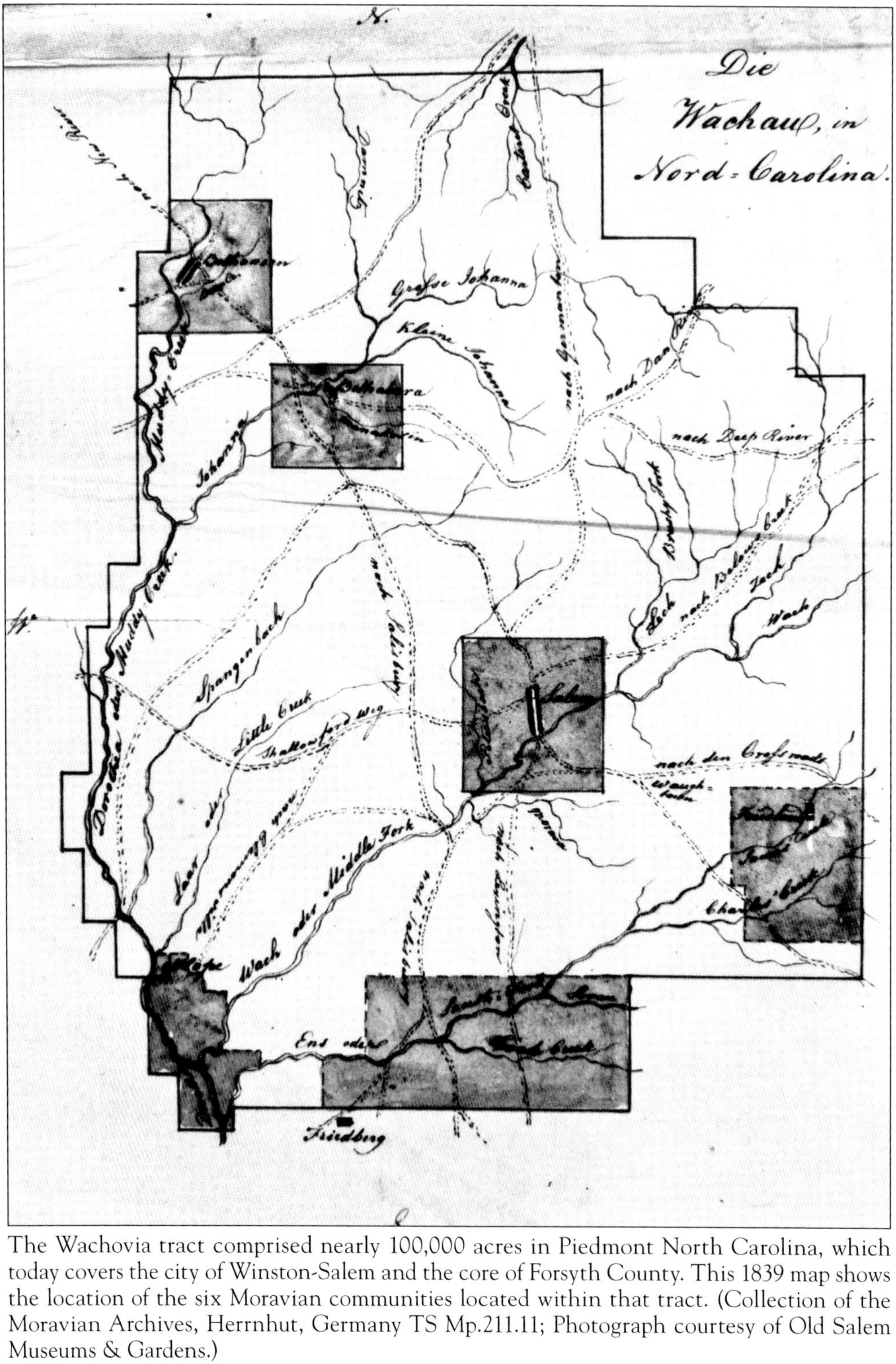

The Wachovia tract comprised nearly 100,000 acres in Piedmont North Carolina, which today covers the city of Winston-Salem and the core of Forsyth County. This 1839 map shows the location of the six Moravian communities located within that tract. (Collection of the Moravian Archives, Herrnhut, Germany TS Mp.211.11; Photograph courtesy of Old Salem Museums & Gardens.)

PREFACE

There are over 4,000 historical photographs within the combined collections of Old Salem Museums & Gardens and the Wachovia Historical Society. All of these historical images have been rephotographed and placed on file in the Old Salem Research Center. The research center also contains photographic copies of images from private collections and various institutions. Photographs within the collection, and those held on file, range from early daguerreotypes to 20th-century prints and negatives. The majority of photographs relate specifically to Salem, Winston, and the surrounding area; however, the images are quite diverse and contain a variety of subject matter. It is from this variety that many of the images were drawn for this publication. This book is not intended to be a history of the Moravians in North Carolina but rather an outlet by which these photographs can be enjoyed by a broad audience. Although the museum strives to document each image accurately, there may be an instance in which a person is listed as "unidentified" or a name is spelled incorrectly. Old Salem is delighted to share these photographs and hopes that by doing so more information will be gleaned on each one of these remarkable images. We hope you will enjoy the photographs that have been selected for this publication and welcome your comments and corrections. Please address any correspondence relating to these photographs or photographers to:

Jennifer Bean Bower, Manager of Photographic Resources
Old Salem Museums & Gardens
P.O. Box 10310
Winston-Salem, NC 27108-0310
(336) 721-7373—phone
(336) 721-7367—fax
jbean@oldsalem.org

ACKNOWLEDGMENTS

This publication was possible because of the many families who preserved and donated their photograph collections to Old Salem Museums & Gardens, the Wachovia Historical Society, and the Moravian Archives in Winston-Salem. I am deeply thankful for their sense of history and their efforts to preserve local heritage. I am also indebted to the families who allowed Old Salem to make copies of their original photographs for research purposes.

Special thanks must be given to Bradford L. Rauschenberg, senior fellow emeritus at Old Salem, who, nearly 12 years ago, gave me the task of researching the photographs and categorizing them for our files. It was through his guidance and support that I entered into an exciting and fulfilling career working with these amazing images. Thank you, Brad. I am forever grateful.

Many of my colleagues at Old Salem provided invaluable assistance in preparing this book: Wes Stewart, Old Salem's photographer extraordinaire, who printed each of the photographs illustrated in this book; Paula Locklair, who initiated this publication and whose guidance and support have been very much appreciated; John Caramia, who gave approval to the project; John Larson, David Bergstone, Paula Locklair, and Johanna Brown, for being such insightful caption readers; Gary Albert, for his ever-needed assistance in proofreading and editing; Mo and Martha Hartley, for their quick answers to my many questions; Erica Douglas, for her assistance in copying and scanning images; and Abigail Linville, for patiently listening to my ideas and issues concerning this publication. Thank you for your support.

Thank you to the staff of the Moravian Archives in Winston-Salem, who are always willing to assist with my research. Thanks especially to Richard Starbuck, who spent time assisting me with the "At Worship" chapter, and to Nicole Blum, who has always assisted with my memoir needs. Thank you both so much.

Thank you also to Maggie Bullwinkel, acquisitions editor at Arcadia Publishing, whose help and assistance with this project was greatly needed and much appreciated.

And finally, to my husband, Larry, and to my mother and father, thank you for believing in everything I do.

INTRODUCTION

The Moravians who settled in North Carolina traced their faith to the Bohemian priest John Hus, who was burned at the stake in 1415 for challenging the authorities and principles of the Catholic Church. Hus's followers formed the Unitas Fratrum, or Unity of the Brethren, which spread throughout Bohemia, Moravia (hence the term "Moravians"), and Poland. Because of religious persecution, the Unitas Fratrum went into hiding but eventually found refuge on the estate of a Saxon nobleman, Count Nicolas Ludwig von Zinzendorf, during the 18th century. It was on his estate that their religion was renewed and the Moravian community of Herrnhut was created. Not long after establishing themselves in this new community, the Unity, or Moravians, began sending colonists to America and other locations throughout the world.

The Moravians' first American Colonial settlement was in Georgia; however, it was soon abandoned. The settlers then moved to Pennsylvania, where they established Bethlehem as their central town. There they quickly earned a reputation for being peaceful and industrious colonists. Because of this reputation, John Carteret, the Earl of Granville, a proprietor of the Royal Province of Carolina, offered to sell the Moravians close to 100,000 acres of land in North Carolina. This tract of land, what now makes up the core of Forsyth County, was named Wachau and later latinized to Wachovia. In 1753, the first group of Moravians, 15 unmarried men, traveled from Pennsylvania to North Carolina. Upon arriving in their newly purchased land, the Moravians celebrated their arrival with a lovefeast and named their new settlement Bethabara. Unfortunately the growth and expansion of Moravian settlements in North Carolina was disrupted by the French and Indian War, which occurred from 1754 to 1760. During this time, a palisade was built around the community of Bethabara and houses were constructed nearby to shelter the influx of refugees seeking safety.

Bethabara operated under an *Oeconomie* system, a communal system of common housekeeping and labor. In 1759, Moravians who wanted to have their own homes and land founded a second community within the Wachovia tract, Bethania, which was located three miles northwest of Bethabara and operated as an independent community that included non-Moravians. In 1760, Bethania was organized as a congregation of the Moravian church.

In 1764, Frederic Wilhelm Marshall, who had been appointed chief officer for material affairs in Wachovia, arrived at Bethabara and announced that the planning of the new town of Salem would finally begin. In 1765, a site located at the center of the Wachovia tract was selected for the Moravians' central town, and in 1766, the first tree was felled for its construction. In November 1771, the Salem congregation was organized, and by April 1772, the general layout of Salem was completed. Salem functioned as a congregation town, which meant that the church was central to all of the activities within the community. The church owned the land but leased lots to individuals for homes and businesses. The congregation itself owned several of the major businesses. As intended, Salem quickly grew and became the center of trade in Piedmont North Carolina.

Salem, however, was not the last Moravian settlement founded within the Wachovia tract. Three more communities would be founded after the settlement at Salem along the southern border of the Wachovia tract. These agricultural communities were: Friedberg, organized in 1773; Friedland, in 1780; and Hope, in 1780. In all of these communities, the Moravians used every aspect of their lives to serve God. They practiced, just as Moravians still do today, a religion that is based on peace and devotion to the common good.

One

Moravian Communities

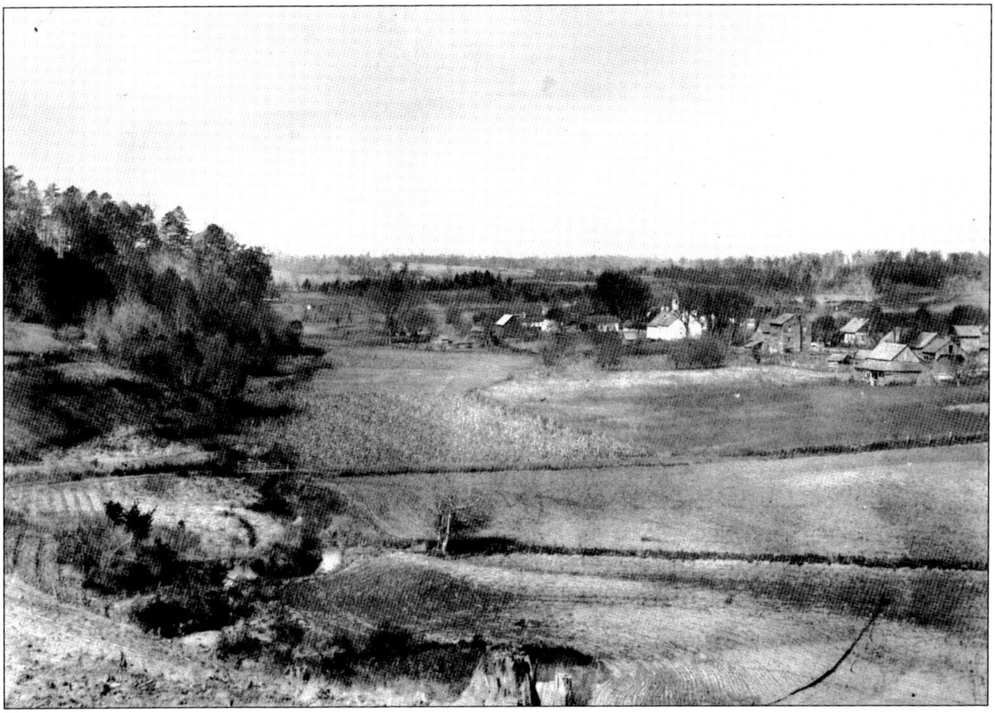

In 1753, fifteen unmarried Moravian men traveled from Pennsylvania to North Carolina to establish a settlement in the newly purchased Wachovia tract. Upon their arrival, they found an abandoned cabin, celebrated their safe arrival, and named their new town Bethabara, meaning "house of passage." This photograph shows the town of Bethabara, 1890–1900. (Collection of Old Salem Museums and Gardens.)

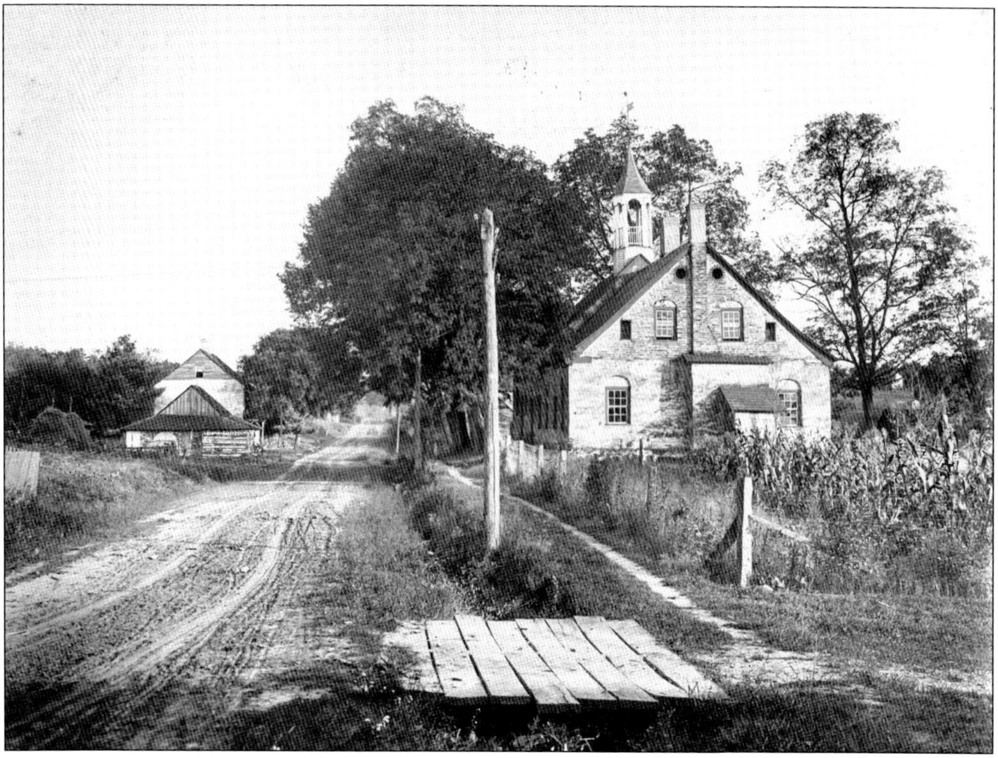

The 1788 Gemein Haus, or congregational meetinghouse, seen right in this *c.* 1900 photograph, was the center of activity in the town of Bethabara. Within its walls was the *Saal* or place of worship, a school, and the living quarters for the minister and his family. (Collection of the Moravian Archives, Winston-Salem, North Carolina; Photograph courtesy of Old Salem Museums & Gardens.)

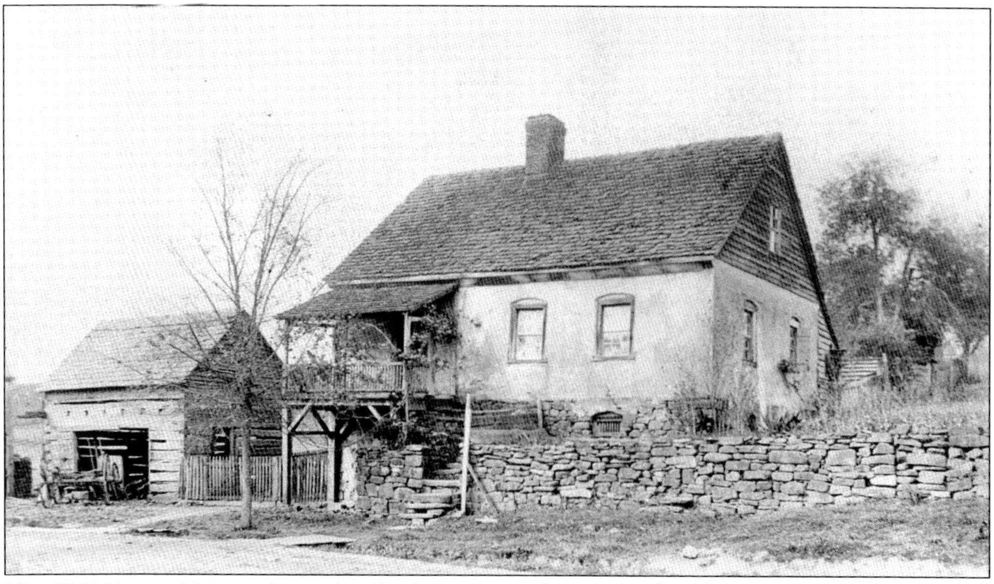

The 1803 Brewers' House, located in Bethabara, was documented in this *c.* 1890 photograph. The building still stands but with some alterations. (Collection of Old Salem Museums & Gardens.)

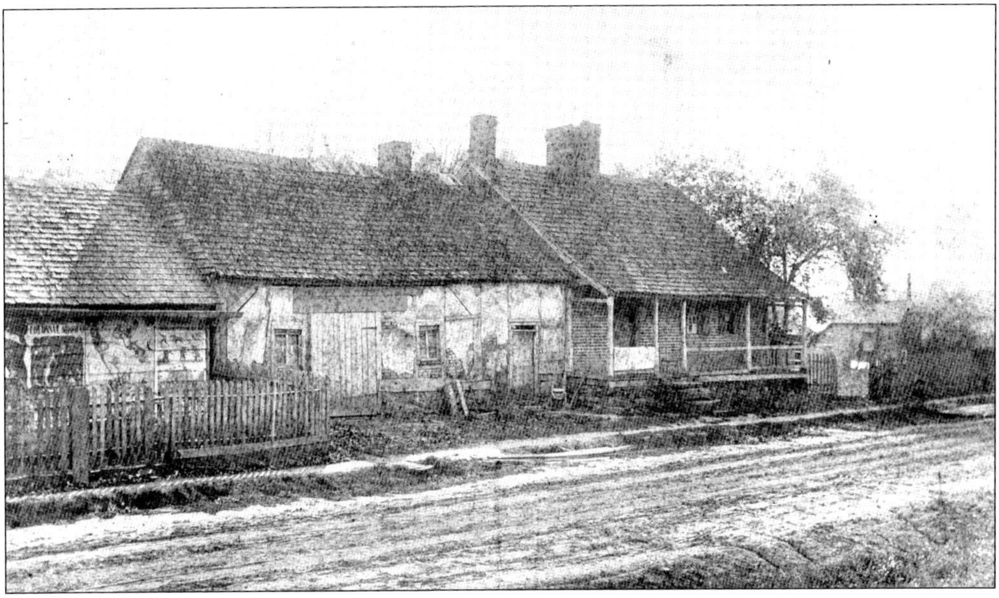

The Gottlieb Krause–John Butner Pottery, located in Bethabara, was photographed *c.* 1890. The brick house, constructed in 1782, still stands, but the half-timbered wing is now gone. (Collection of Old Salem Museums & Gardens.)

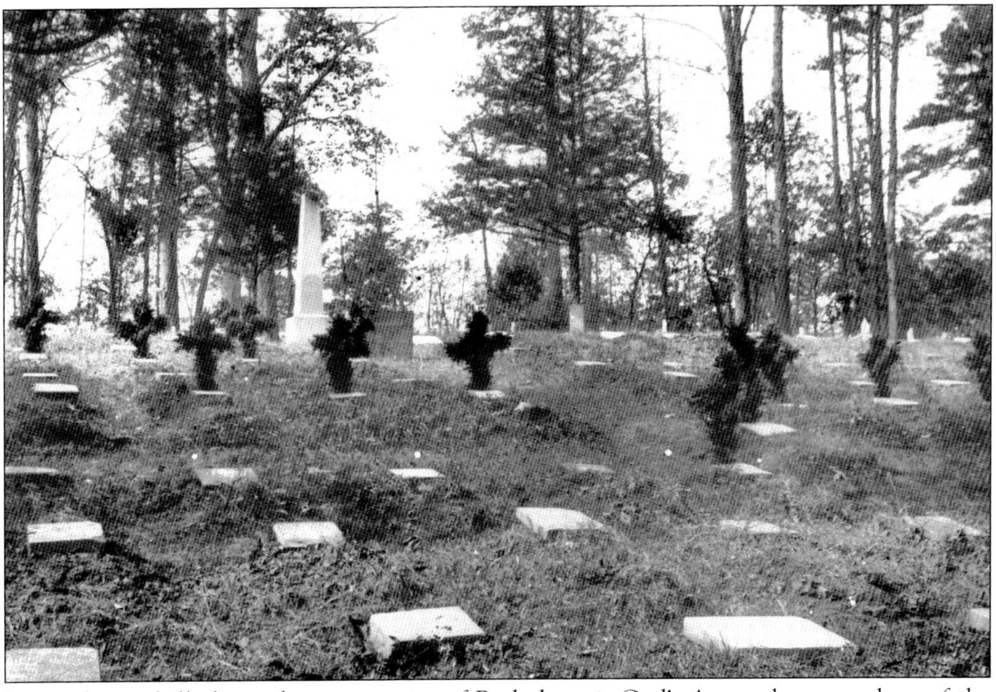

Located on a hill above the community of Bethabara is God's Acre, where members of the Bethabara Moravian Church bury their dead. The simple flat headstones illustrate the Moravian belief that all people are equal in death. The large monument, seen center left in this *c.* 1900 photograph, is a memorial to Moravian missionaries. The crosses decorating the graves appear to have been made from evergreens. (Collection of the Wachovia Historical Society; Photograph courtesy of Old Salem Museums & Gardens.)

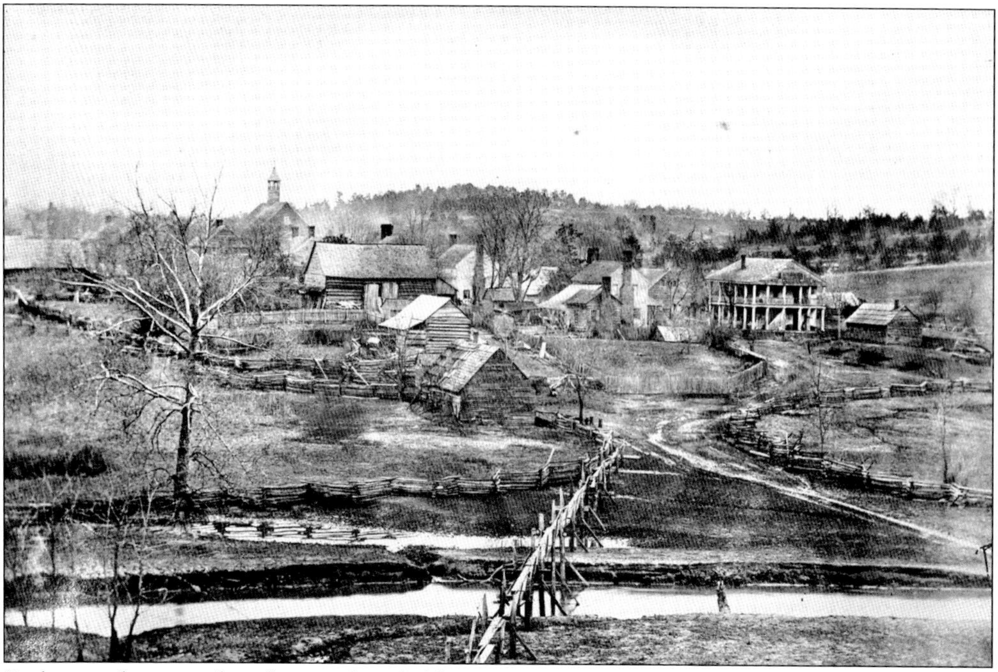

Bethania, the second settlement founded by Moravians in the Wachovia tract, was established in 1759 as a farming and craft community. Located three miles northwest of Bethabara, the town was named after Bethany, a village not far from Jerusalem, which was a place of special significance for Jesus Christ. This photograph shows the town of Bethania c. 1890. (Private collection; Photograph courtesy of Old Salem Museums & Gardens.)

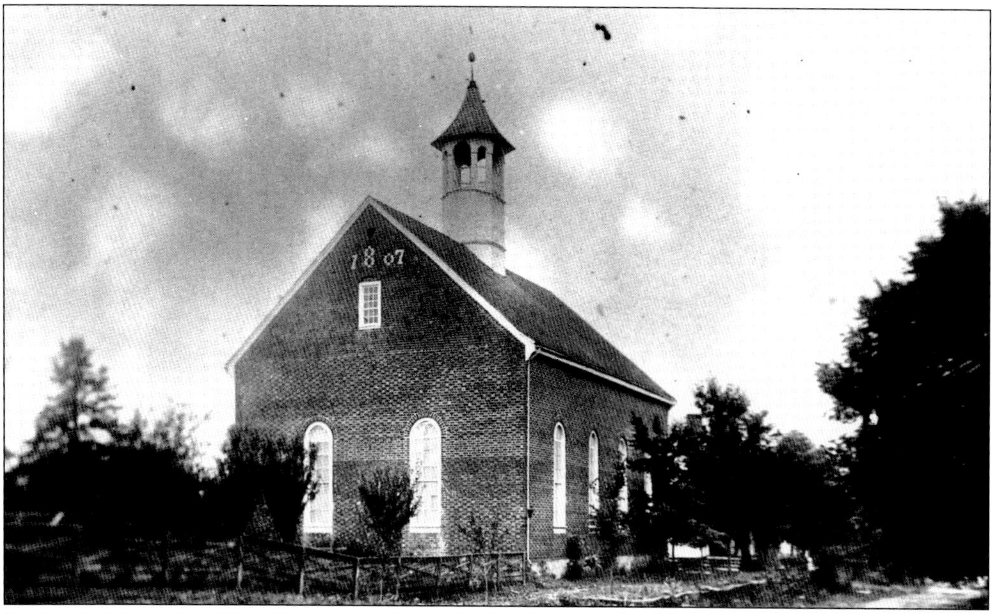

Bethania Moravian Church, seen in this c. 1900 photograph, was erected in 1807. The church interior and roof burned in 1942, but repairs were made, and the church still stands today. (Collection of the Wachovia Historical Society; Photograph courtesy of Old Salem Museums & Gardens.)

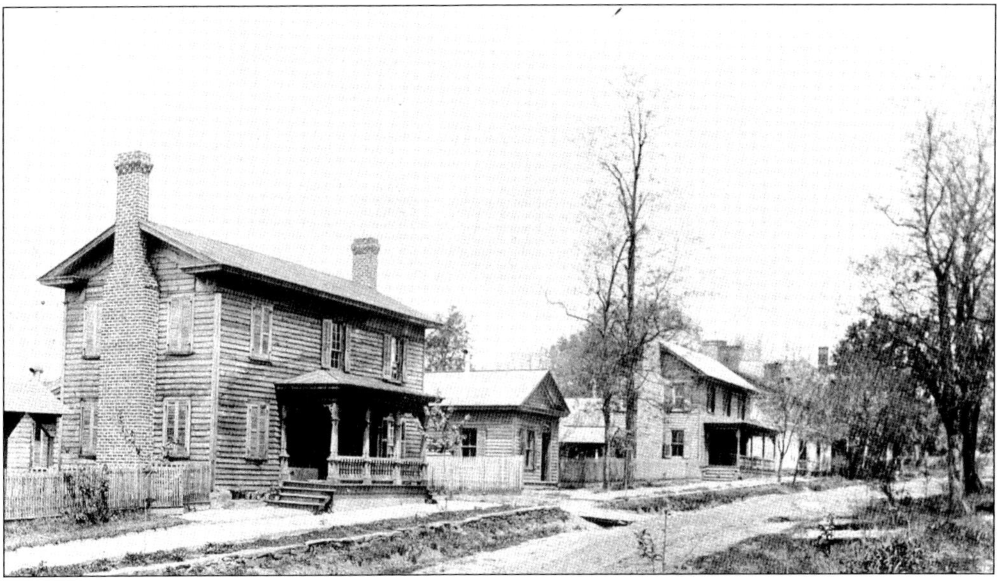

The upper west side of Main Street in Bethania was documented in this *c.* 1900 photograph. Buildings are, from left to right, the Transou house, Dr. Edward F. Strickland's office, the Hauser-Strupe house, and the John Christian Loesch house and store. (Collection of Old Salem Museums & Gardens.)

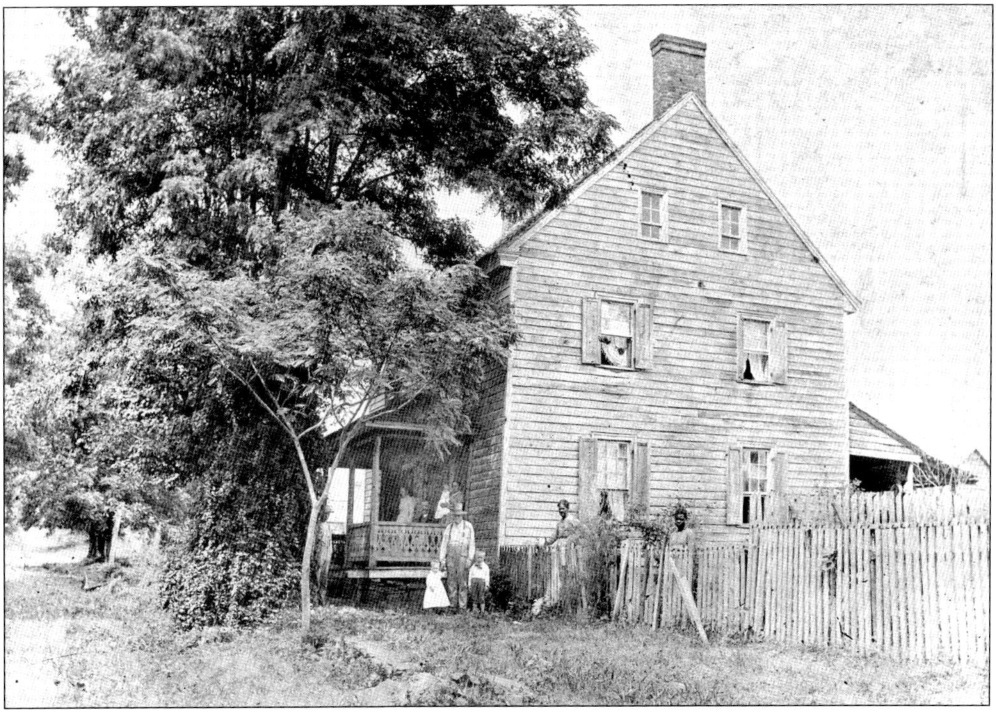

The Reich-Strupe-Butner house was built in Bethania *c.* 1775 and became known as the Cornwallis house after February 9, 1781, when Lt. Gen. Charles Cornwallis spent the night there. The house and its unidentified occupants were captured in this *c.* 1890 photograph. (Private collection; Photograph courtesy of Old Salem Museums & Gardens.)

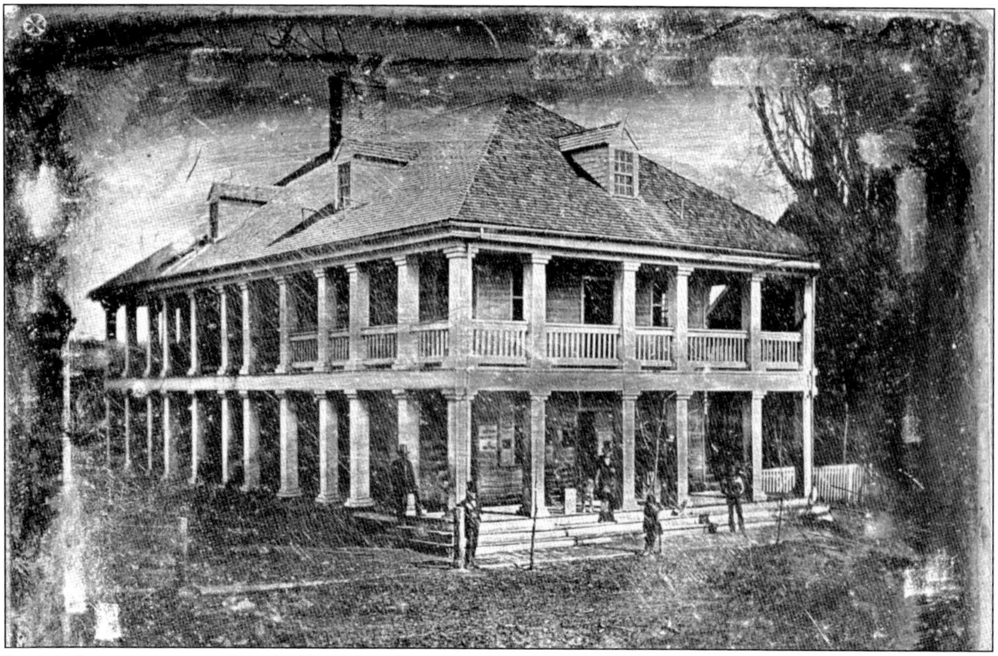

Lash's Store, seen in this 1855–1860 photograph, was an impressive structure that stood on the corner of Main Street and Loesch Lane in Bethania. At the beginning of the Civil War, in April 1861, speakers came to Lash's Store, where they encouraged men to volunteer for the Confederacy. The store was demolished *c.* 1930. (Collection of the Moravian Archives, Winston-Salem, North Carolina; Photograph courtesy of Old Salem Museums & Gardens.)

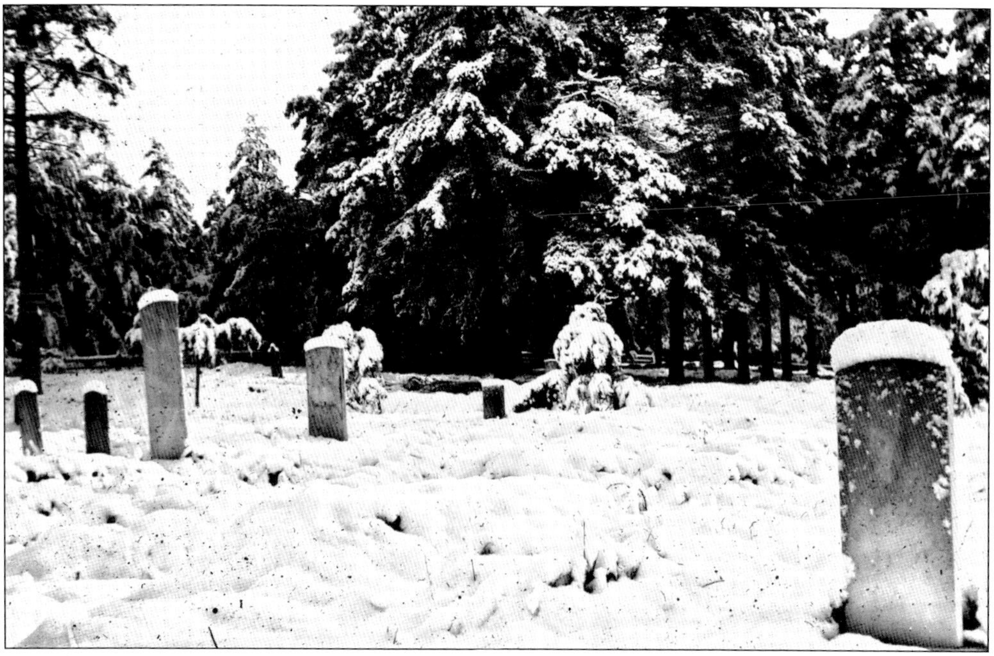

This photograph, taken *c.* 1900, shows a snow-covered God's Acre in Bethania. The standing grave markers, erected during the late 19th century, are not typical of Moravian graveyards. (Collection of the Wachovia Historical Society; Photograph courtesy of Old Salem Museums & Gardens.)

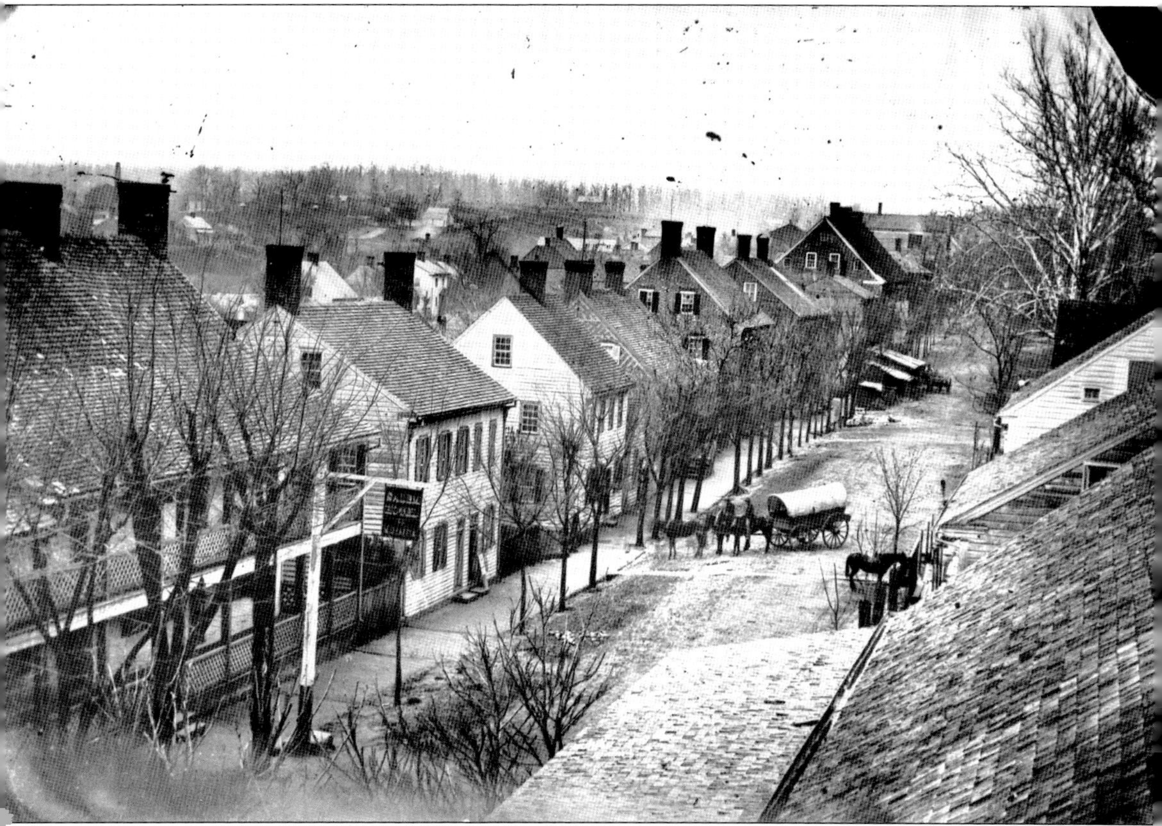

The Moravian settlement of Salem, meaning "peace," was founded in 1766, at the center of the Wachovia tract. The town quickly grew and became the center of trade in Piedmont North Carolina. Henry A. Lineback photographed this partial view of Salem's Main Street 100 years later. (Collection of Old Salem Museums & Gardens.)

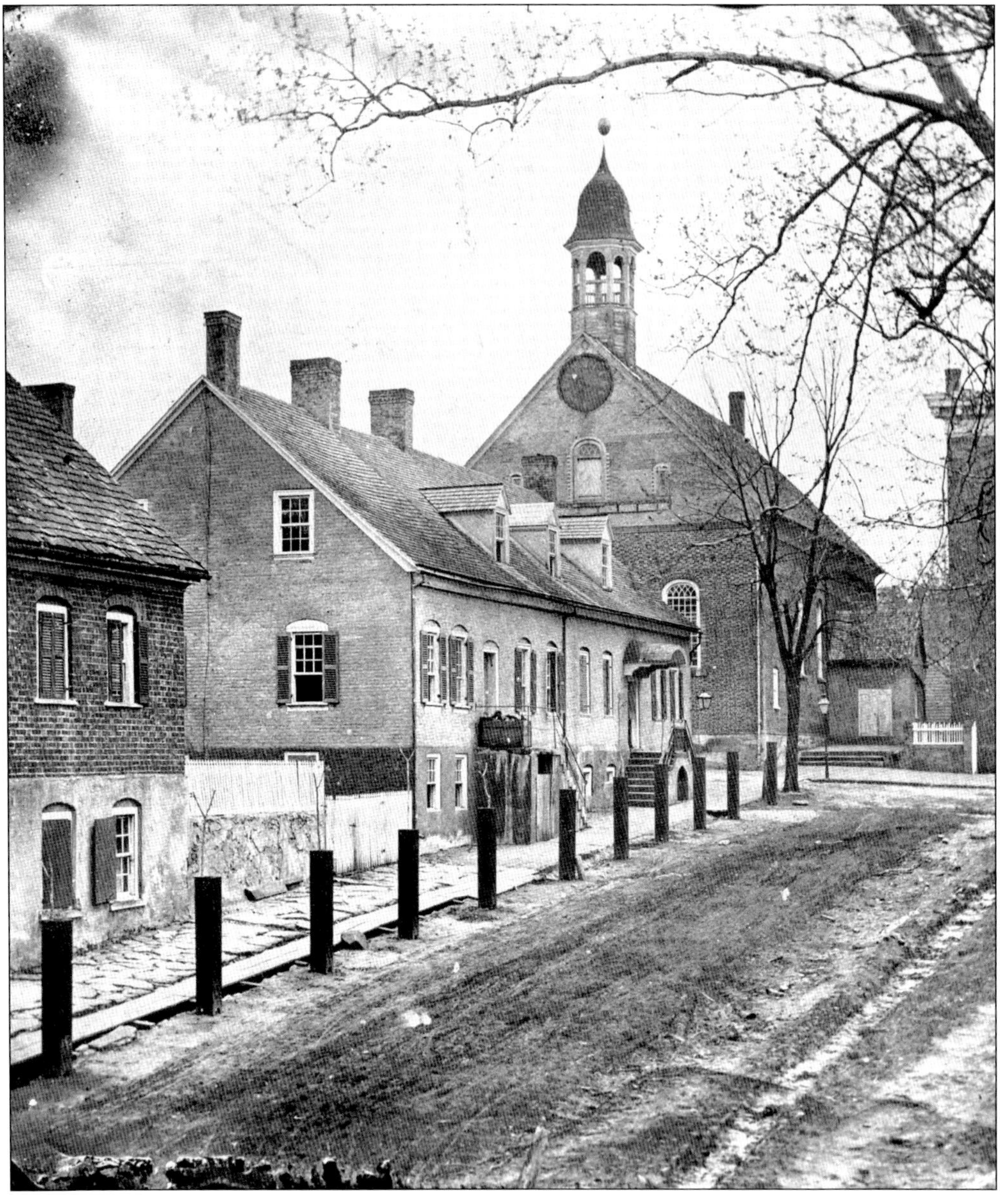

Salem Moravian Church was erected in 1800. It was first called Home Church in 1878, but it took almost 10 years before the name was commonly used. The church and the 1811 Inspectors' House (center left), which was home to the headmaster of the Salem Girls' Boarding School, are seen in this 1870–1875 photograph. (Collection of Old Salem Museums & Gardens.)

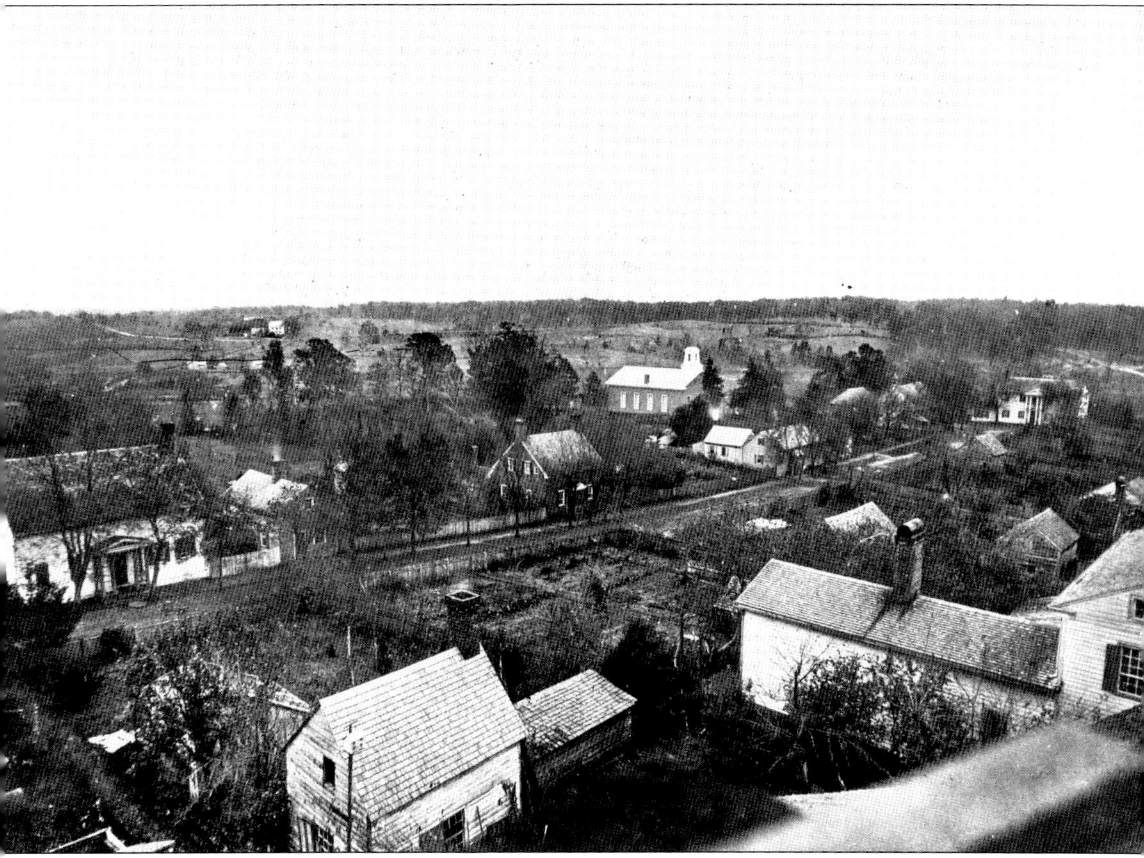

This photograph, taken by Henry A. Lineback *c.* 1866, shows the south end of Church Street in Salem and includes rare images of the African American log church, built in 1823 (seen left of the two-story house with colonnade porches), and the brick church, St. Philip's (center), which replaced the log church in 1861. In these two churches, both Moravian and non-Moravian African Americans worshipped together under the direction of white pastors. (Collection of the Wachovia Historical Society; Photograph courtesy of Old Salem Museums & Gardens.)

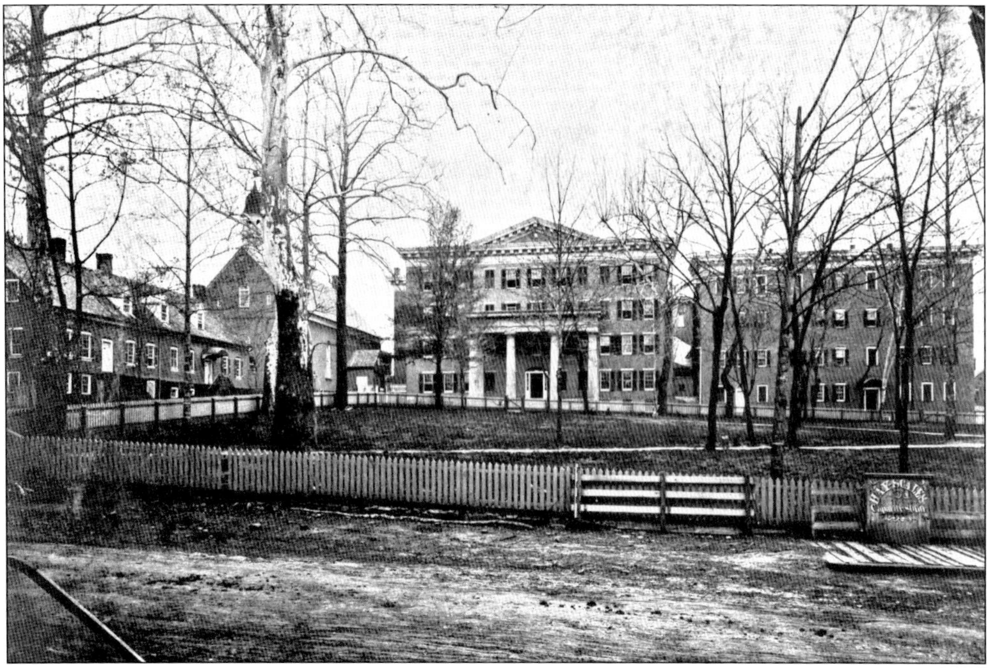

Salem Square, located in the center of Salem, was the location for many community functions. The hay scales (bottom right) were often a center of activity as men waited with wagons to weigh their loads. Henry A. Lineback photographed this view c. 1870. (Collection of Old Salem Museums & Gardens.)

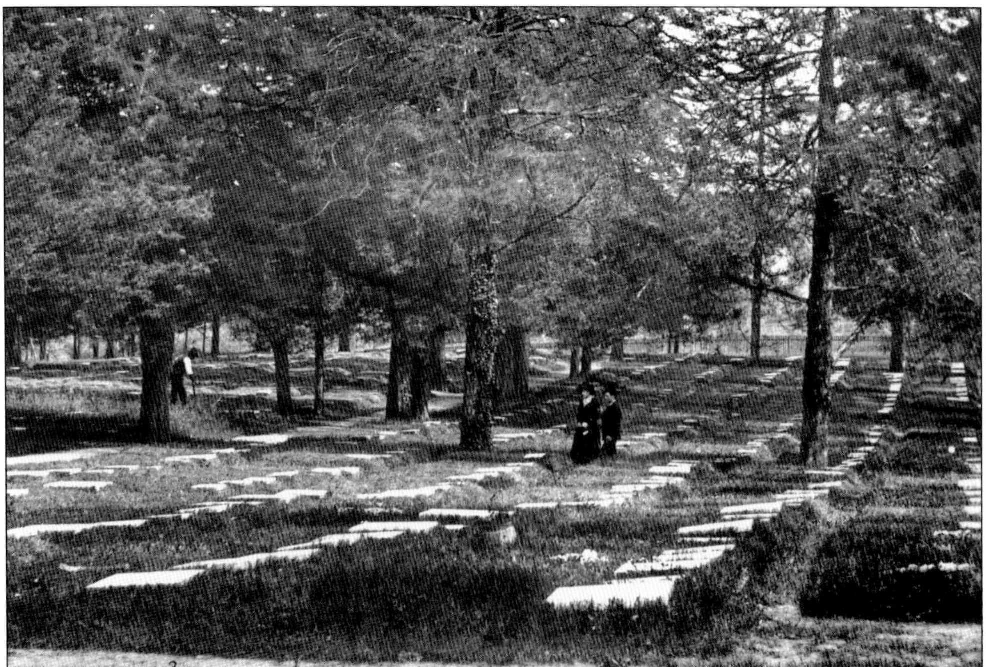

Edward F. Small photographed this view of God's Acre at Salem in 1882. (Collection of Old Salem Museums & Gardens.)

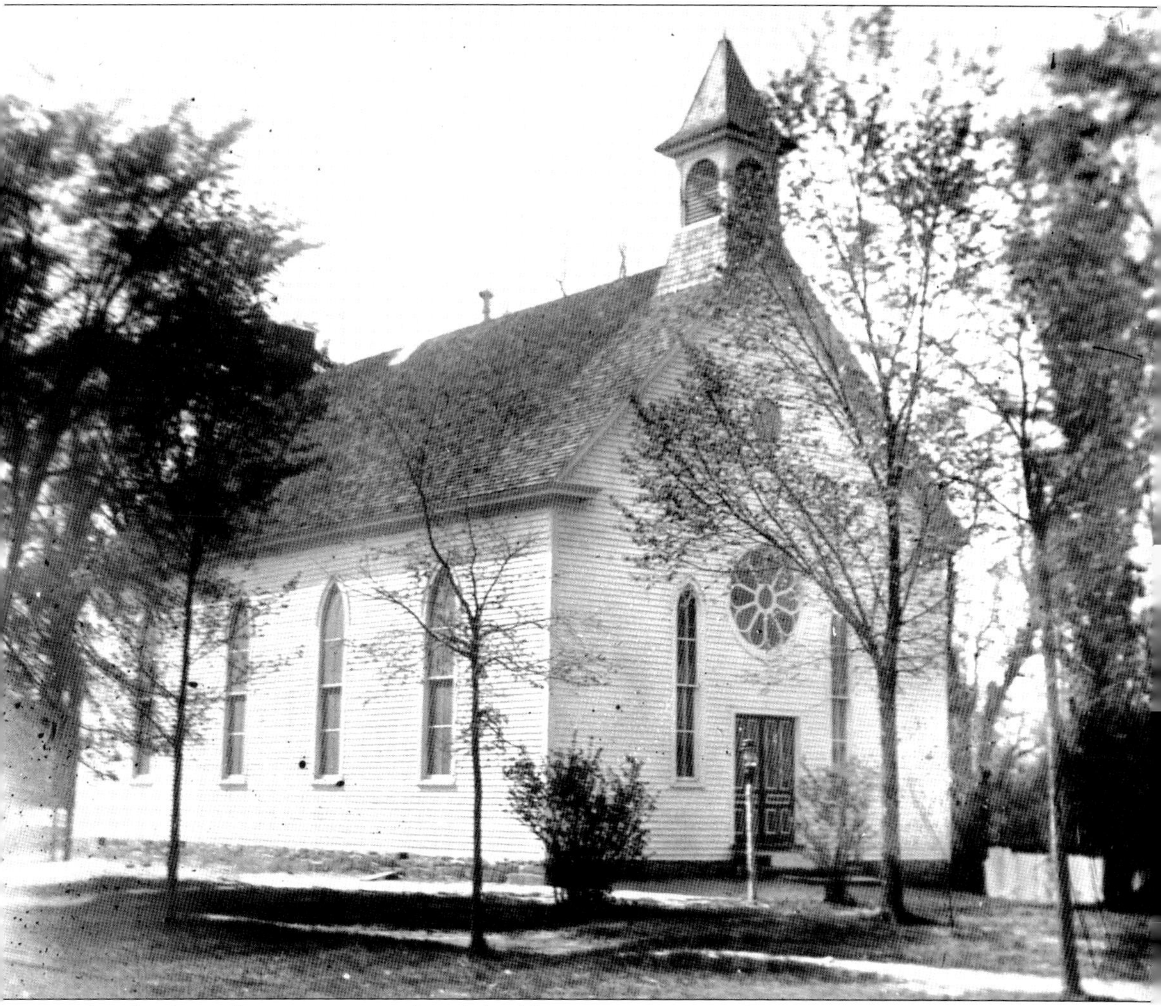

The third Friedberg Moravian church building was consecrated on July 28, 1827, and is seen in this *c.* 1900 photograph. This church served the congregation until 1976, when the current sanctuary was built. (Collection of the Wachovia Historical Society; Photograph courtesy of Old Salem Museums & Gardens.)

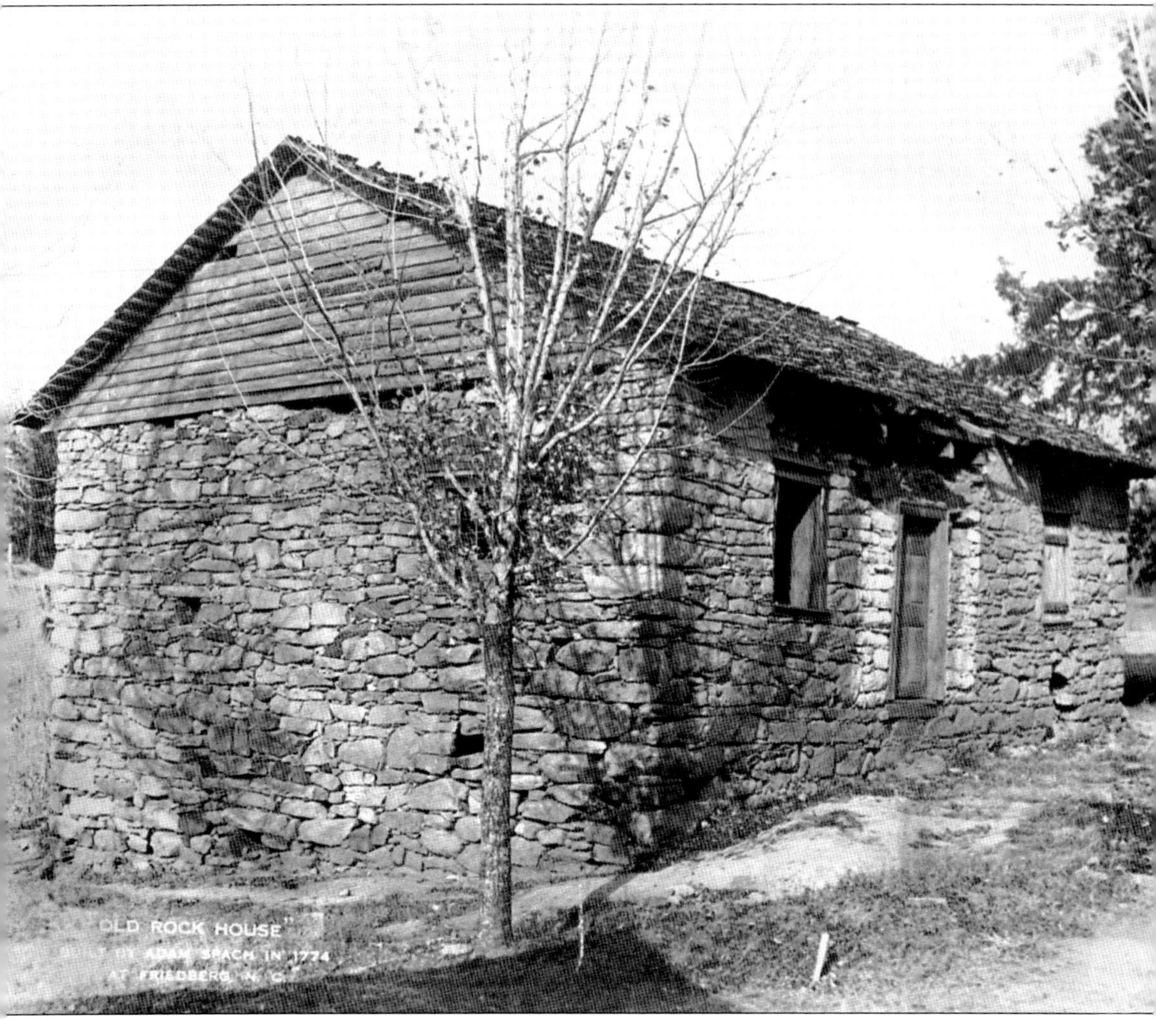

During the 1750s, Adam and Maria Spach traveled 14 miles from their home in the South Fork settlement, near the present-day Davidson/Forsyth County line, to attend worship services at Bethabara. Later, in 1769, a meetinghouse was completed in their community, and in 1773, the congregation was formally organized as Friedberg, meaning "hill of peace." Adam Spach's Rock House, which he built in 1774, is seen in this 1918–1920 photograph taken by Walker Stroud. (Collection of the Wachovia Historical Society; Photograph courtesy of Old Salem Museums & Gardens.)

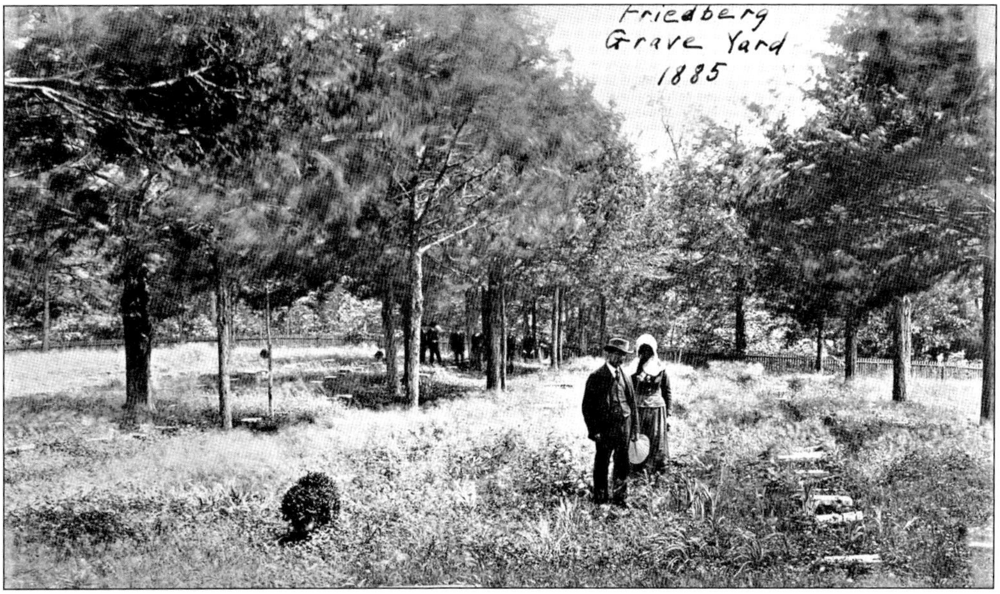

This photograph, showing God's Acre at Friedberg, was taken in 1885. (Collection of the Moravian Archives, Winston-Salem, North Carolina; Photograph courtesy of Old Salem Museums & Gardens.)

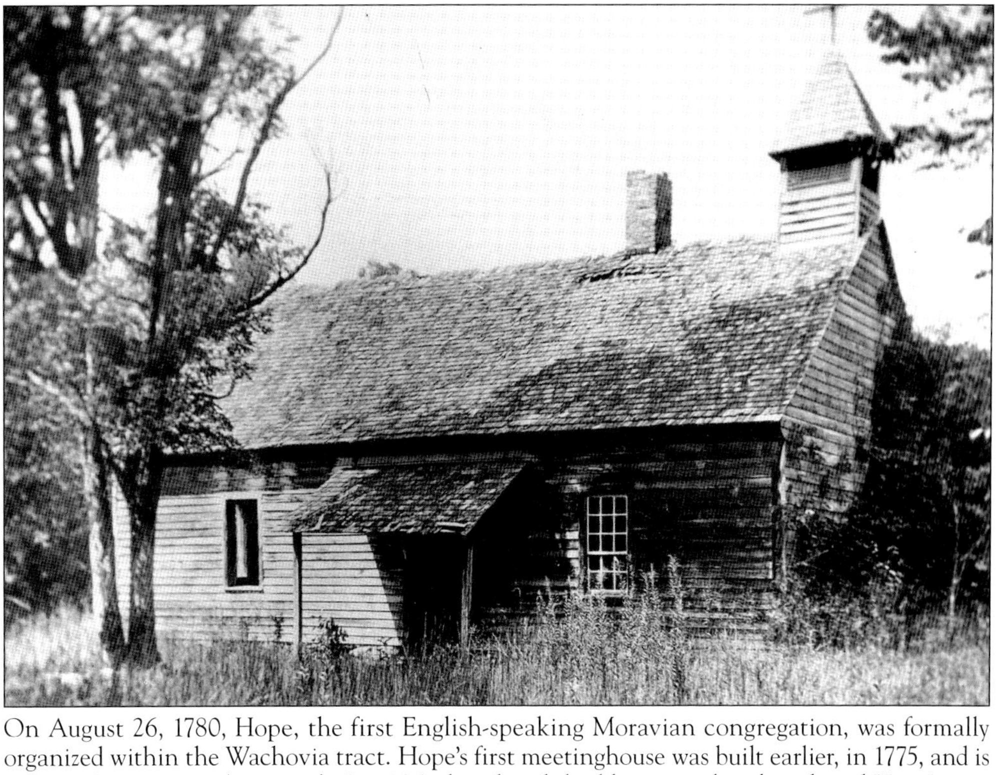

On August 26, 1780, Hope, the first English-speaking Moravian congregation, was formally organized within the Wachovia tract. Hope's first meetinghouse was built earlier, in 1775, and is seen in this *c.* 1900 photograph. In 1896, this church building was abandoned, and Hope's new church was consecrated. (Collection of the Wachovia Historical Society; Photograph courtesy of Old Salem Museums & Gardens.)

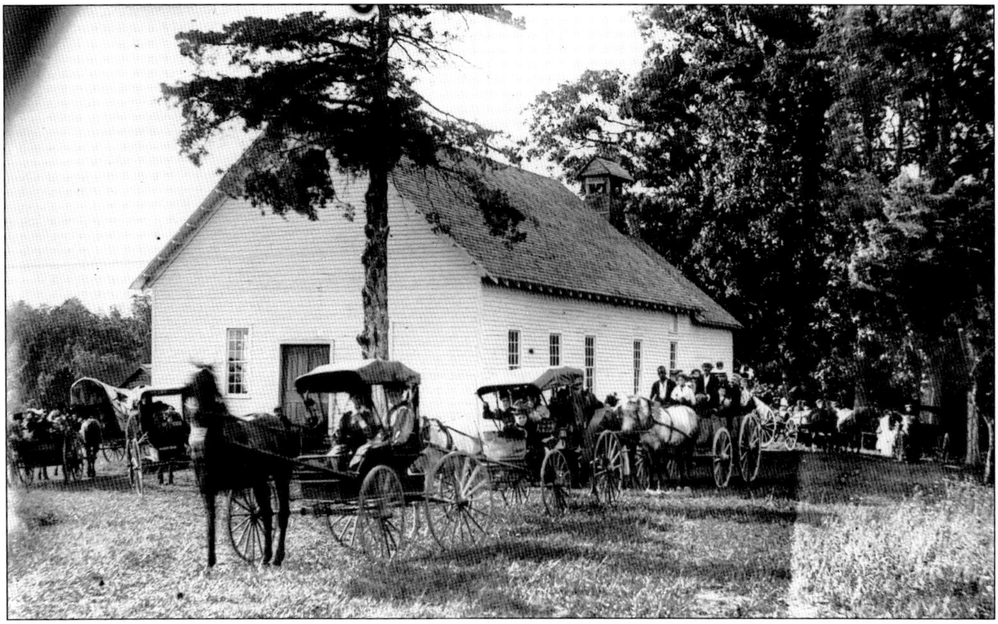

Settlers from Broadbay, Maine, led by their Moravian pastor, George Soelle, arrived in Wachovia in 1769 and 1770. In 1771, the community they established was given the name Friedland, meaning "land of peace," and, on September 3, 1780, was formally organized as a congregation of the Moravian Church. This photograph shows Friedland Moravian Church, c. 1895. (Collection of the Wachovia Historical Society; Photograph courtesy of Old Salem Museums & Gardens.)

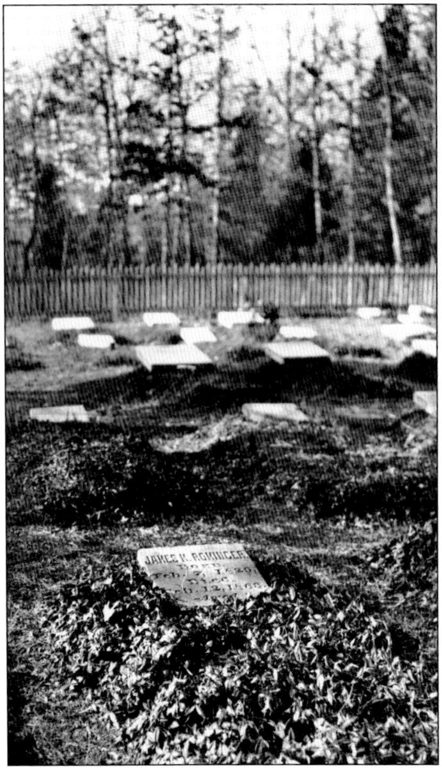

God's Acre at Friedland was photographed c. 1925. (Collection of Old Salem Museum & Gardens.)

Two

AT SCHOOL

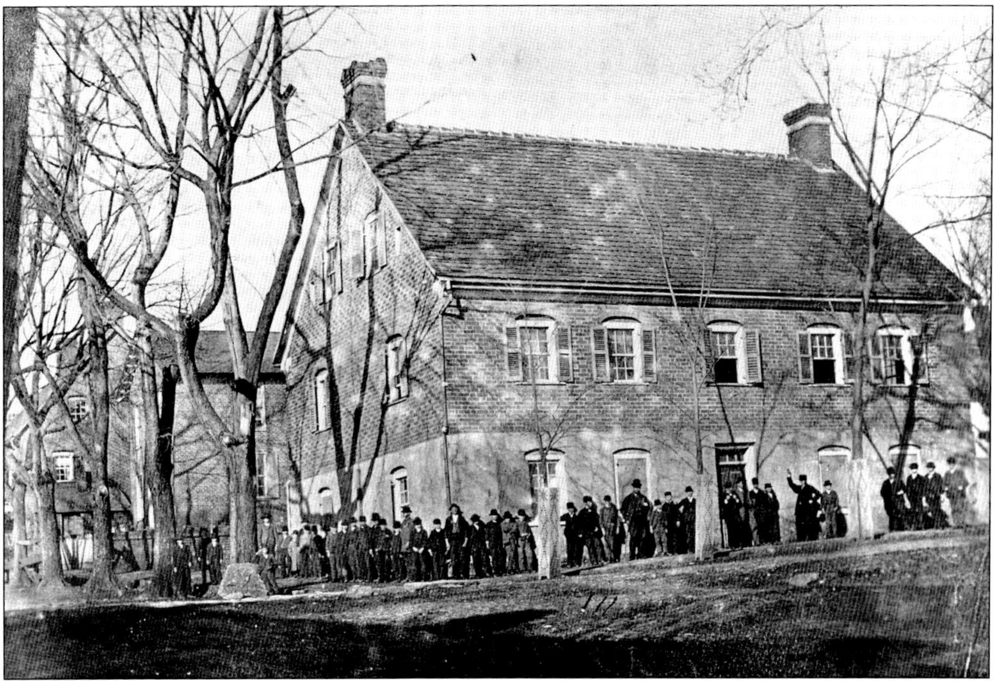

Salem boys between the ages of 6 and 14 were educated at the Salem Boys' School, where they were taught in the Germanic tradition of academic work and discipline. Built in 1794, this building functioned as the school until 1896, when the new Salem Boys' School was opened. In 1897, the Wachovia Historical Society began operating the old Boys' School building as a museum. The 1794 school building was captured by Edward F. Small in 1882. (Collection of Old Salem Museums & Gardens.)

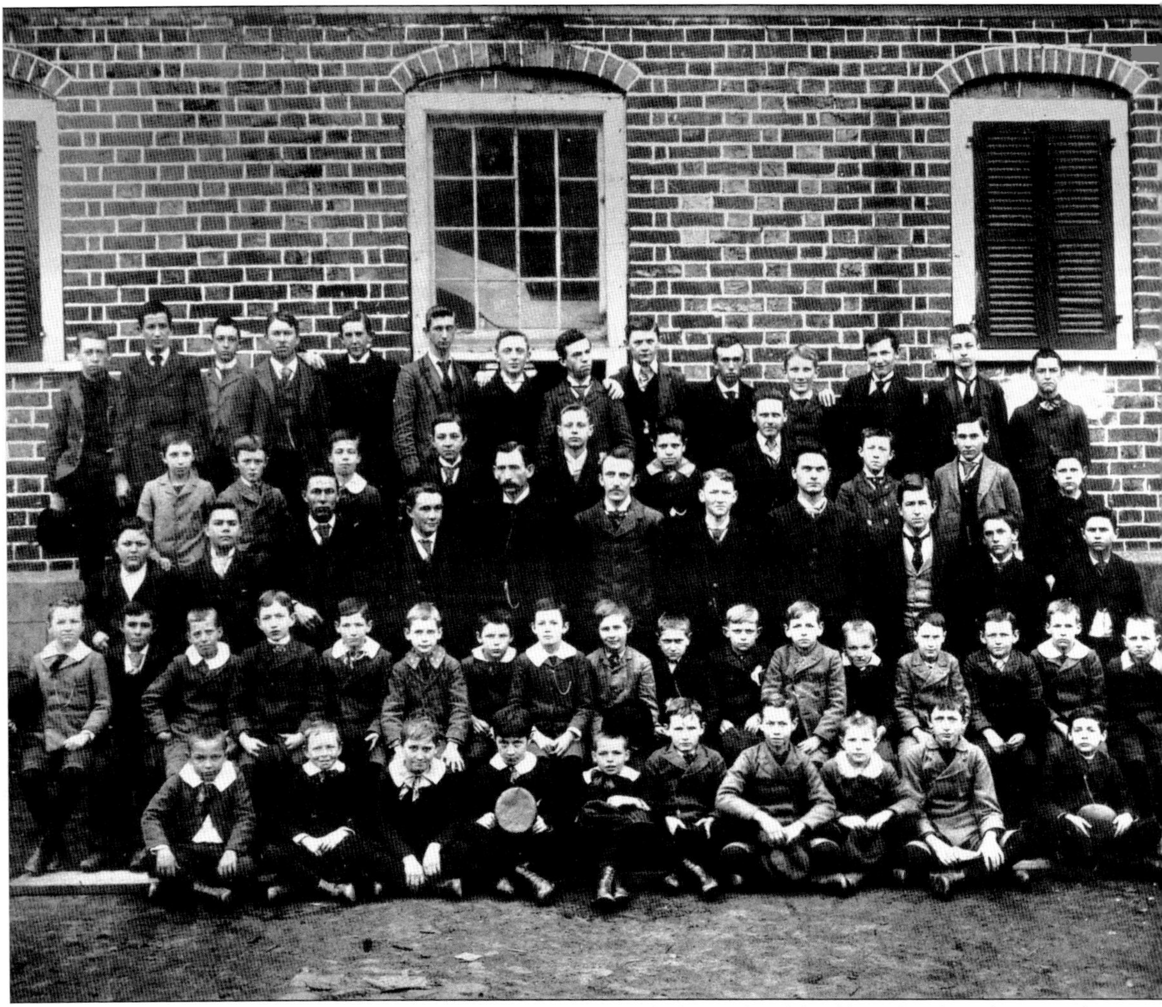

Students from the Salem Boys' School posed behind their school building for this photograph taken *c.* 1890. Pictured from left to right are (first row) Fred Lassiter, Robah Gray, Will Fetter, Percival Hall, Wilson Gray, Ralph Siewers, Robert Mickey, Sam Welfare, John Gibbons, and Robert Lichtenthaeler; (second row) Bill Whitaker, Lorenzo Frazier, Harvey Ebert, Fred Nissen, unidentified, Fred Brower, Bernie Tesh, Clarence Clewell, Robert Grunert, Paul Fogle, Fred Sheets, Fred Fogle, Harry Taylor, Orestes Keehln, Carl Harris, Francis Rogers, and unidentified; (third row) Zach Barton, Judson Vipperman, Virgil Robinson, John Frazier, Prof. James F. Brower, Howard Rondthaler, Lee Lamb, unidentified, Tom Tise, Will Watkins, and unidentified; (fourth row) Charlie Johnson, Fred Lemly, Robert Frederick Lineback, Ernest Pfohl, Will Goslen, Howard Shore, Henry Masten, Harry Reid, Hugh Brown, and Henry Meinung; (fifth row) Fred Tise, Will O'Brien, Will Reich, unidentified, Henry Shelton, unidentified, George Stockton, Frank Reid, two unidentified, Cam Buxton, Charles Siewers, Harry Hough, and unidentified. (Collection of Old Salem Museums & Gardens.)

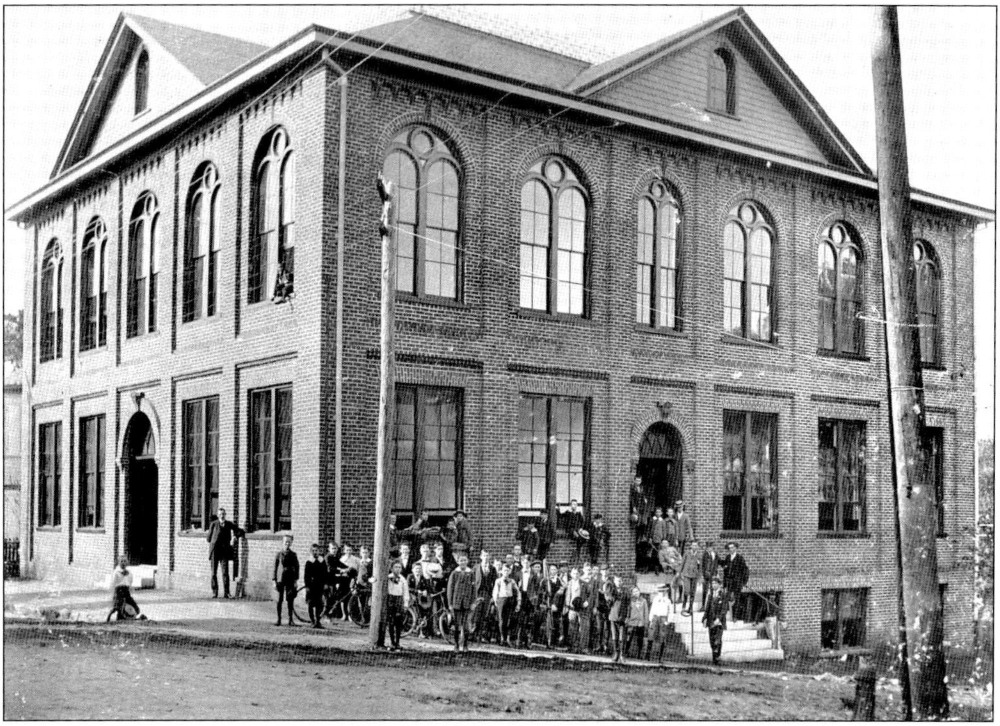

The second Salem Boys' School was built in 1896 and opened for students in August that same year. This photograph shows the students and Prof. James F. Brower (leaning against the building at left), 1897–1900. (Collection of the Moravian Archives, Winston-Salem, North Carolina; Photograph courtesy of Old Salem Museums & Gardens.)

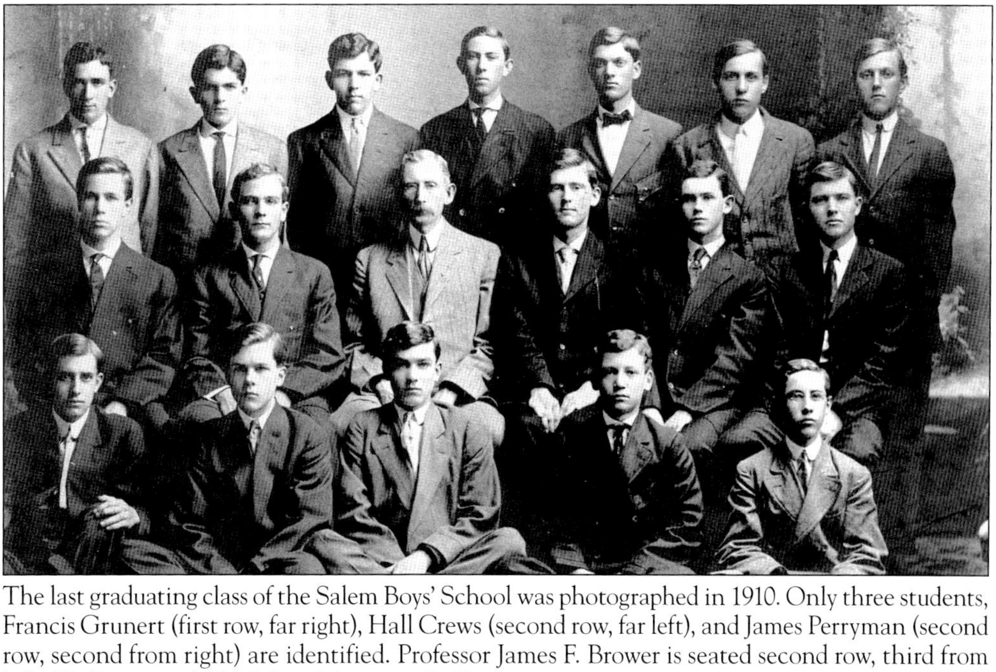

The last graduating class of the Salem Boys' School was photographed in 1910. Only three students, Francis Grunert (first row, far right), Hall Crews (second row, far left), and James Perryman (second row, second from right) are identified. Professor James F. Brower is seated second row, third from left. (Collection of Old Salem Museums & Gardens.

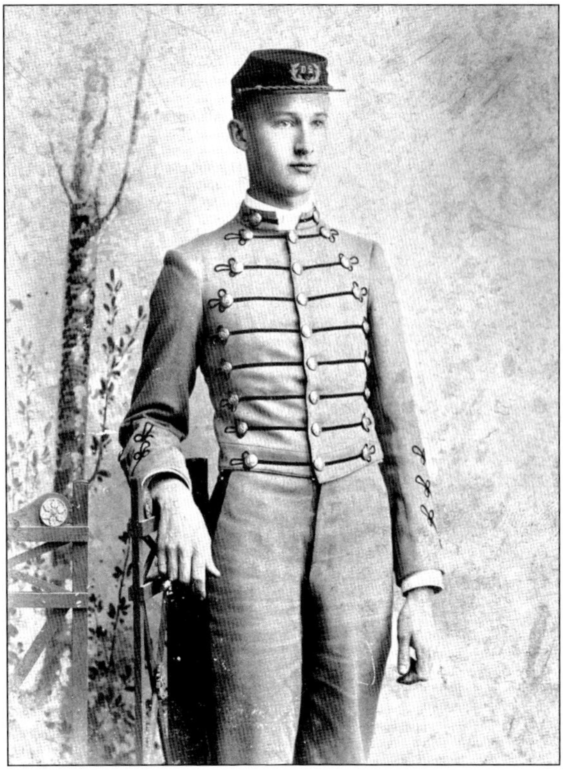

Many Moravian men attended the Davis Military School in Winston, including James E. Peterson, who was photographed in his Davis school uniform at the studio of Sylvester E. Hough, 1890–1892. Davis Military School moved to Winston from Lenoir, North Carolina, in 1890 and remained until 1909, when the property became the Methodist Children's Home. (Collection of the Wachovia Historical Society; Photograph courtesy of Old Salem Museums & Gardens.)

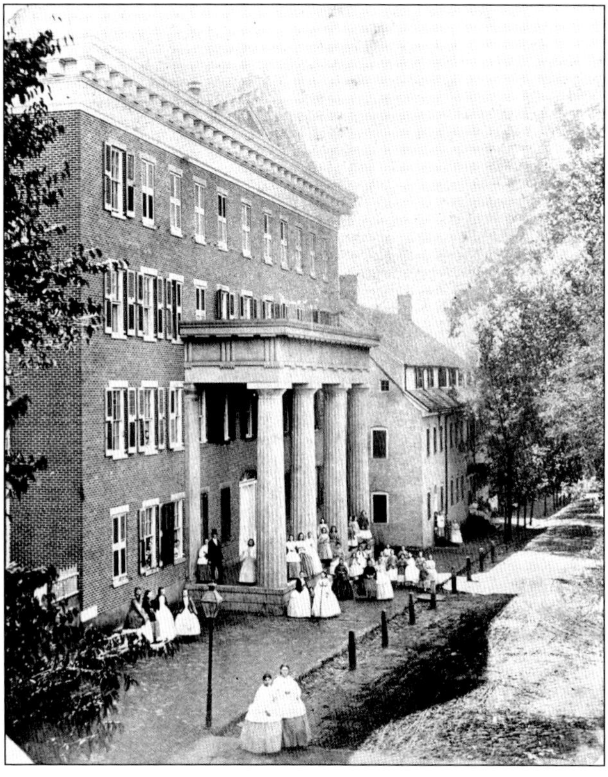

Salem Academy and College students gather around Main Hall, and peer from its windows, in this c. 1858 photograph captured by the photographers Hough and Welfare. (Collection of Old Salem Museums & Gardens.)

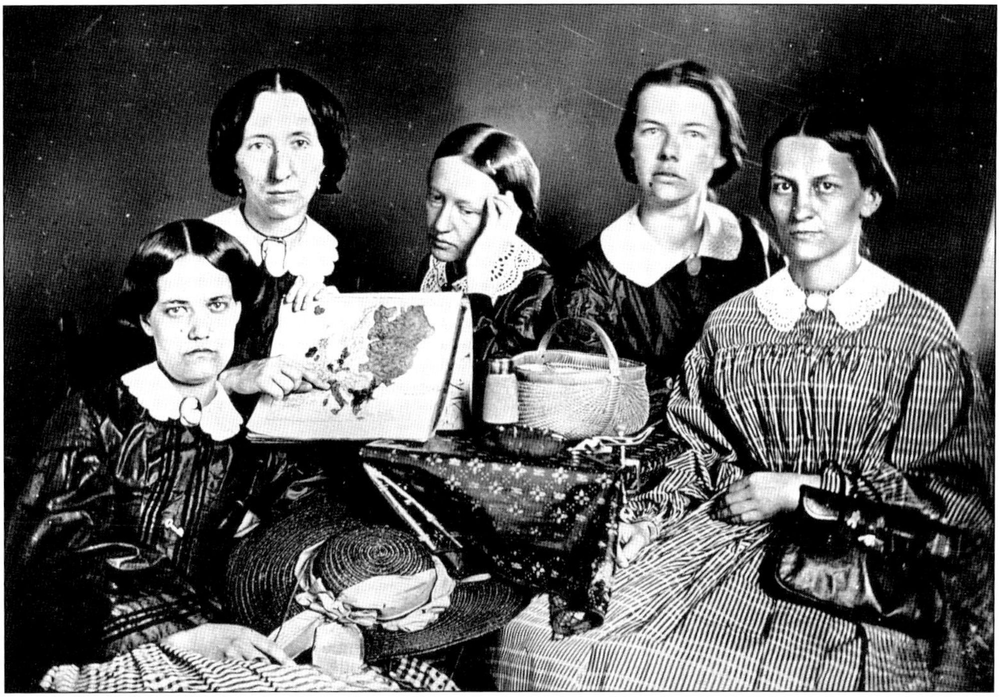

Numerous Moravian women taught at Salem Academy and College, and for many, their careers at the institution lasted more than 10 years. Five of those teachers, and the dates they taught at the school, are, from left to right, Elizabeth Chitty (1856–1878), Louisa Herman (1849–1860), Olivia Warner (1844–1856), Theophilia Welfare (1852–1863), and Maria Vogler (1853–1882). These teachers sat for their portrait *c.* 1856. (Collection of the Wachovia Historical Society; Photograph courtesy of Old Salem Museums & Gardens.)

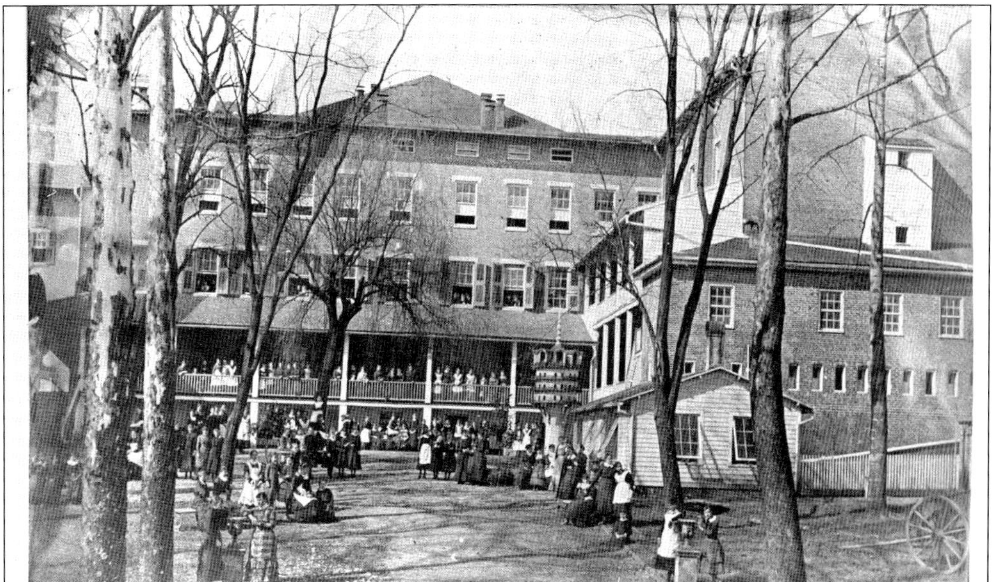

Edward F. Small captured the courtyard behind Salem Academy and College's Main Hall building in 1882. (Collection of Old Salem Museums & Gardens.)

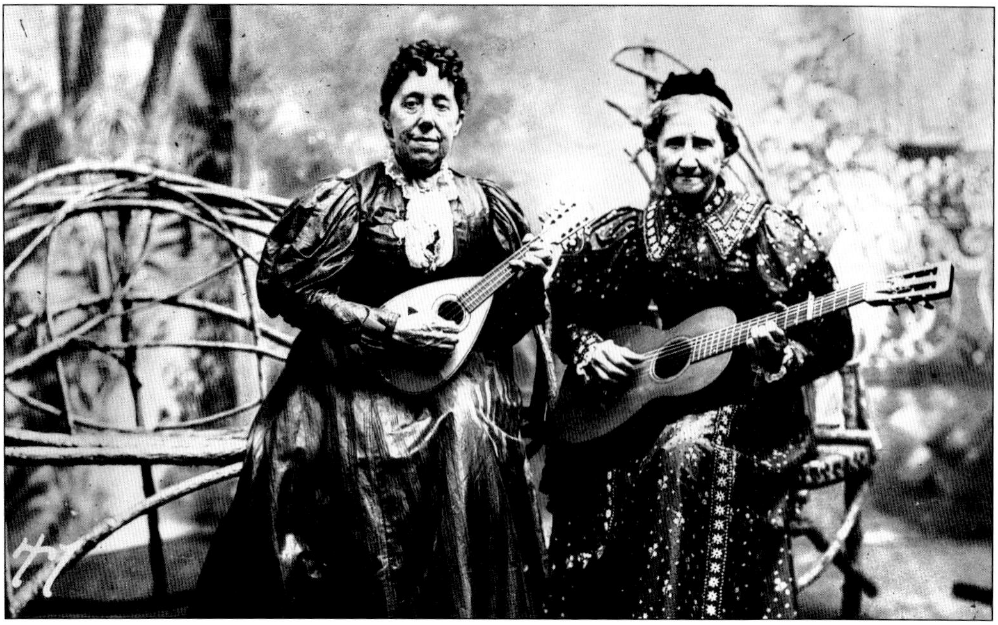

Sisters Amelia "Amy" (left) and Louisa "Lou" Van Vleck were music teachers at Salem Academy and College. Amy taught for 50 years (1859–1909), and Lou taught for 51 years (1851–1902). The sisters played duets on both the piano and guitar, sang, composed music, and were in constant demand to entertain the residents of Salem. Amy and Lou are seen in the studio of Thomas C. Hege, who captured their portrait *c.* 1895. (Collection of Old Salem Museums & Gardens.)

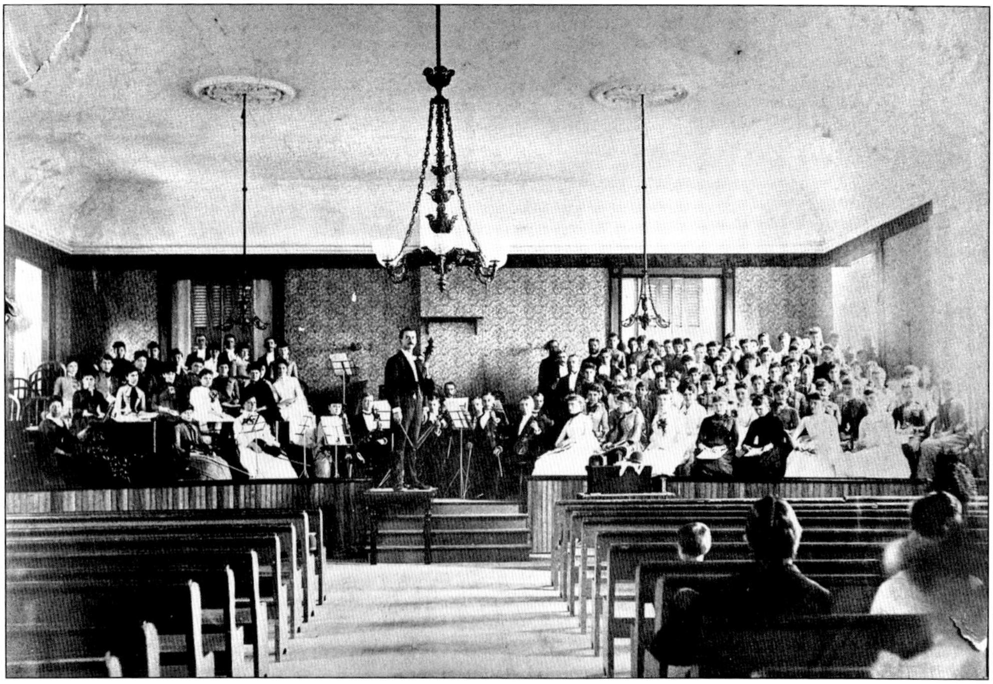

A photograph of Salem Academy and College's music hall was taken *c.* 1890. Amelia "Amy" Van Vleck can be seen seated at the piano (bottom left). (Collection of the Moravian Archives, Winston-Salem, North Carolina; Photograph courtesy of Old Salem Museums & Gardens.)

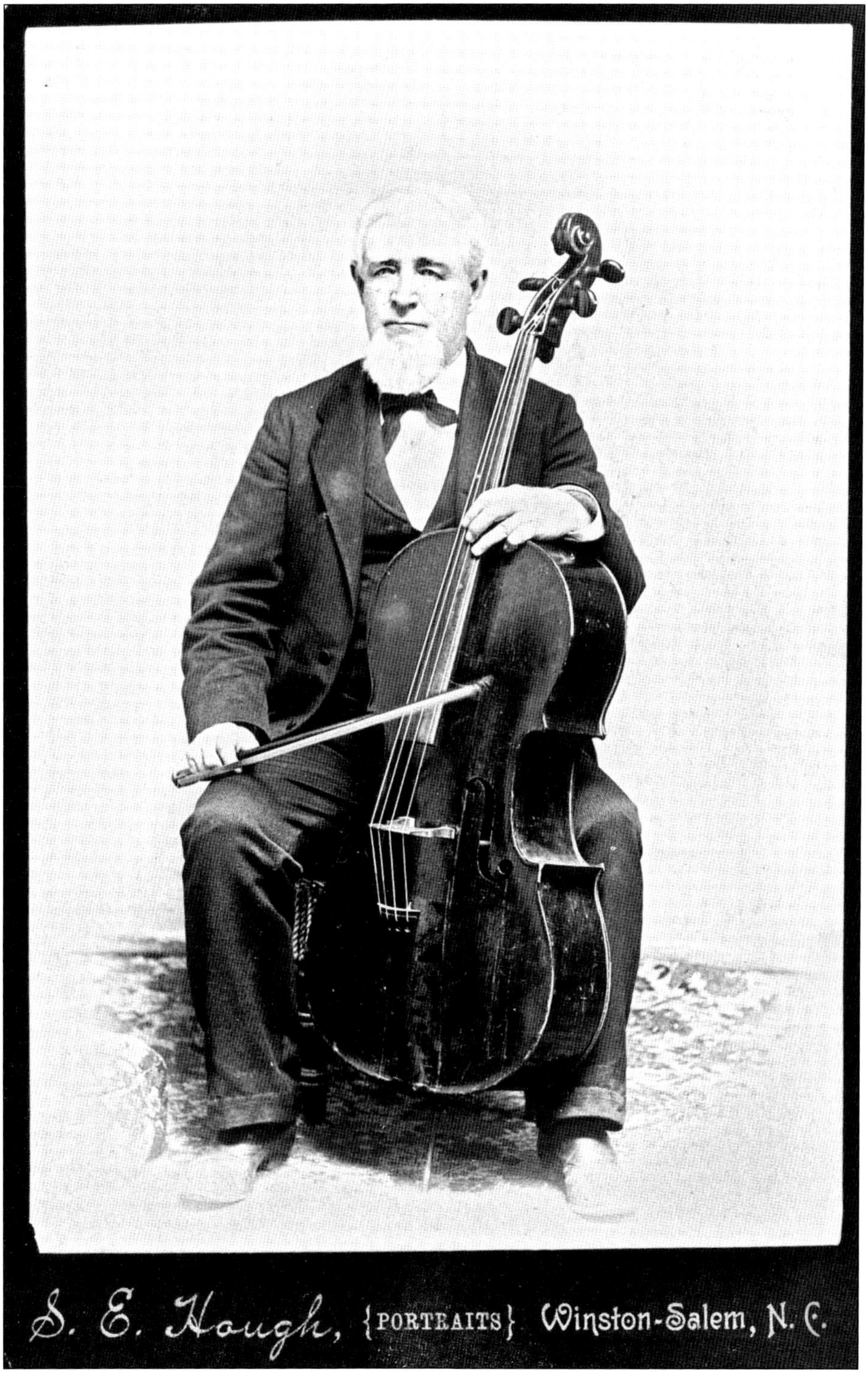

Edward W. Lineback taught music at Salem Academy and College during the years 1856–1877. Edward is seen *c.* 1890 in the studio of Sylvester E. Hough. (Collection of the Moravian Archives, Winston-Salem, North Carolina; Photograph courtesy of Old Salem Museums & Gardens.)

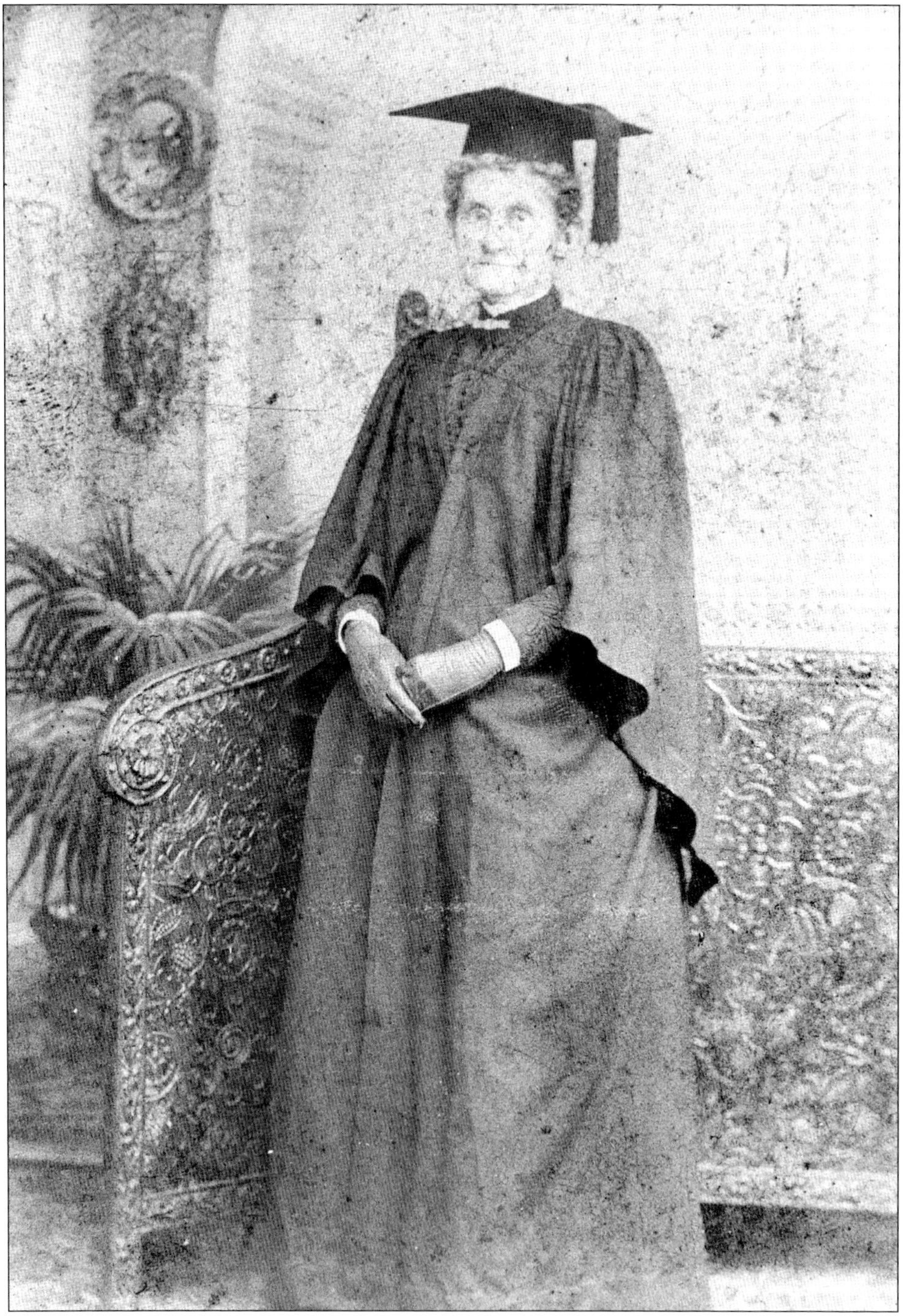

Emma A. Lehman taught English at Salem Academy and College from 1864 to 1916. She also pursued a study of plants and other natural sciences. As an amateur botanist, she discovered an unidentified plant at Roaring Gap, North Carolina, in 1903. The state botanist of New York named the plant Monotropsis Lehmani in her honor in 1906. Emma is seen, in her academic robes, in this 1896 photograph taken by Sylvester E. Hough. (Collection of the Moravian Archives, Winston-Salem, North Carolina; Photograph courtesy of Old Salem Museums & Gardens.)

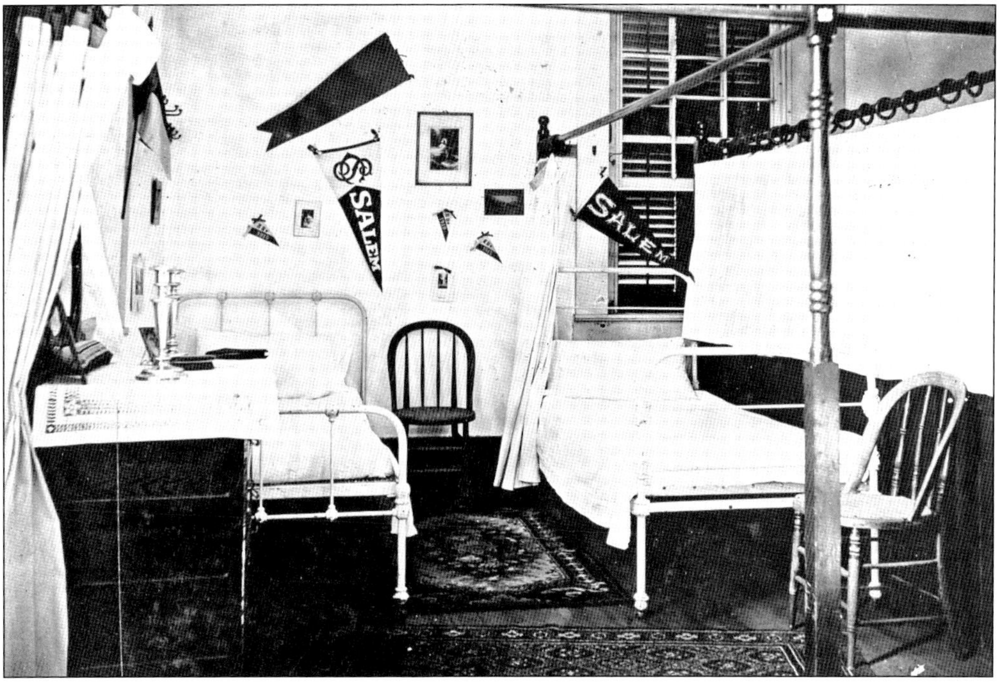

This photograph, taken *c.* 1910, shows part of a sleeping hall inside Salem Academy and College. The sleeping halls were divided by curtains, which allowed for privacy. (Private collection; Photograph courtesy of Old Salem Museums & Gardens.)

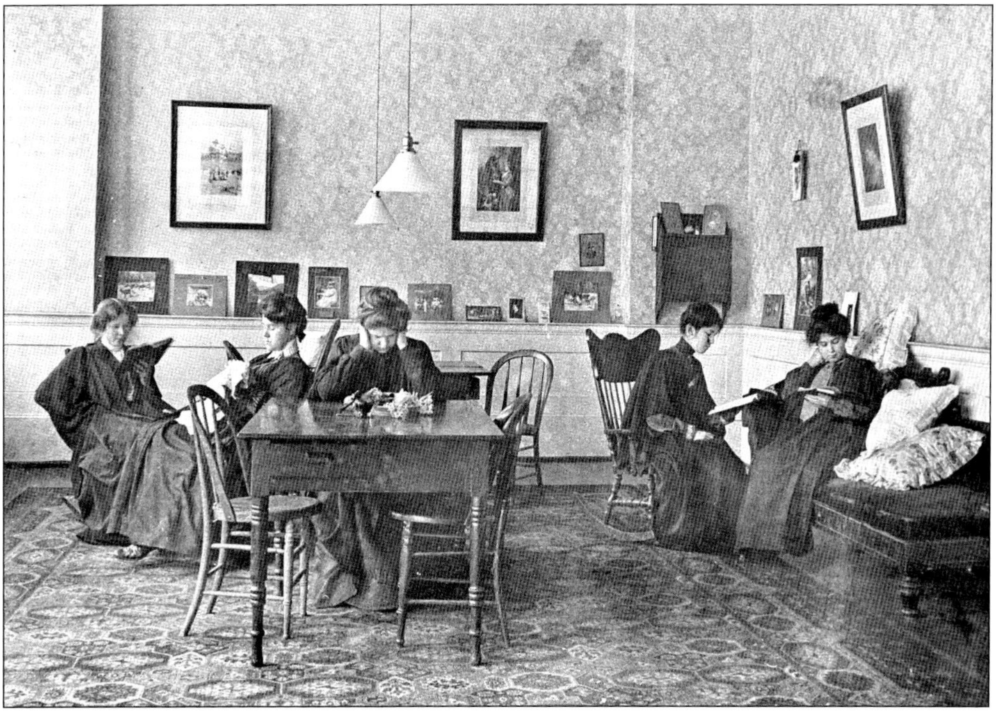

The "Senior Study Parlor," at Salem Academy and College is seen in this photograph taken *c.* 1910. (Collection of Old Salem Museums & Gardens.)

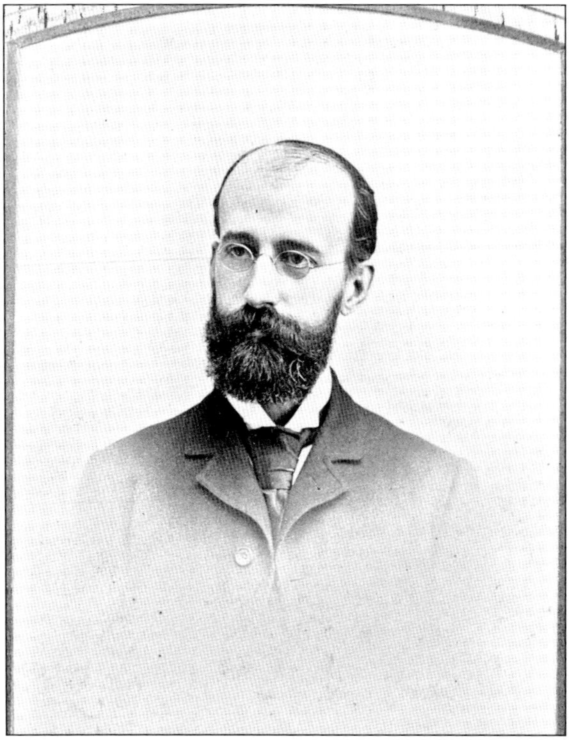

In 1888, Rev. John H. Clewell became the president of Salem Academy and College. Two years later, in 1890, he had the honor of awarding seven graduates the institution's first bachelor of arts degree. Reverend Clewell is seen in this *c.* 1895 photograph taken by Sylvester E. Hough. (Collection of the Moravian Archives, Winston-Salem, North Carolina; Photograph courtesy of Old Salem Museums & Gardens.)

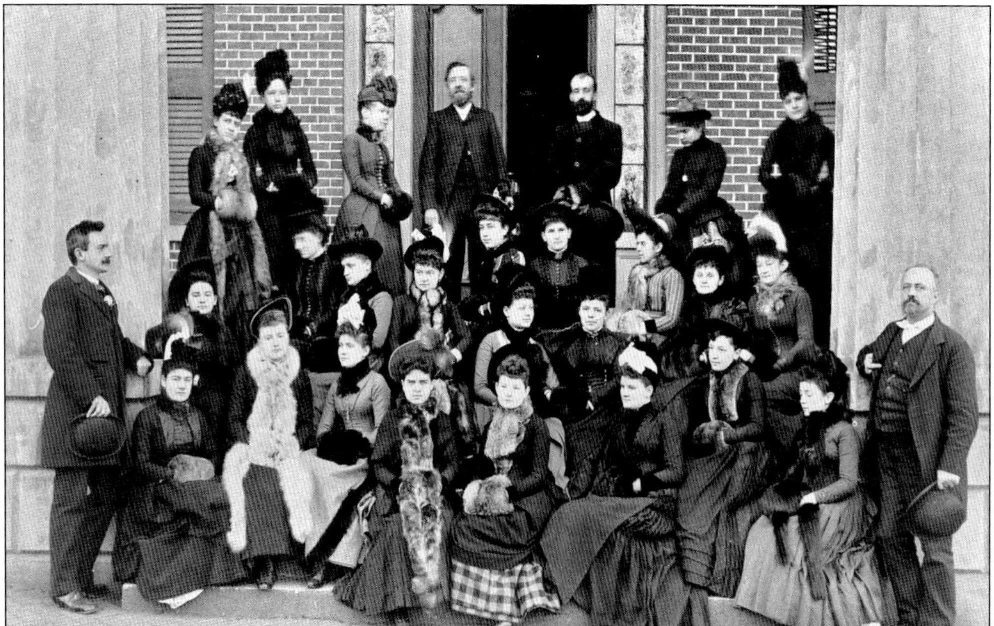

Salem Academy and College students posed for their photograph on the steps of Main Hall in 1889. The two men standing in the doorway are Dr. Edward Rondthaler (left) and Rev. John H. Clewell (right). The only identified student is Mary E. Fries (second row, third from right). This particular graduating class had the distinction of being welcomed at the White House by President Harrison. (Collection of Old Salem Museums & Gardens.)

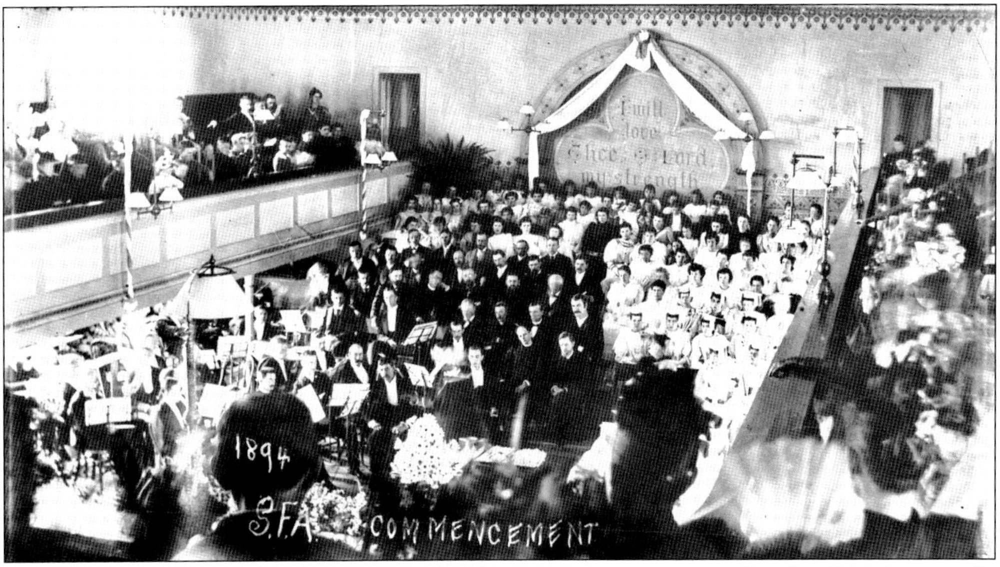

The commencement of Salem Academy and College graduates was captured in this 1894 photograph. (Collection of the Wachovia Historical Society; Photograph courtesy of Old Salem Museums & Gardens.)

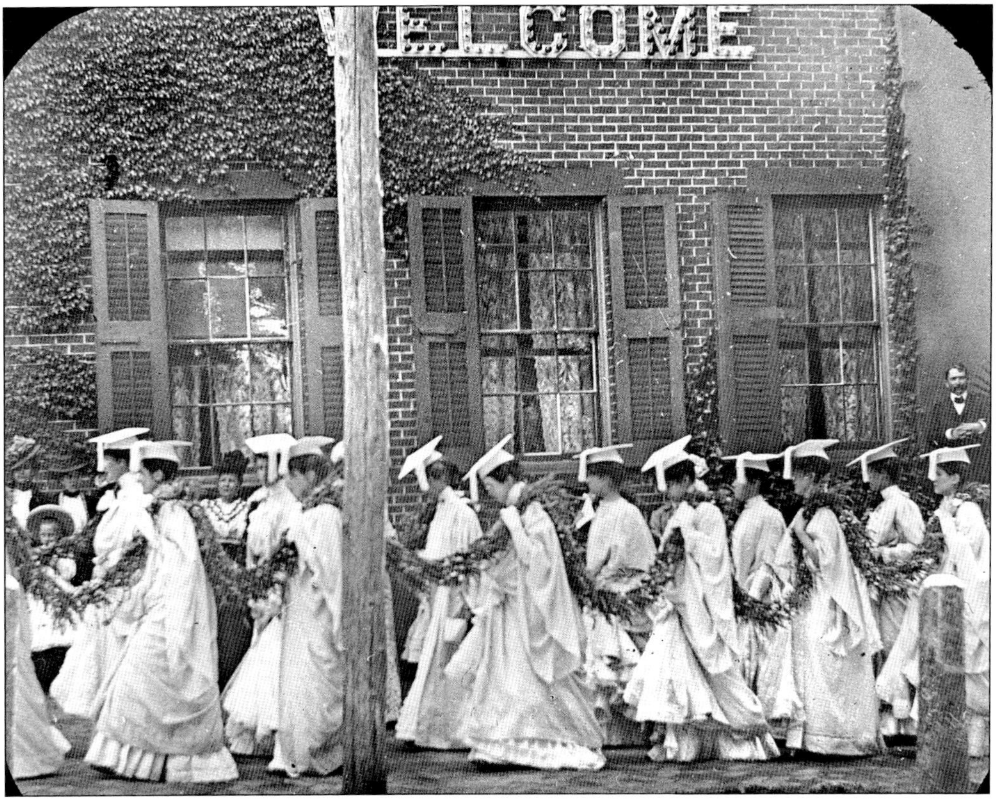

Salem Academy and College students marched with their daisy garlands, or "chains," underneath a lighted "WELCOME" sign during the 1902 commencement. (Collection of the Wachovia Historical Society; Photograph courtesy of Old Salem Museums & Gardens.)

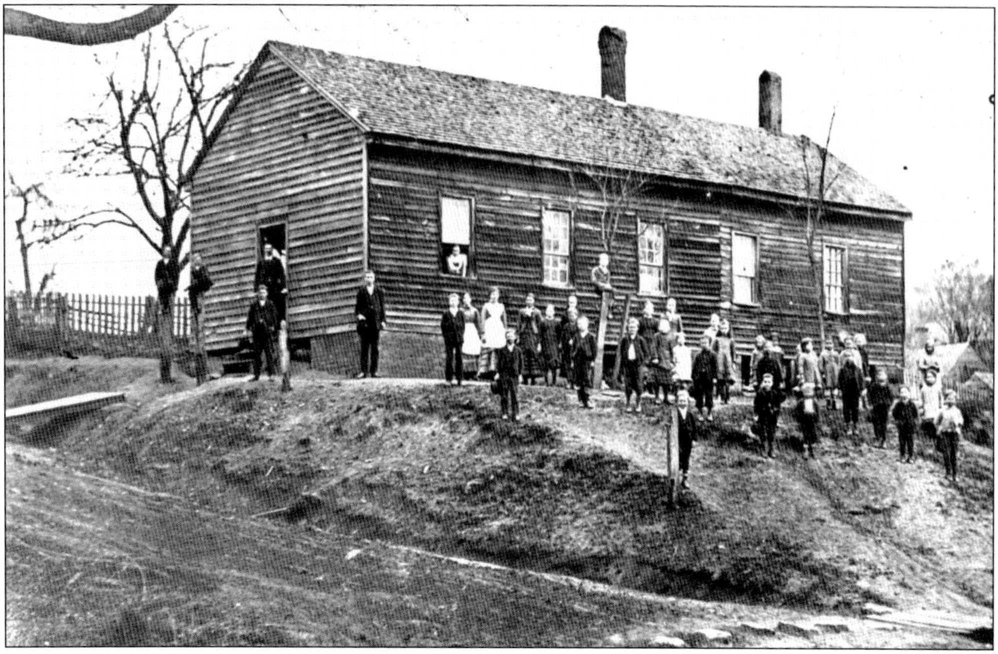

Edward F. Small documented students at the Elm Street Sunday School and Chapel in 1882. The building was located in Salem on the corner of Academy Street and what is now Factory Row. (Collection of the Wachovia Historical Society; Photograph courtesy of Old Salem Museums & Gardens.)

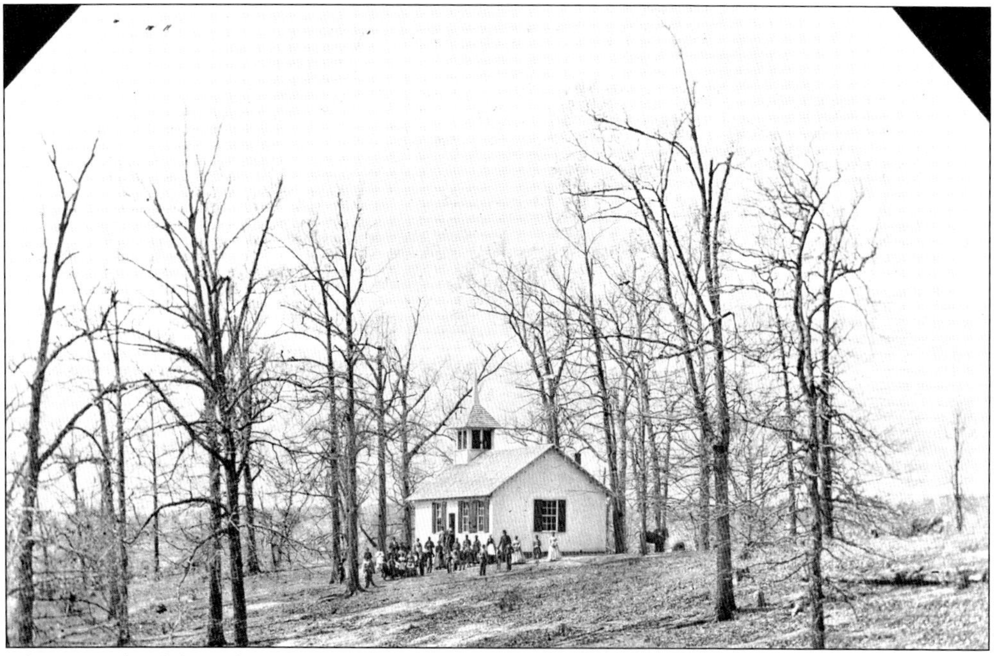

The first school for African Americans in Forsyth County was built near Salem in 1867 and is seen in this *c.* 1870 photograph. The school was located on Moravian lands south of Salem Creek near the Great Plank Road and the current Happy Hill community. (Collection of the Wachovia Historical Society; Photograph courtesy of Old Salem Museums & Gardens.)

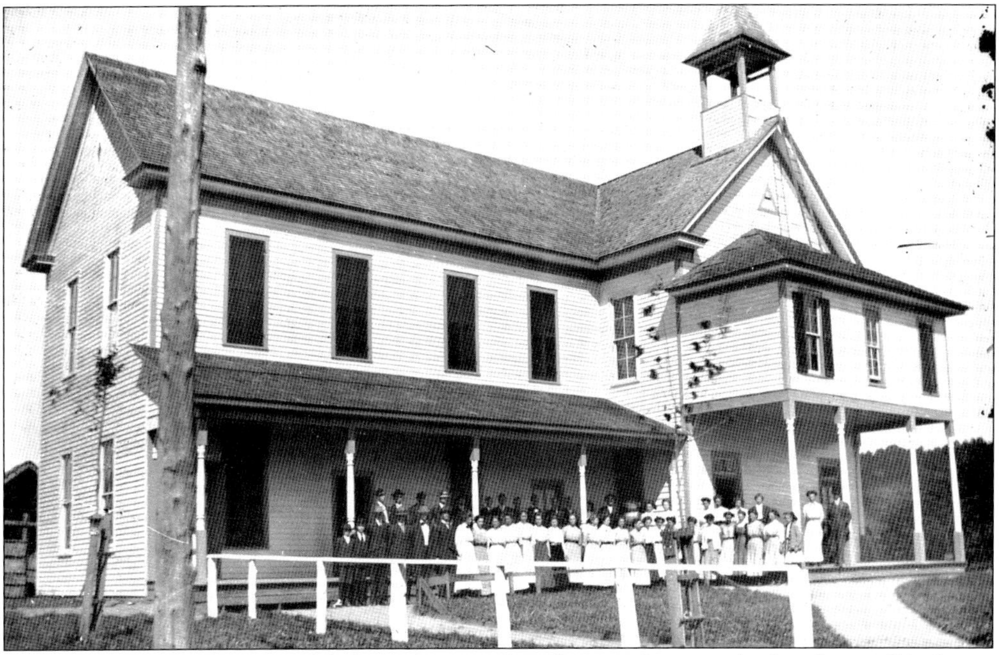

A group of men and women, likely students and staff, were photographed in front of Bethania High School *c.* 1910. The school was organized in 1908 and remained in operation until 1924. (Collection of the Wachovia Historical Society; Photograph courtesy of Old Salem Museums & Gardens.)

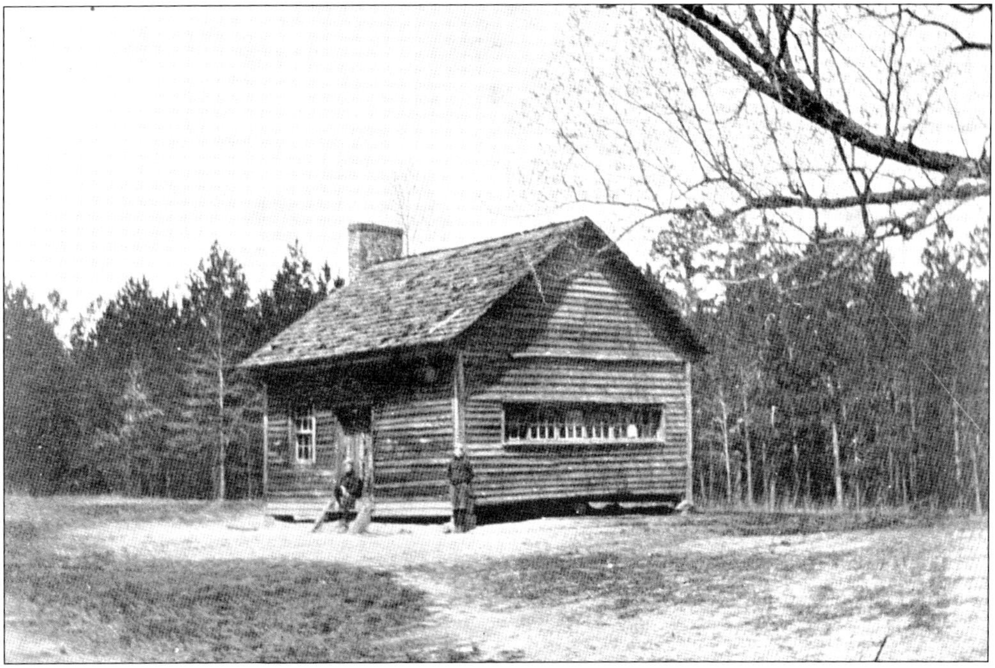

This photograph, labeled "old school house Friedberg," was taken *c.* 1895. (Collection of the Moravian Archives, Winston-Salem, North Carolina; Photograph courtesy of Old Salem Museums & Gardens.)

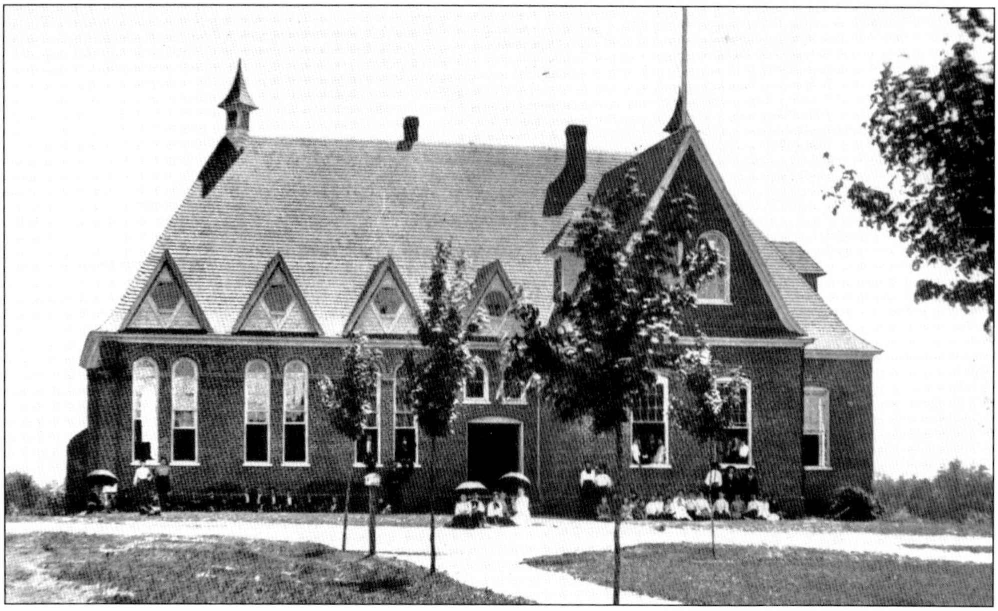

Clemmons School, founded by Edwin T. Clemmons through provisions in his will, was a school for both boys and girls. Students were taught practical life skills and academics that prepared them for college. The school, which was under management of the Moravian Church, is seen in this *c.* 1907 photograph. The building is now part of Clemmons Moravian Church. (Collection of the Wachovia Historical Society; Photograph courtesy of Old Salem Museums & Gardens.)

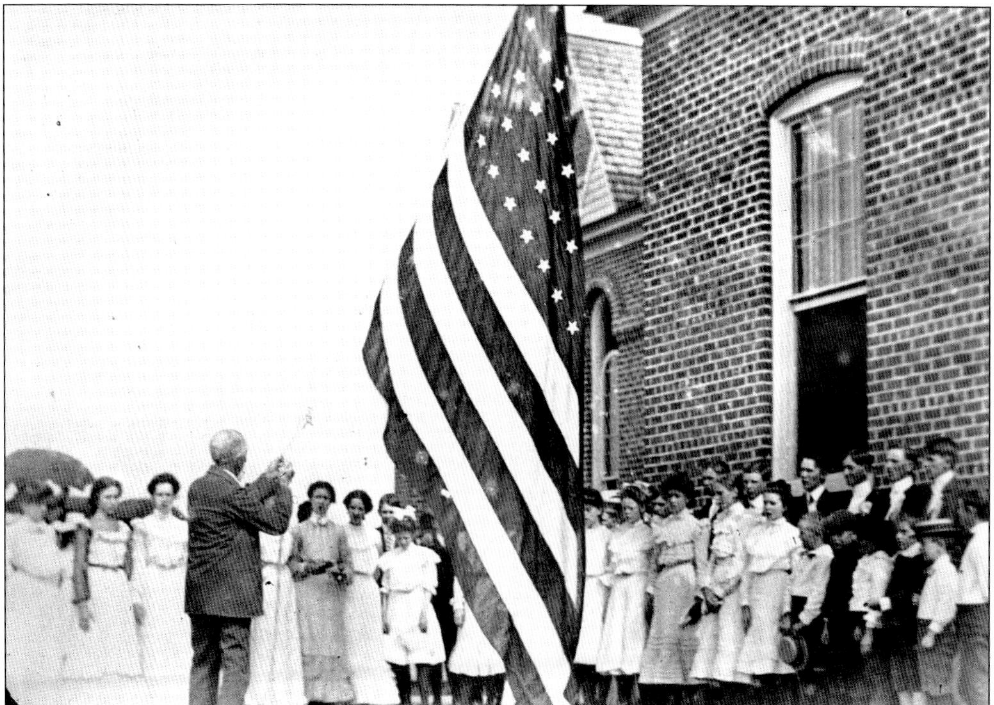

Students watch as the American flag is raised at Clemmons School *c.* 1915. (Collection of the Wachovia Historical Society; Photograph courtesy of Old Salem Museums & Gardens.)

Three
AT WORK

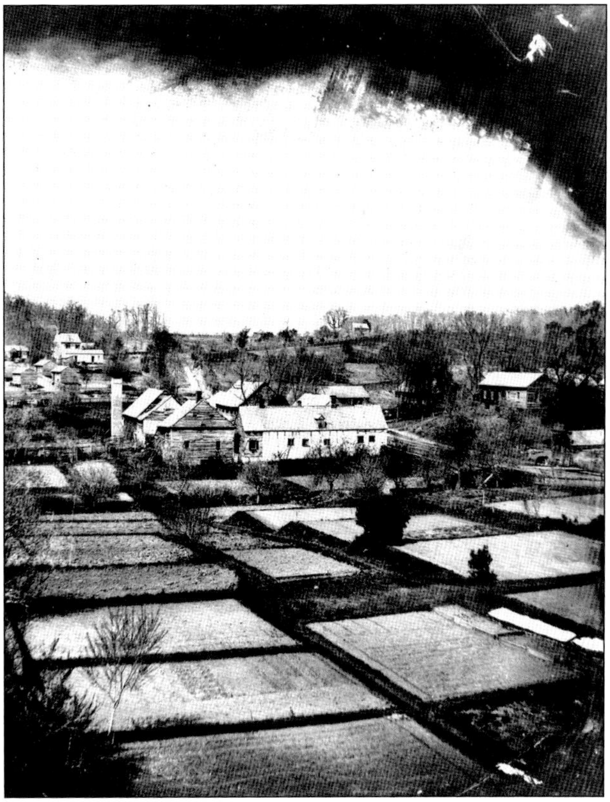

The Single Brothers' garden in Salem, looking west from South Main Street, can be seen in this late-19th-century photograph. The buildings in the center of the photograph include the slaughterhouse, the brewery, and the tannery. (Collection of the Wachovia Historical Society; Photograph courtesy of Old Salem Museums & Gardens.)

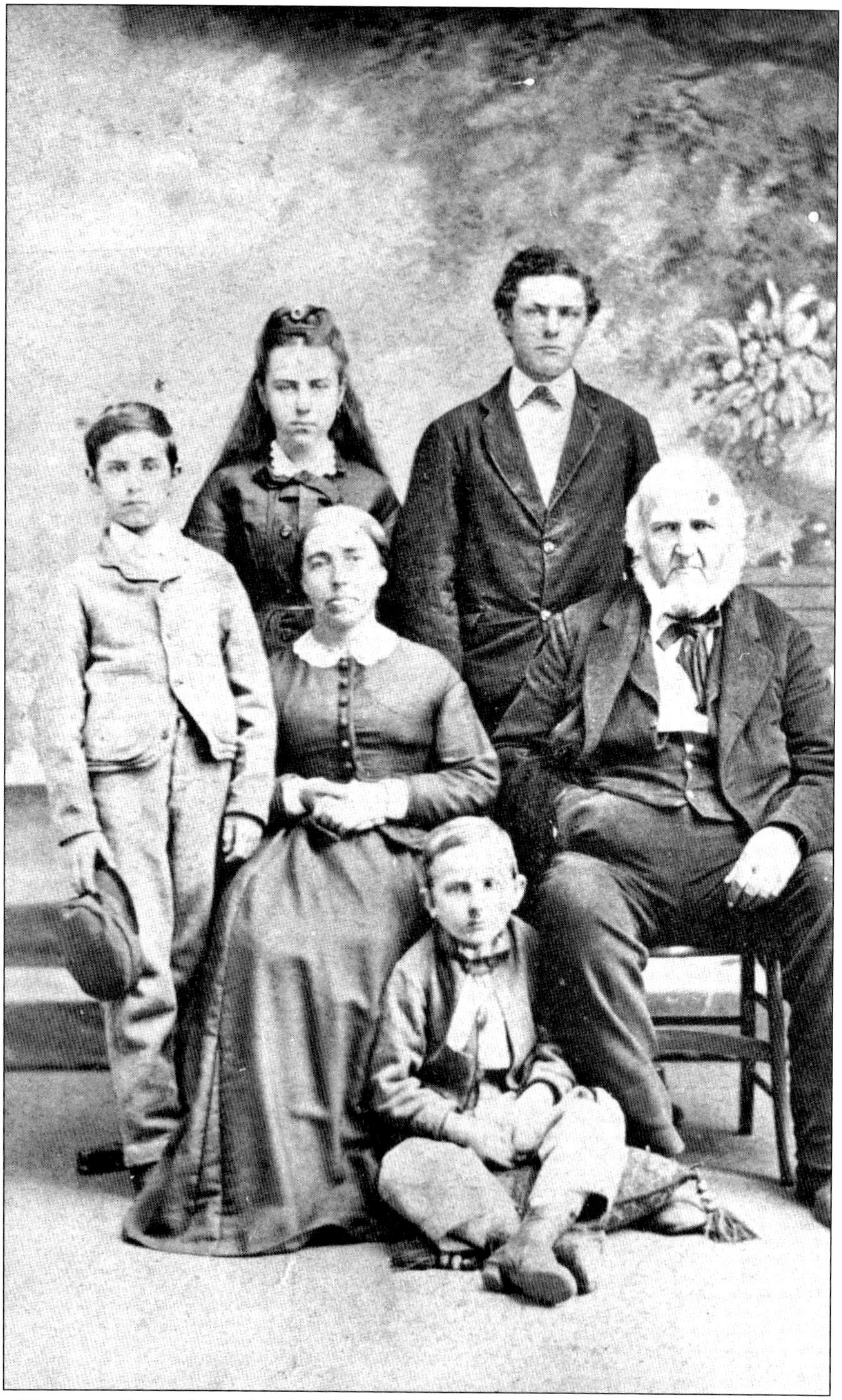

Charles Gustavus Brietz (seated right), his wife, Margaret Morrow (seated left), and four of his children are seen in this photograph taken by Henry A. Lineback *c.* 1875. Brietz, who was a tanner by trade, operated the Salem tannery for many years. In 1856, he became the first mayor of Salem. (Collection of Old Salem Museums & Gardens.)

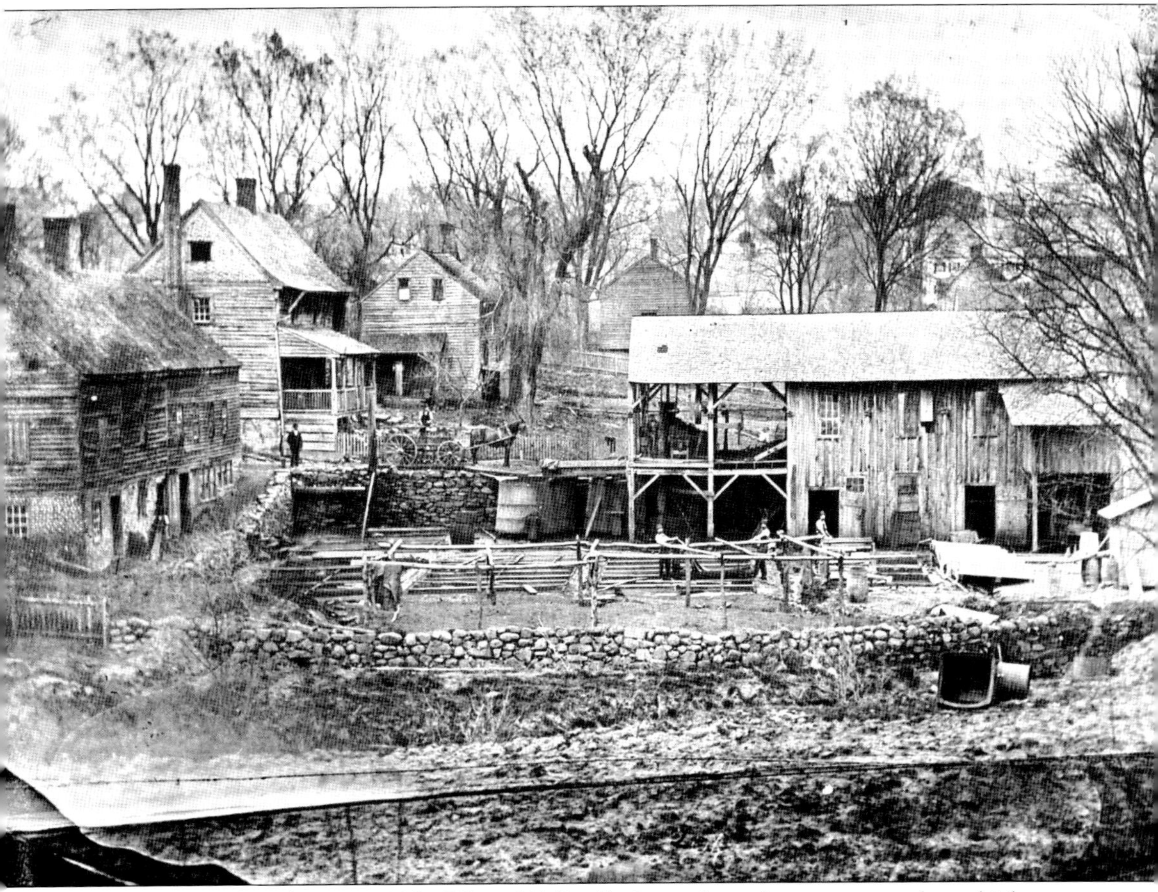

This photograph, taken in 1882 by Edward F. Small, shows the red tannery complex, which was a highly successful business in Salem. The large house on the left is the building in which hides were scraped prior to being tanned. The building to the right is the tannery itself. Two vats, where hides were kept, can be seen at the center of the photograph, as well as the bark mill (underneath the covered part of the tannery) where bark was ground for use in the tanning vats. (Collection of Old Salem Museums & Gardens.)

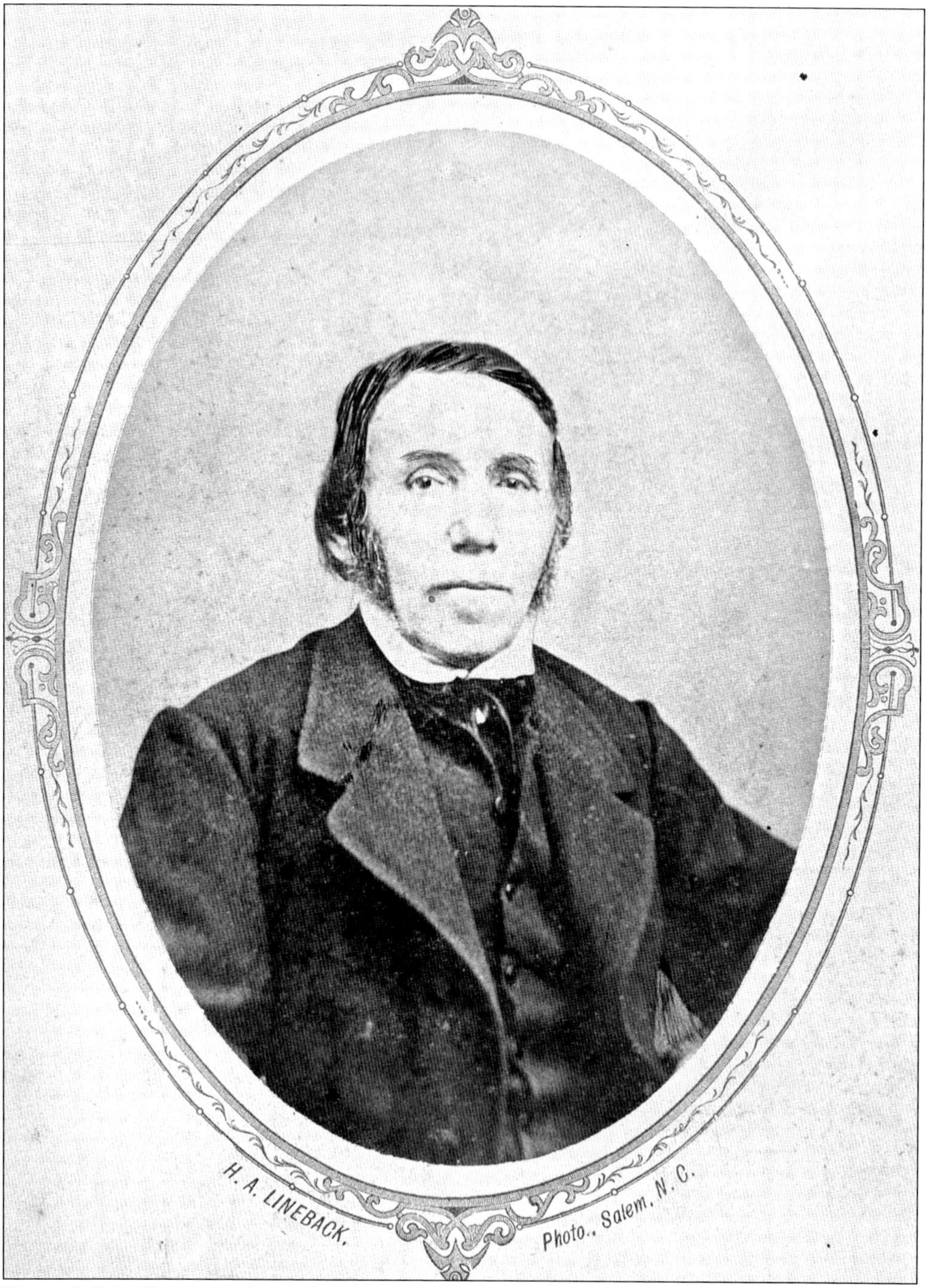

Heinrich Schaffner arrived in Salem from Neuwied, Germany, in 1833 and became a journeyman potter under John Holland. In April 1834, Schaffner received permission to operate his own shop. Many years later, while working as a master potter, Schaffner took the young man Daniel Krause into his shop, where he taught him the potter's trade. Before his death, Heinrich Schaffner turned his business over to Daniel Krause, who became the last potter in Salem. Henry A. Lineback took this photograph of Heinrich Schaffner *c.* 1875. (Collection of Old Salem Museums & Gardens.)

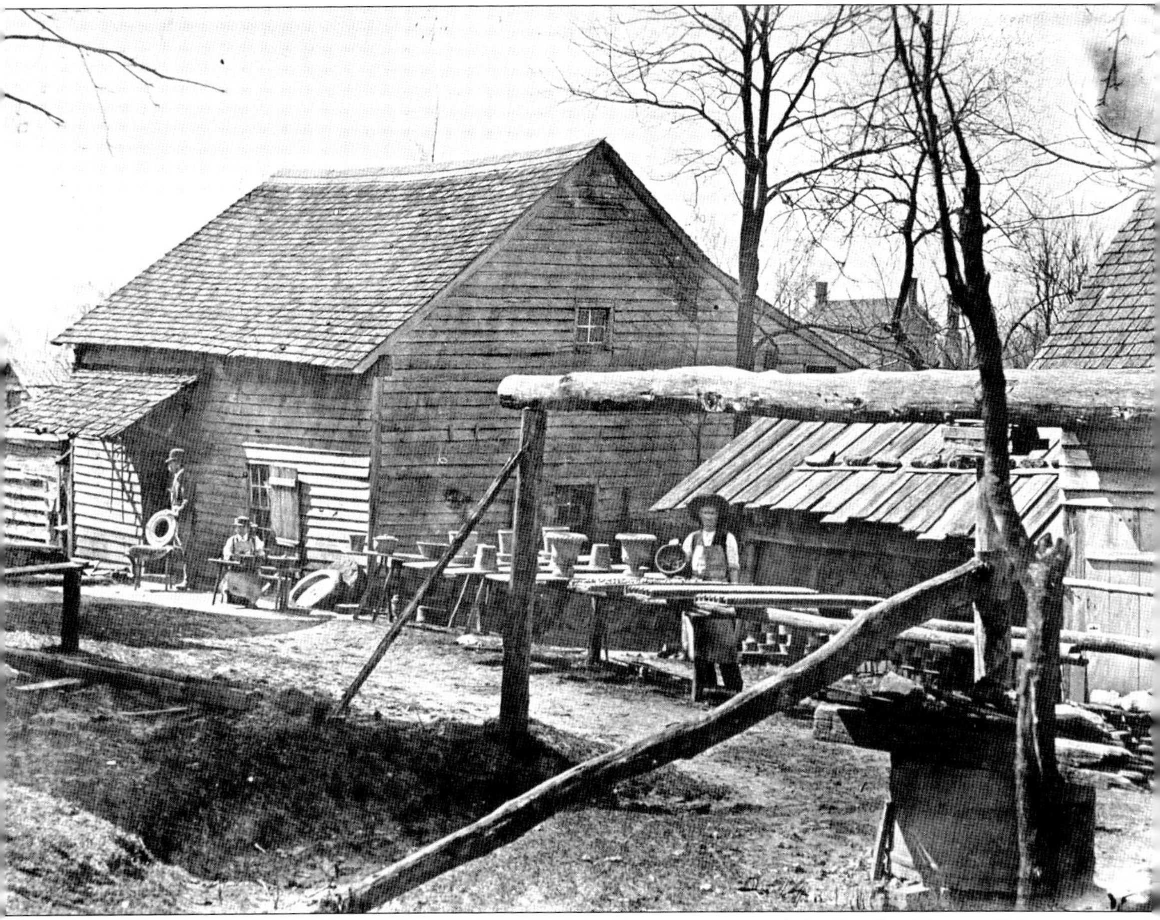

The Heinrich Schaffner–Daniel Krause pottery in Salem incorporated the first building in Salem, the 1766 Builders' House. Moravian pottery, which was Salem's largest commercial enterprise, was in high demand throughout North Carolina, as it was known to be durable and attractive. The photographer Edward F. Small documented these potters in 1882. (Collection of Old Salem Museums & Gardens.)

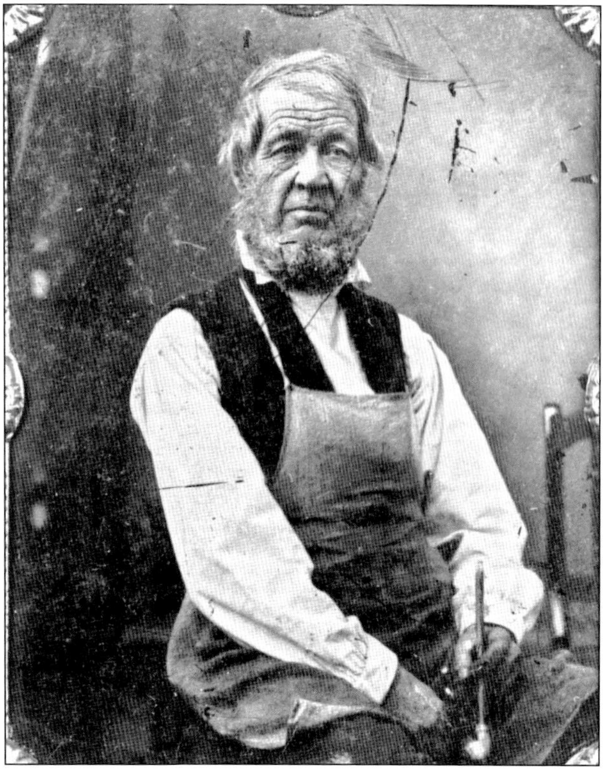

John Henry Lineback was a shoemaker who operated his business from his home on Main Street in Salem. He was also an avid gardener and beekeeper. Henry Alexander Lineback, John Henry's son, likely took this photograph 1867–1870. (Collection of Old Salem Museums & Gardens.)

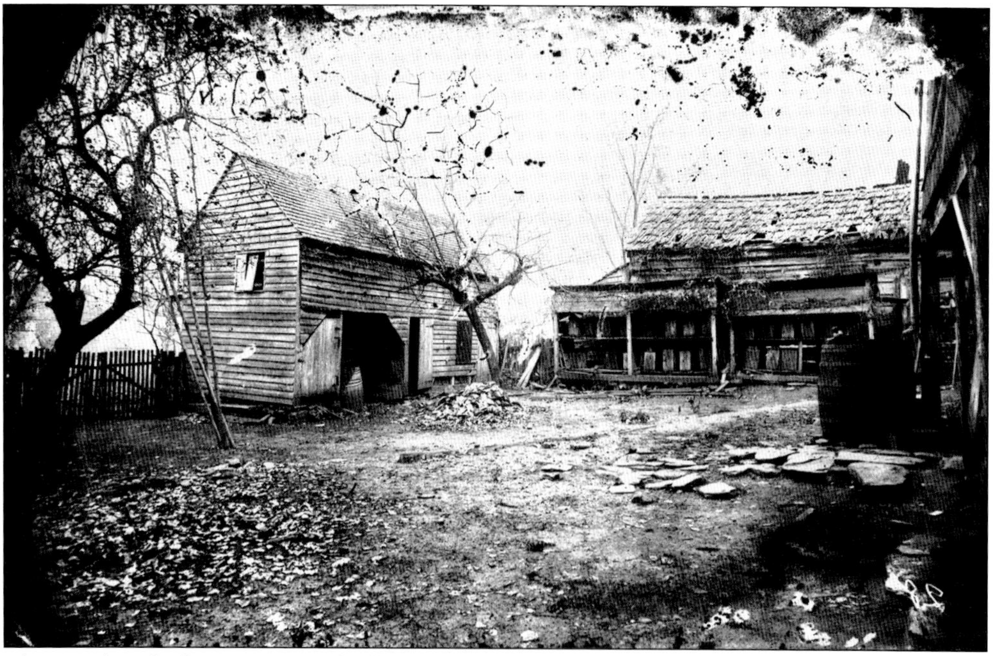

The rear lot of John Henry Lineback's house, located on Main Street in Salem, can be seen in this photograph, attributed to his son, Henry, *c.* 1867. John Henry's beehives (the square wooden boxes) can be seen in the center right of the photograph. (Collection of the Wachovia Historical Society; Photograph courtesy of Old Salem Museums & Gardens.)

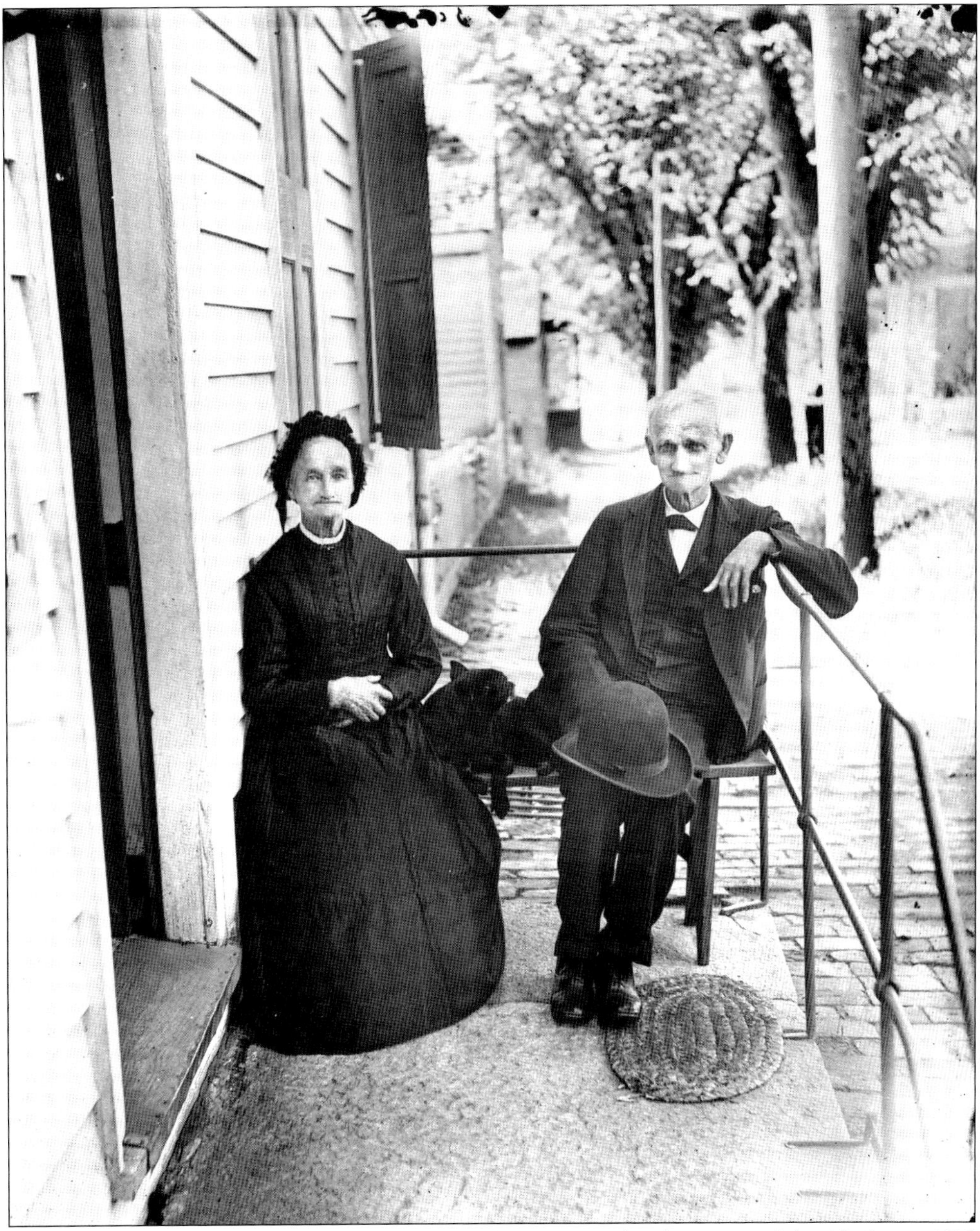

Timothy Vogler was born in Salem in 1806 and apprenticed to his cousin John Vogler in 1819 to learn the trade of a gunsmith. In 1831, Timothy established himself as a master gunsmith and married Charlotte Horton. Dedicated to his profession, Timothy was still practicing his trade at the age of 72. Timothy and his wife, Charlotte, are seated on the front porch of their house, located on Main Street in Salem, in this *c.* 1895 photograph. (Collection of the Wachovia Historical Society; Photograph courtesy of Old Salem Museums & Gardens.)

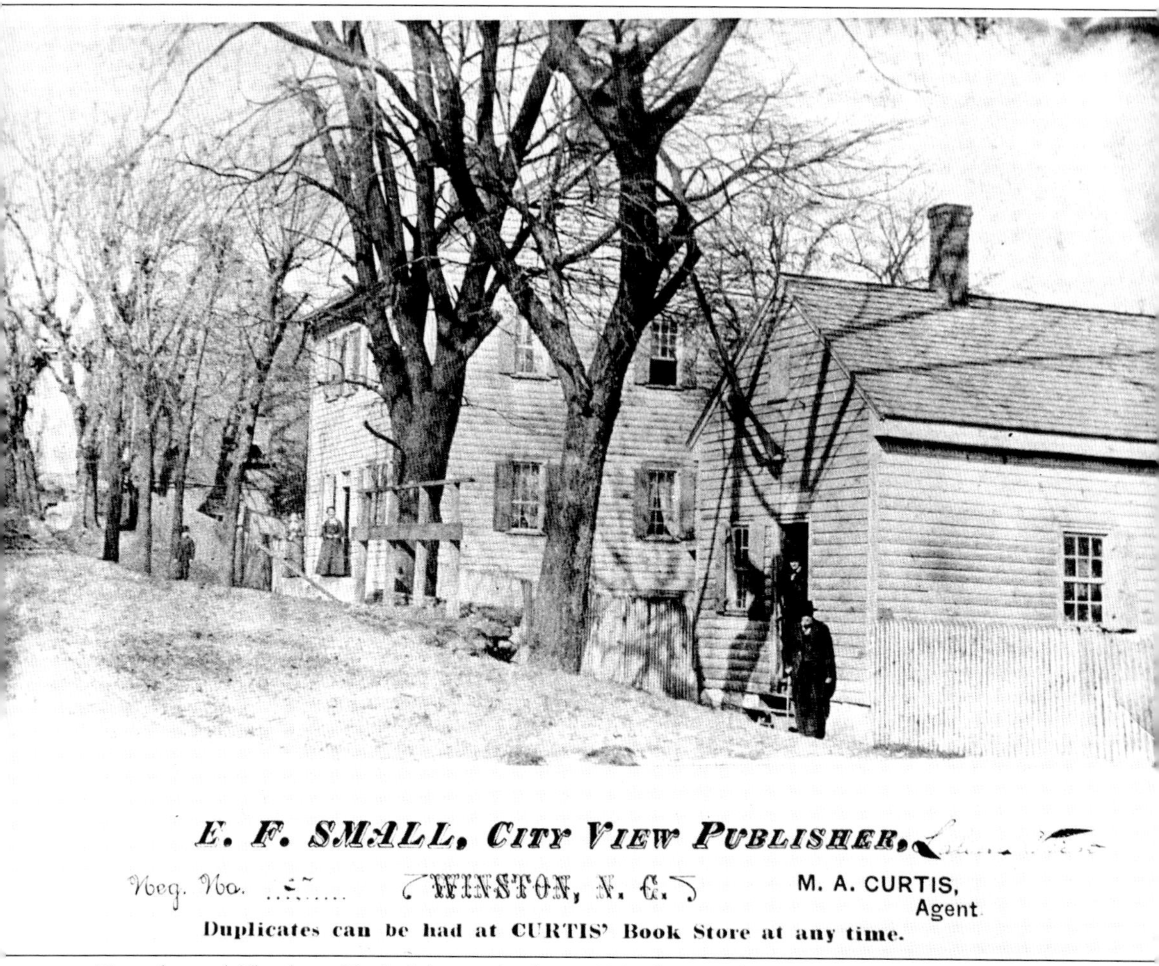

Timothy and Charlotte Vogler's house, built in 1832, along with Timothy's gunsmith shop, built in 1831, can be seen in this photograph taken by Edward F. Small c. 1882. Surviving today, the gunsmith shop is the earliest and best-documented gunsmith shop remaining in the United States. Note the gun, used as Vogler's shop sign, hanging above the shop door. (Collection of Old Salem Museums & Gardens.)

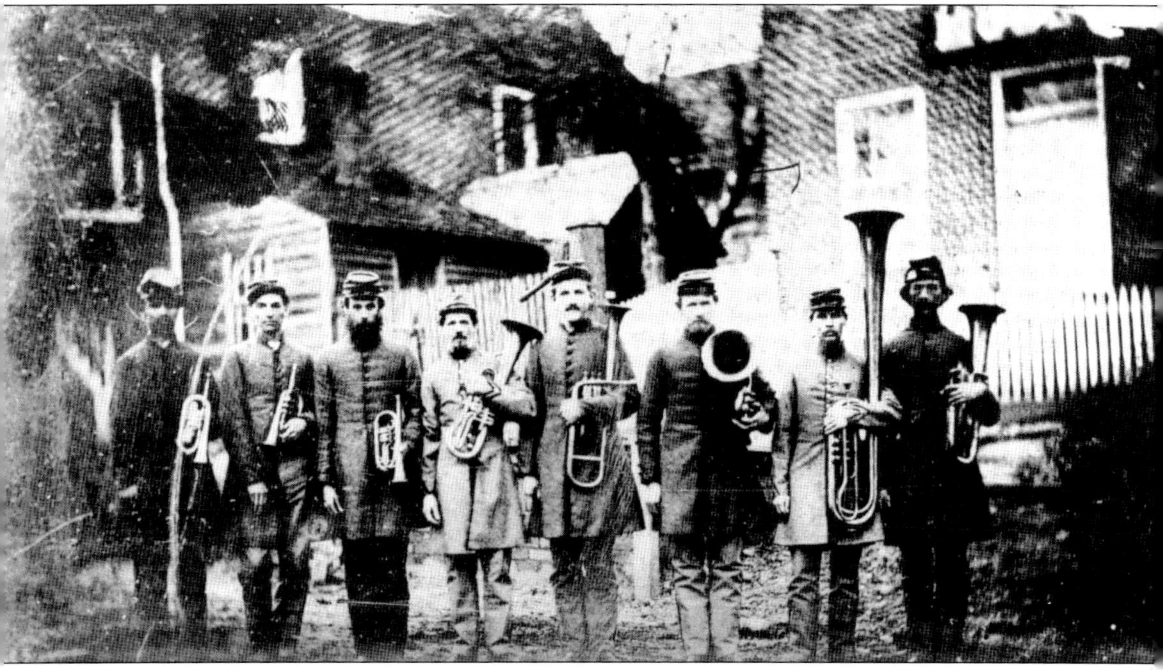

Members of the Salem Moravian Church Band joined the Confederacy and marched with the 26th North Carolina Regiment throughout the Civil War. This photograph was taken in July or August 1862, while the soldiers were on furlough at Salem. The band members are, from left to right, Samuel T. Mickey, A. P. Gibson, J. O. Hall, W. H. Hall, A. L. Hauser, Daniel T. Crouse, Julius A. Leinbach, and James M. Fisher. Fisher had served with the band prior to the war, but did not serve in the regiment. Alexander C. Meinung was also a member of the regimental band but was not present for the photograph. (Collection of Old Salem Museums & Gardens.)

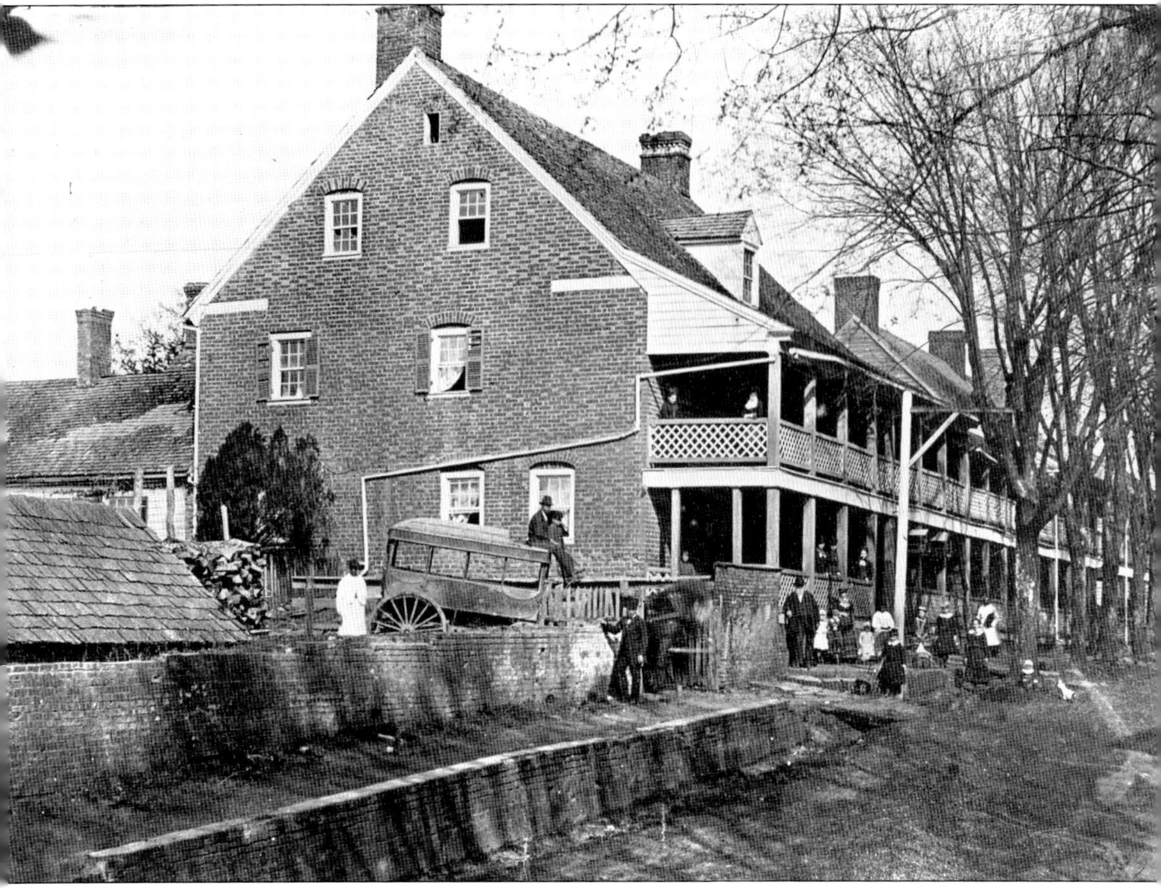

The Salem tavern, located on Main Street and built in 1771, was one of the first public buildings constructed in Salem and became known throughout the Southeast for its excellent hospitality and service. The tavern was important to Salem's business interests as it provided lodging and food for travelers; one of those was George Washington, who visited Salem in 1791. The original tavern was destroyed by fire in 1784 but was quickly rebuilt. The tavern is seen in this 1882 photograph taken by Edward F. Small. (Collection of the Wachovia Historical Society; Photograph courtesy of Old Salem Museums & Gardens.)

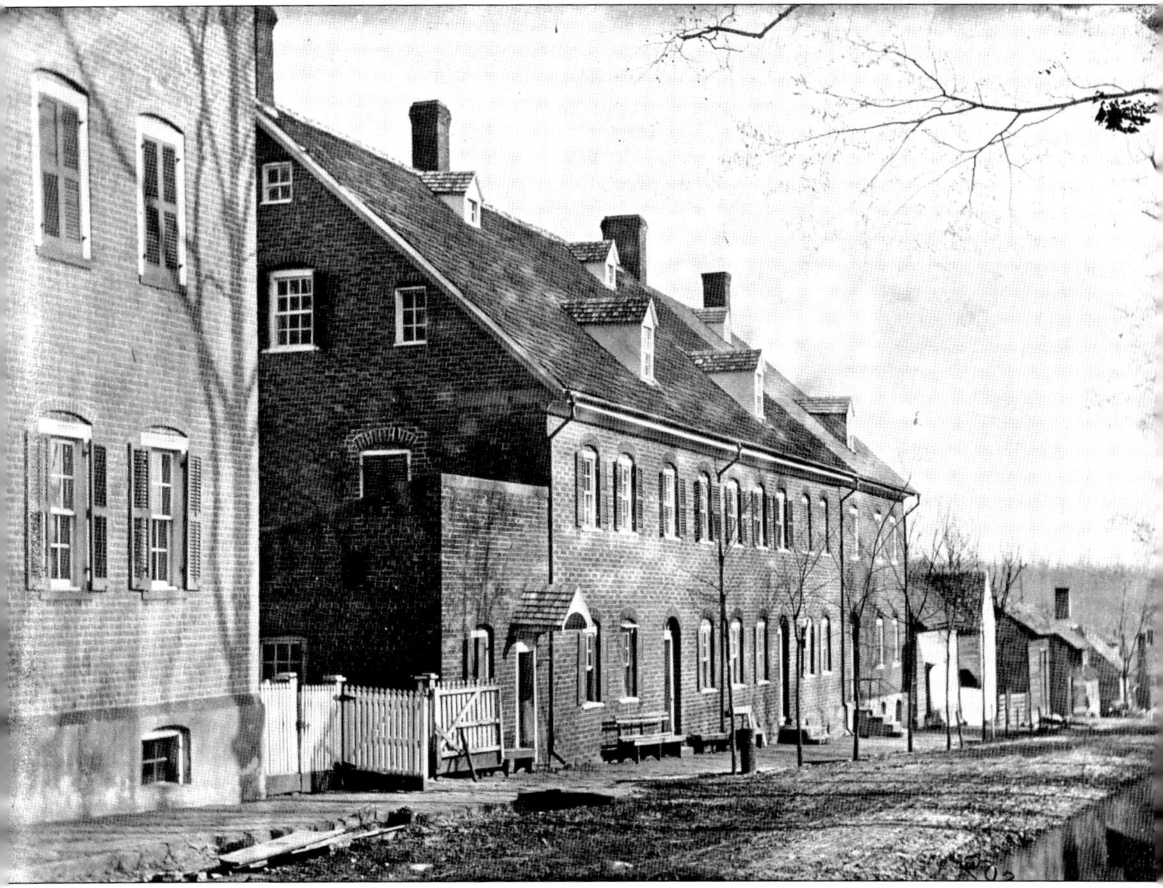

The Single Sisters' House was built in Salem in 1785 and was expanded in 1819. Here single sisters worked together to provide for their own needs and for those of the community. Earning income for the services they provided, the single sisters contributed greatly to the economy of Salem. This photograph, taken by Edward F. Small, shows the Single Sisters' House in 1882. The building is now part of Salem College. (Collection of Old Salem Museums & Gardens.)

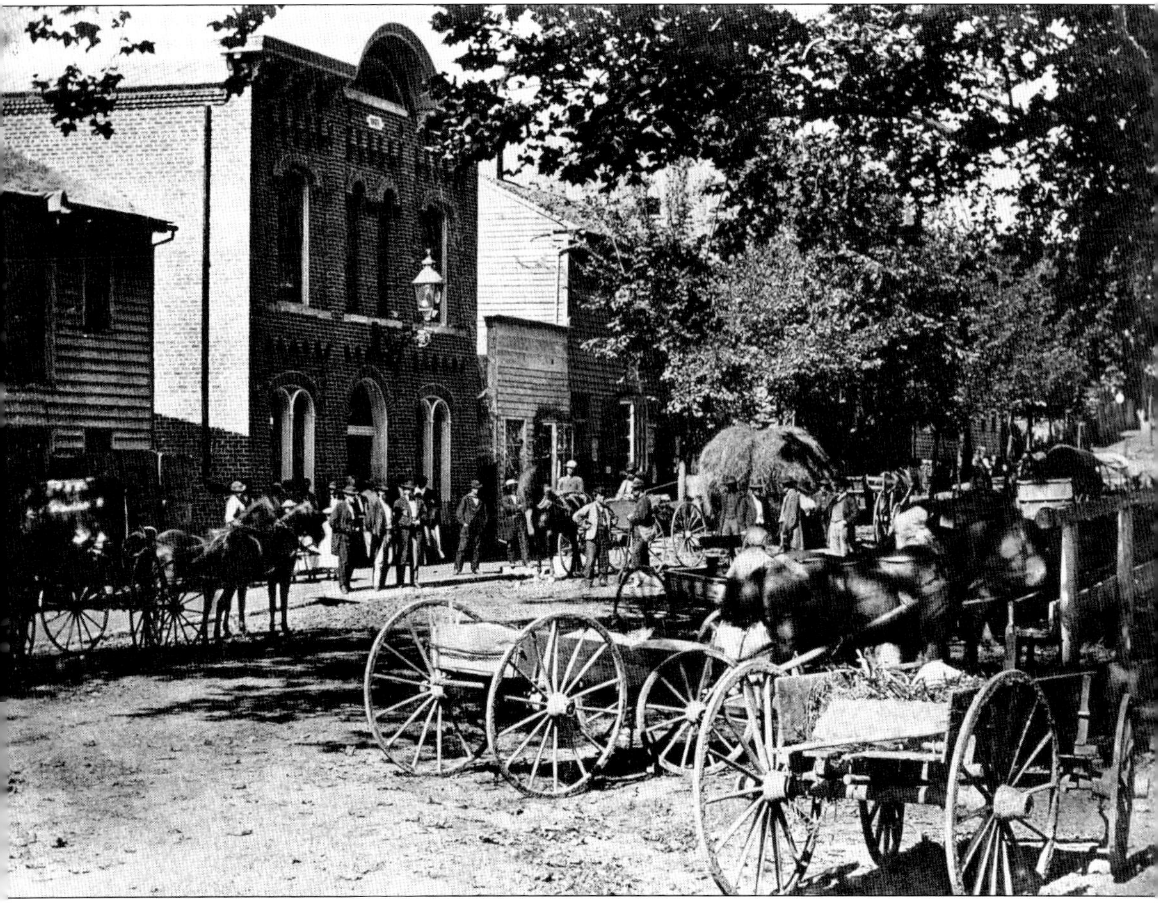

Businessmen can be seen congregating on Salem's Main Street in this c. 1870 photograph. A wagon filled with hay likely waits to use the hay scales, which were located on the corner of Salem Square. (Collection of the Wachovia Historical Society; Photograph courtesy of Old Salem Museums & Gardens.)

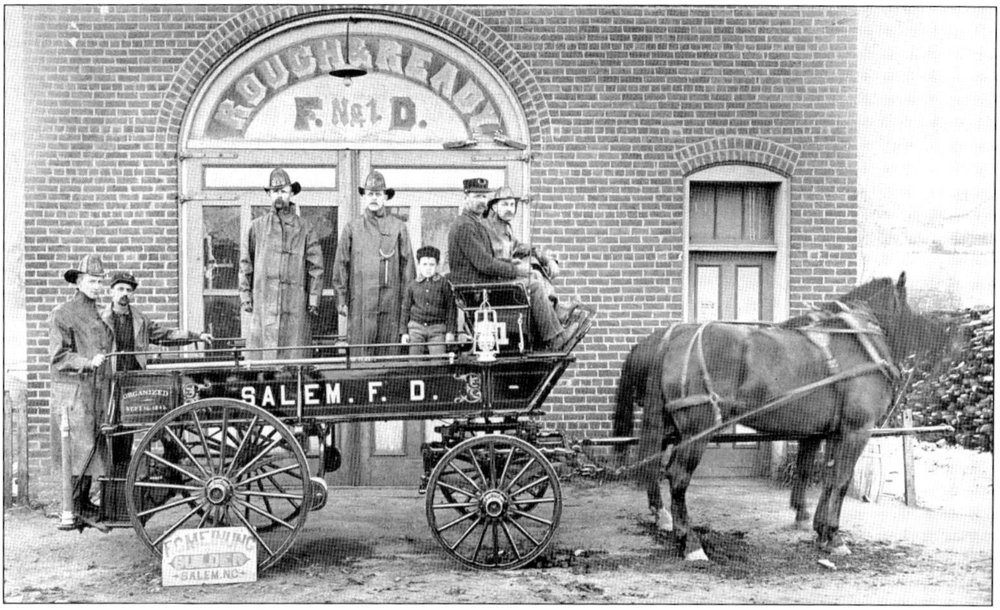

Salem's Rough and Ready Fire Department was organized in 1843. The firemen, photographed by Salem resident Edmund V. Patterson in 1893, are, from left to right, James Peterson, Chief F. C. Meinung, Emmanuel Tesh, Frank Vogler, Lindsay Meinung, James Petree, and Capt. Shirley Rogers. (Collection of Old Salem Museums & Gardens.)

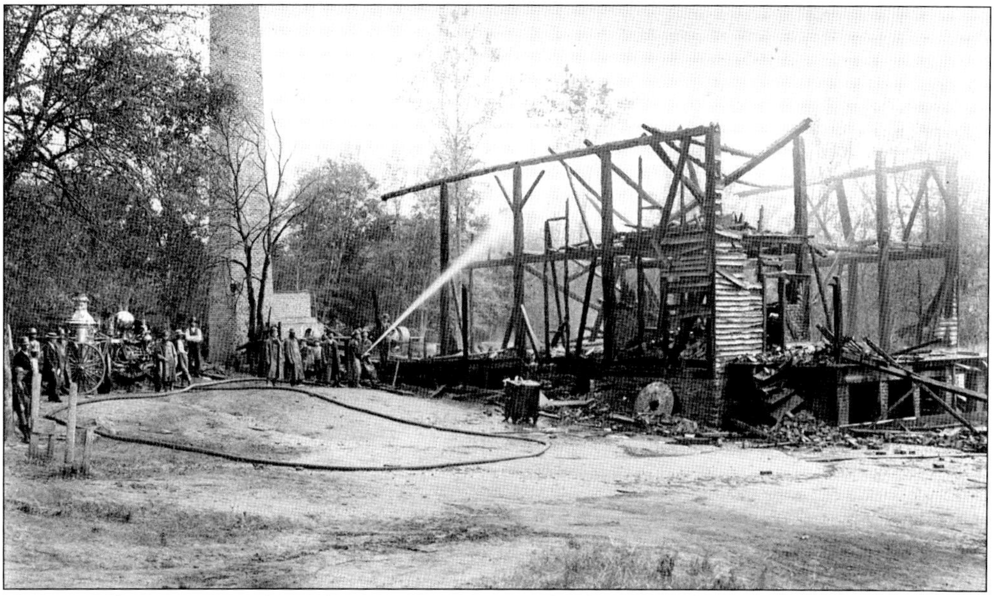

On December 18, 1902, Edmund V. Patterson captured Salem's Rough and Ready Fire Department working to extinguish the blaze that destroyed the Salem Mill. (Collection of the Moravian Archives, Winston-Salem, North Carolina; Photograph courtesy of Old Salem Museums & Gardens.)

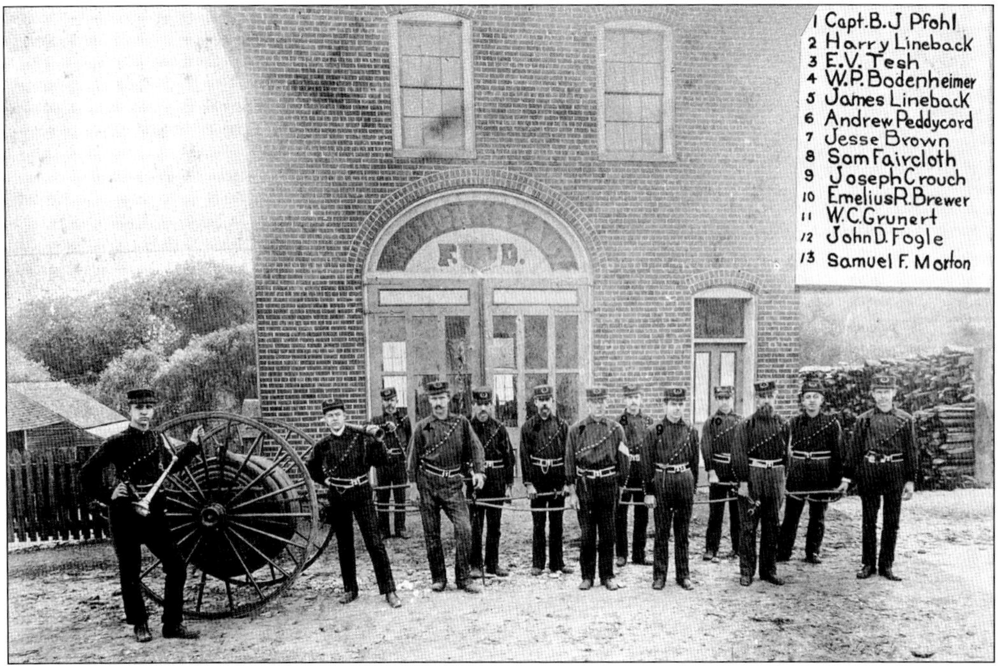

Members of Salem's Rough and Ready Fire Department posed for their photograph c. 1890. The fire department was located on Liberty Street. (Collection of the Wachovia Historical Society; Photograph courtesy of Old Salem Museums & Gardens.)

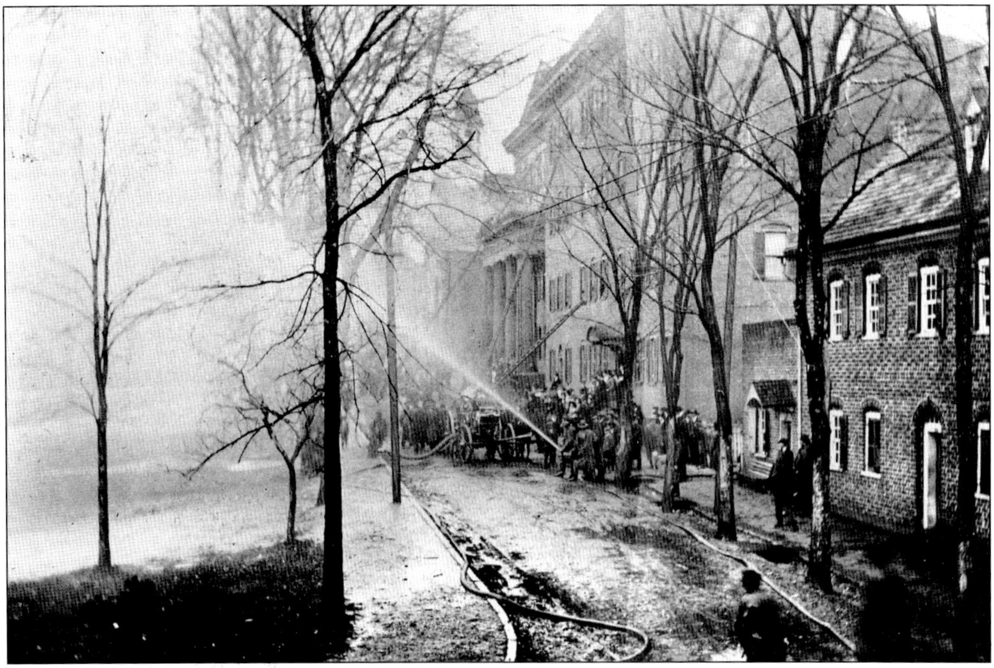

Salem's Rough and Ready Fire Department is seen in a training exercise that occurred c. 1900. Look closely and you can see a man scaling a ladder above the columns of Salem Academy and College's Main Hall building. (Private collection; Photograph courtesy of Old Salem Museums & Gardens.)

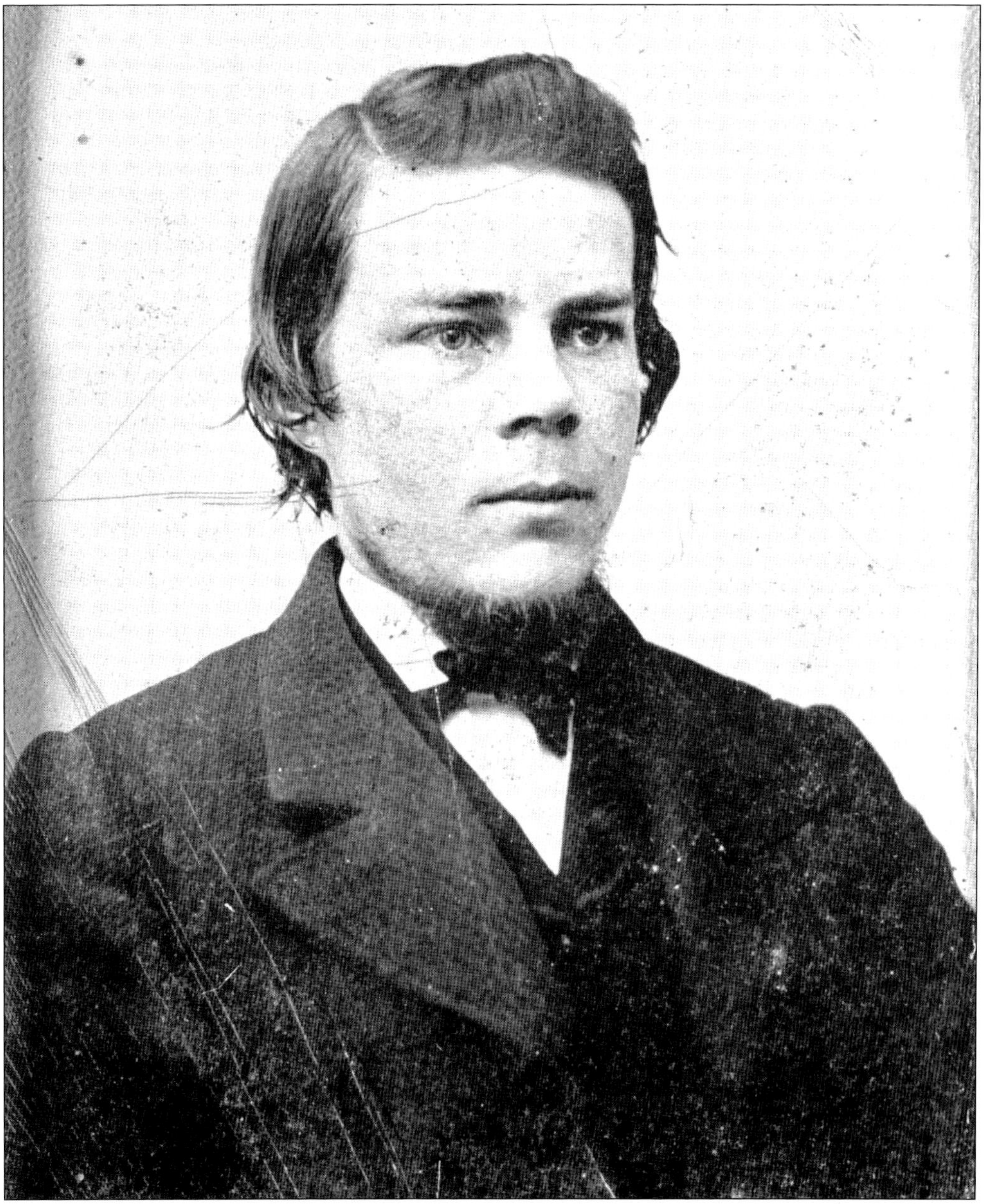

Henry Alexander Lineback was Salem's "pioneer photographer" who worked in the business for over 50 years. Henry built his first photography studio on the north end of his father's house on Main Street in 1867. By 1889, he had moved his entire business to the corner of Fourth and Liberty Streets in Winston. He drew patronage from far and near and was even called upon to take postmortem photographs of the famous Siamese twins Chang and Eng Bunker. Henry is seen in this 1866 photograph that was taken during his trip to Philadelphia, Pennsylvania, where he studied the art of photography. (Collection of Old Salem Museums & Gardens.)

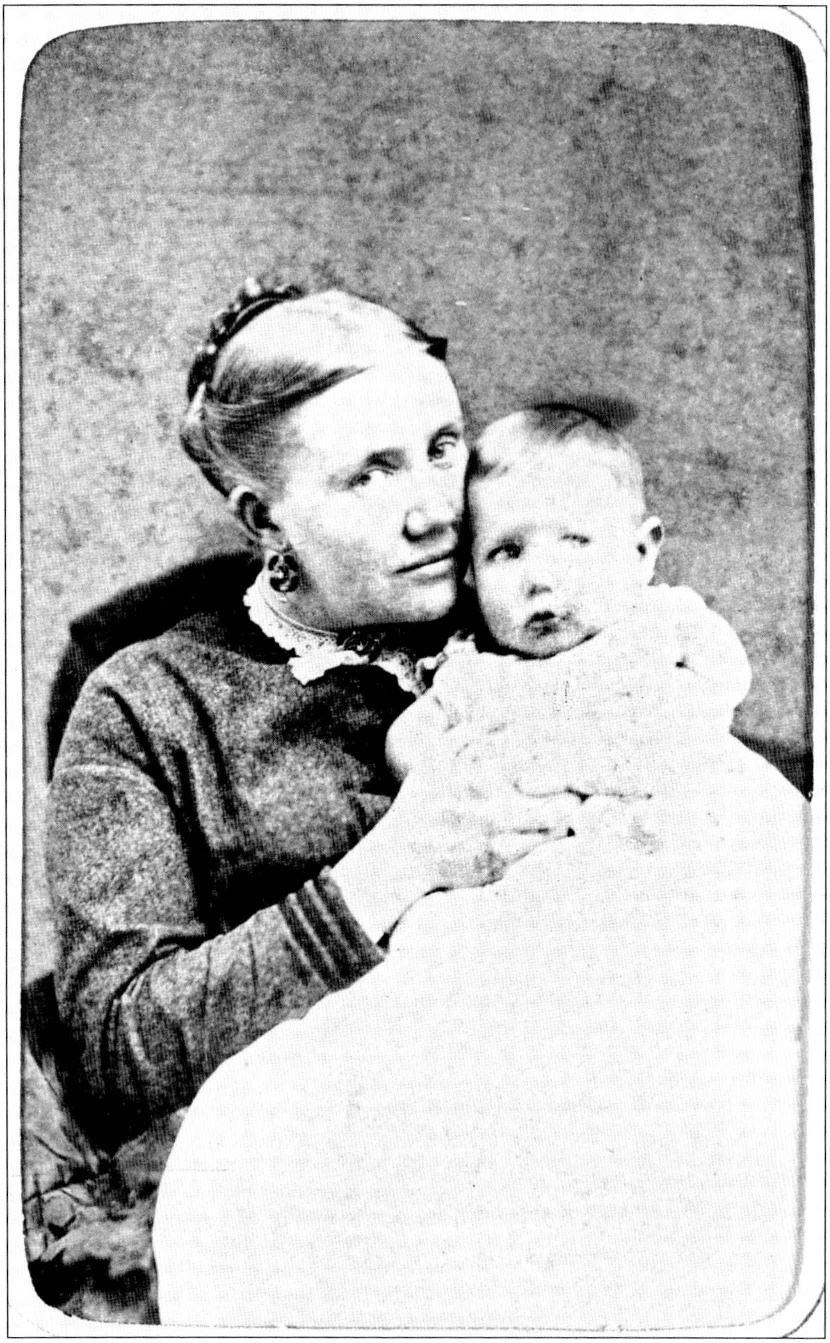

Caroline Louisa Fries Shaffner was an active member of many civic and charitable organizations in Salem and Winston. During the Civil War, she worked to provide comfort and welfare to soldiers of the Confederacy. She was one of the organizers and teachers of the East Salem Sunday School and Chapel, a charter member and treasurer of the Twin City Hospital Association, and a charter member of the Dorcas Circle, which directed the activities of the Salem Home. Caroline is seen, with an unidentified child, in this *c.* 1870 photograph taken by Henry A. Lineback. (Collection of Old Salem Museums & Gardens.)

Dr. Theodore Felix Keehln was a well-known and respected doctor who practiced in Salem and the surrounding areas for more than 30 years. Dr. Keehln is seen in this photograph taken by Henry A. Lineback *c.* 1875. (Collection of Old Salem Museums & Gardens.)

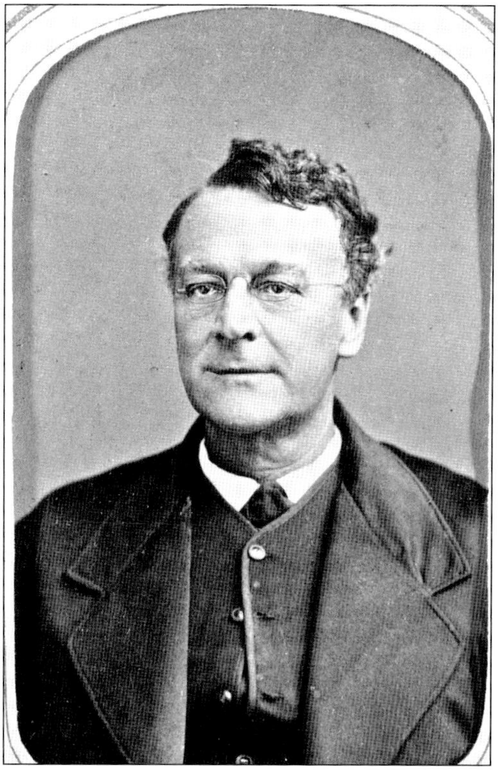

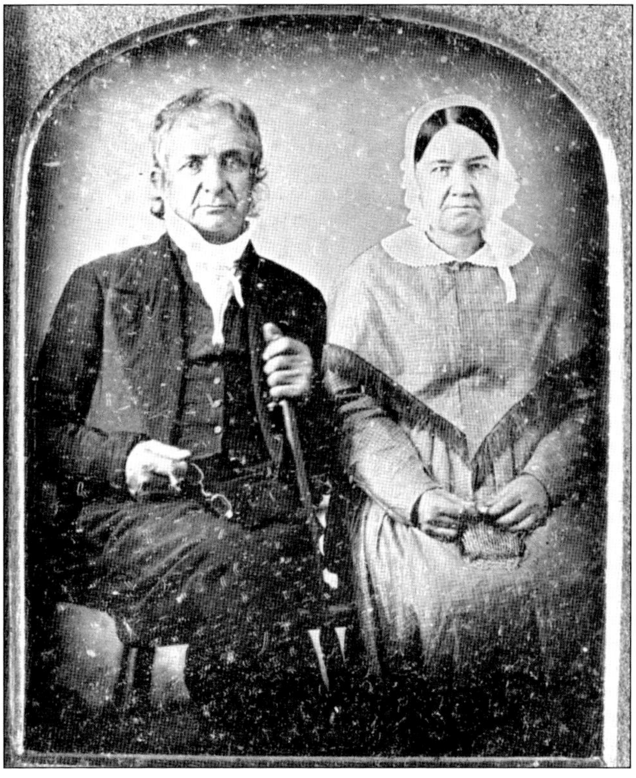

John Vogler was a widely known businessman of Salem. He was a skilled gunsmith, jeweler, and silversmith and was identified with most of the enterprises in Salem. Vogler was a financial supporter of the Salem Flouring Mills, Cotton Manufactory, and Water Works. John and his wife, Christina, are seen in this 1851 photograph. (Collection of Old Salem Museums & Gardens.)

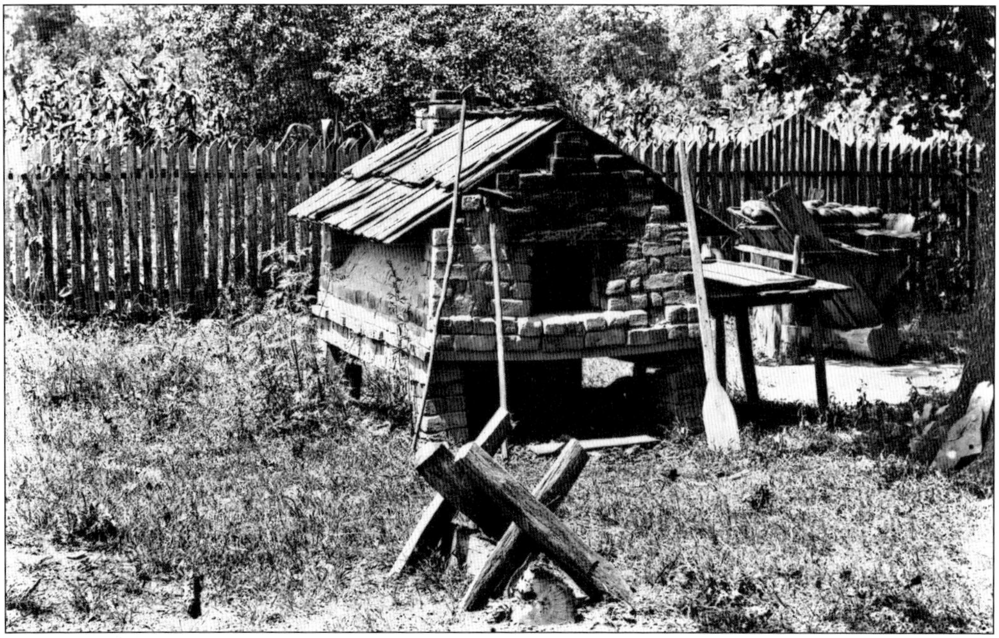

Bake ovens like this one were used in Moravian communities for the baking of lovefeast rolls and other foods. This photograph, likely taken in Bethania, shows a bake oven as it sat in the early 20th century. Apparently it was still in use as a sheet of baked rolls can be seen on the right. (Collection of Old Salem Museums & Gardens.)

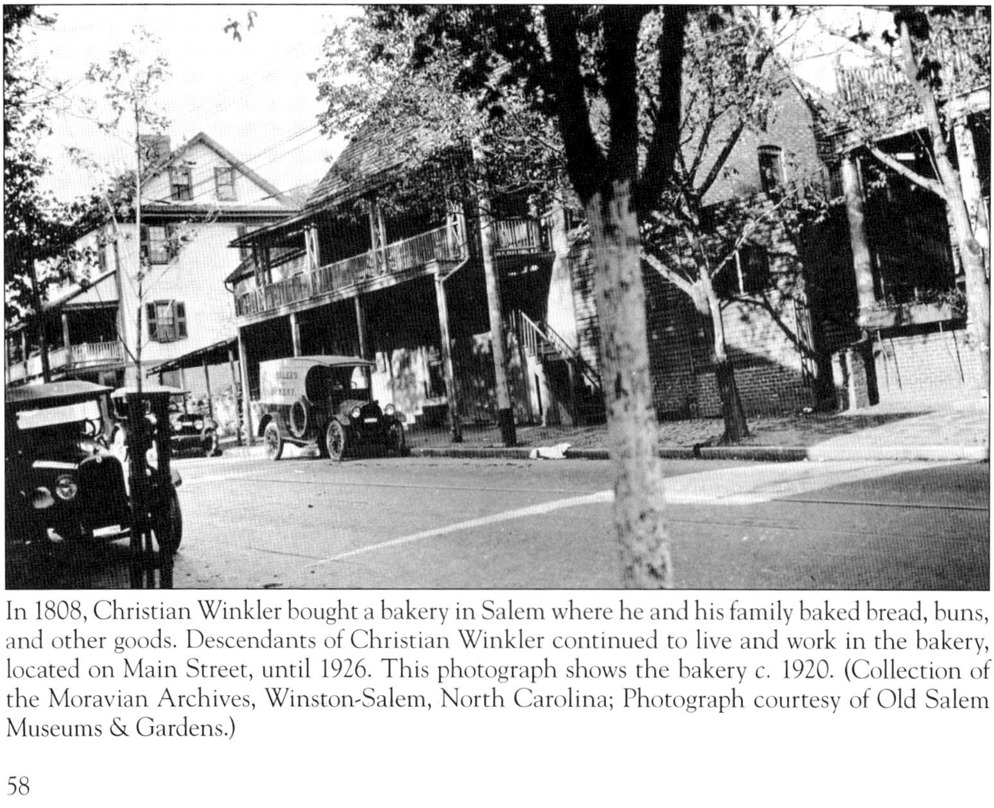

In 1808, Christian Winkler bought a bakery in Salem where he and his family baked bread, buns, and other goods. Descendants of Christian Winkler continued to live and work in the bakery, located on Main Street, until 1926. This photograph shows the bakery c. 1920. (Collection of the Moravian Archives, Winston-Salem, North Carolina; Photograph courtesy of Old Salem Museums & Gardens.)

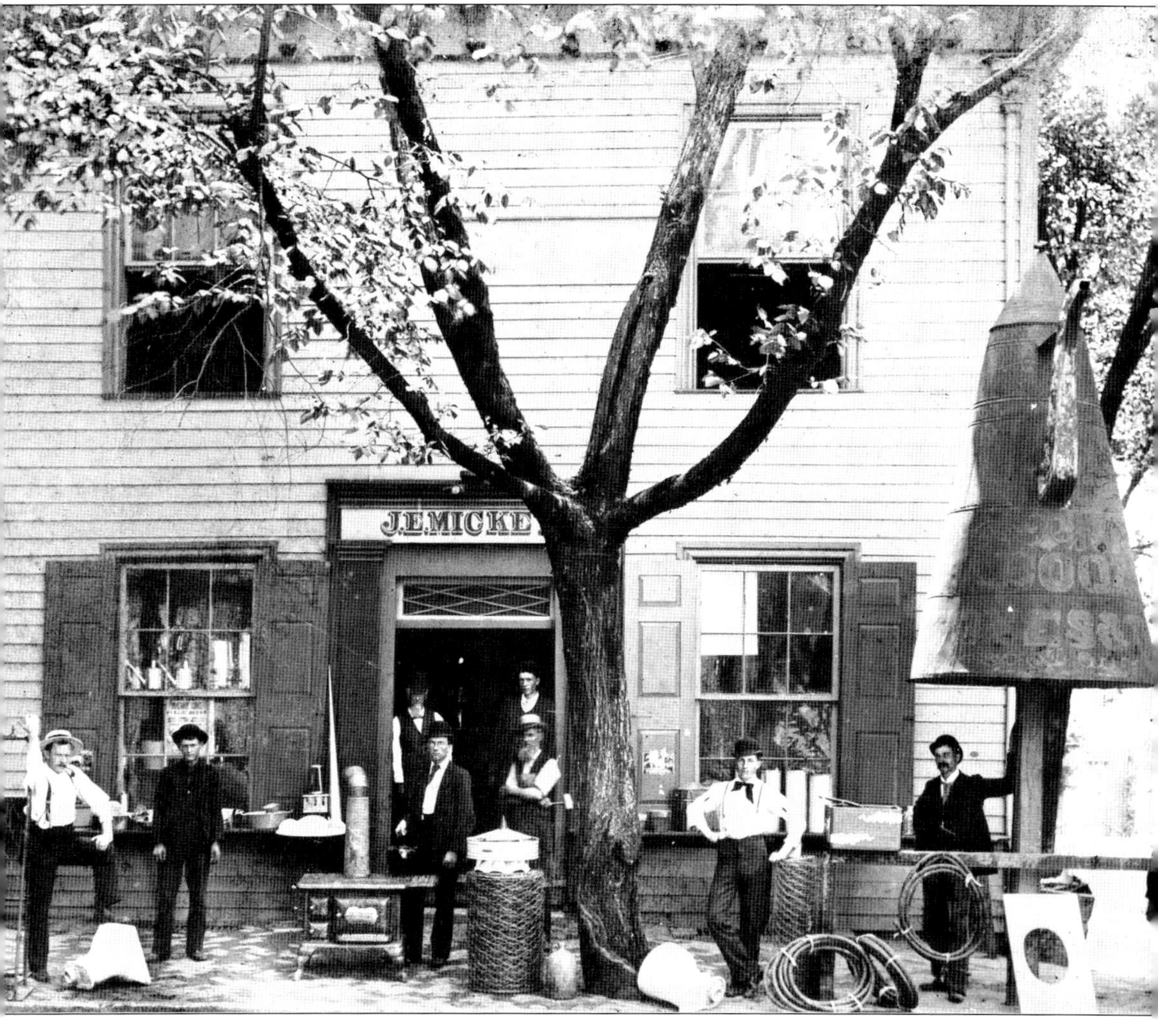

The tin shop of Julius E. Mickey was photographed *c.* 1895 by Edmund V. Patterson. Julius Mickey (bottom right) and his brother Samuel (top left) can be seen standing in the doorway. The large coffeepot, one of Winston-Salem's best-known landmarks, was made by the two brothers in 1858 as their shop sign. About 1960, the shop was claimed by Interstate 40 (now Business 40) and the coffeepot was moved to its current location at the intersection of Main Street and Old Salem Road. (Collection of Old Salem Museums & Gardens.)

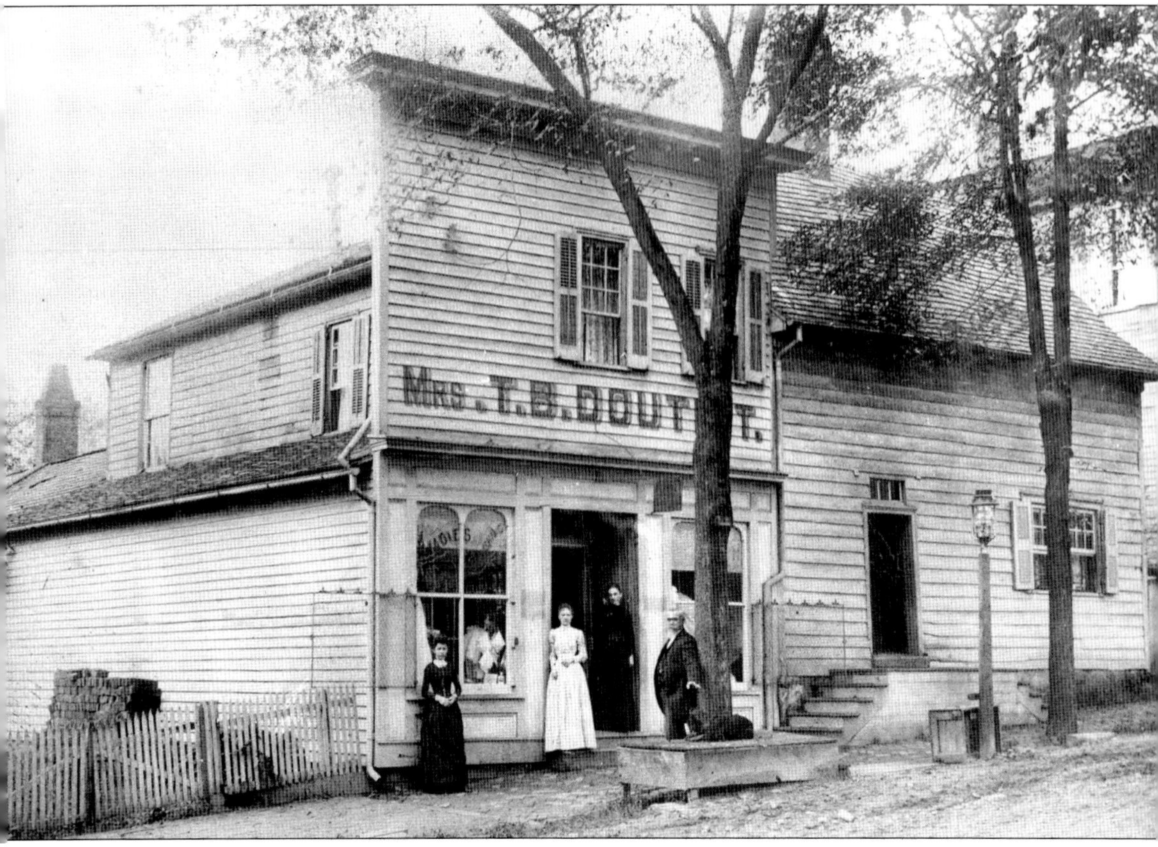

Mrs. T. B. Douthit (Julia C. Jenkins) began operating a millinery and fancy goods store near the northwest corner of Main and Academy Streets in Salem around 1867. This photograph shows her store *c.* 1890. Standing in front of the store are, from left to right, Annie Strupe, Mattie Winkler Crist, Julia Douthit, Thomas Douthit, and Bravo the dog. (Private collection; Photograph courtesy of Old Salem Museums & Gardens.)

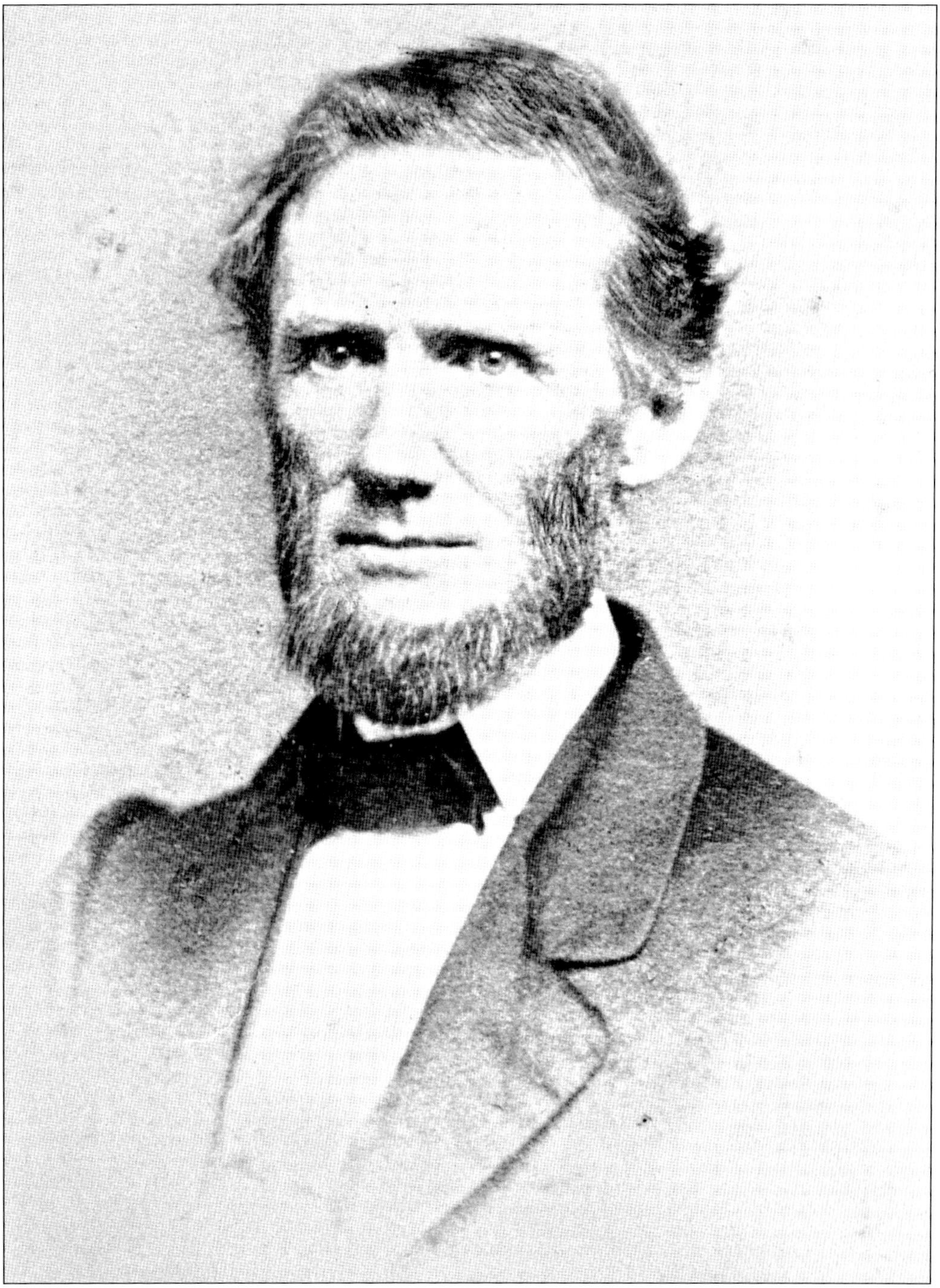

Francis Levin Fries, seen in this *c.* 1860 photograph, was an industrialist who operated a successful wool and cotton mill on New Shallowford Street, present-day Brookstown Avenue, in Salem. Fries also taught in the Salem Boys' School, oversaw the building of Main Hall at Salem Academy and College, was active in the Moravian Church, was a promoter and director of a North Carolina railroad, served on numerous county commissions, and was once mayor of Salem. (Collection of Old Salem Museums & Gardens.)

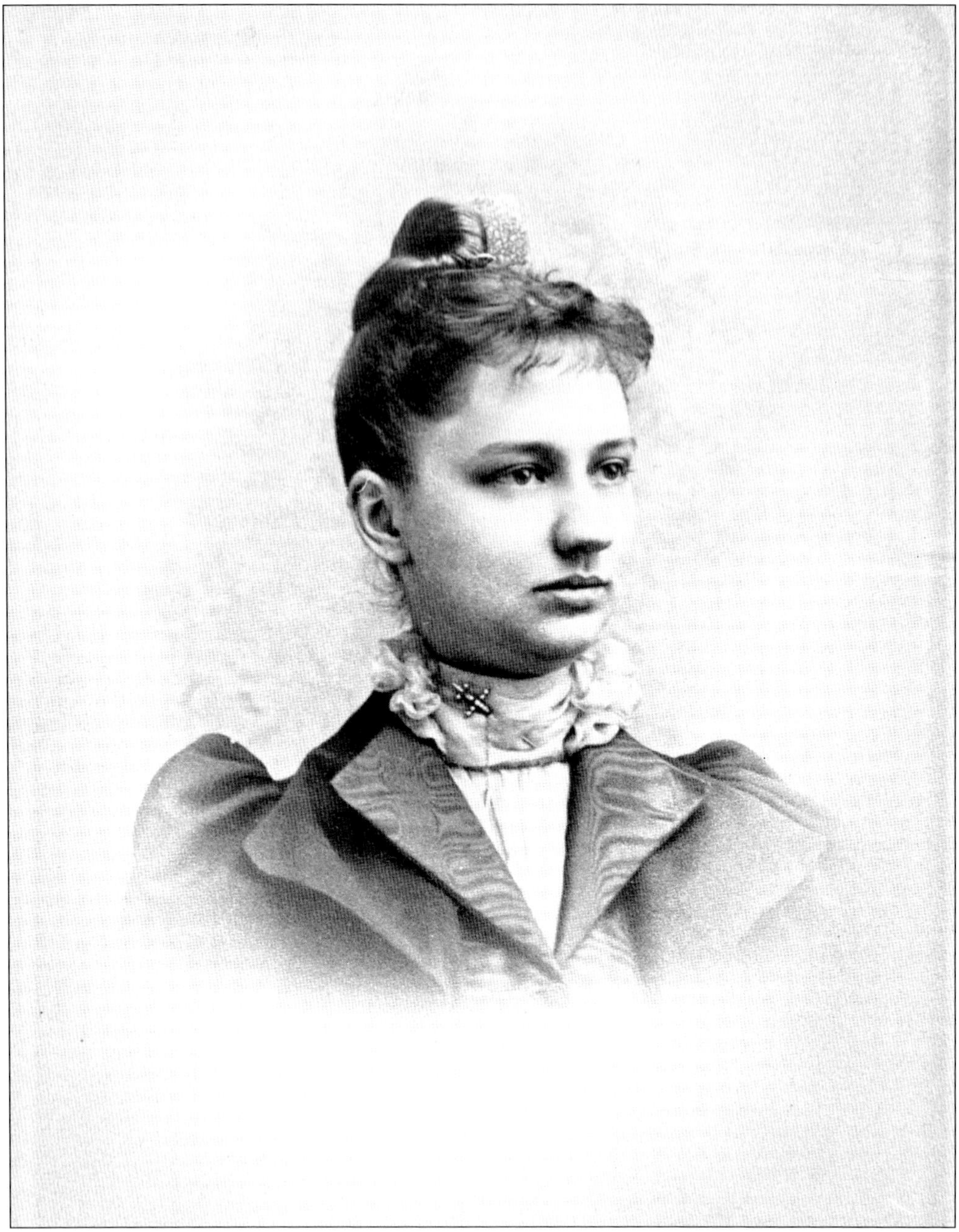

Born in Salem, Adelaide Lisetta Fries dedicated her life to the preservation of the history of her church and community. She received both her bachelor and master of arts degrees at Salem Academy and College. She also received honorary doctor of letters degrees from the Moravian College, Wake Forest College, and the University of North Carolina. Appointed archivist for the Moravian Church, Winston-Salem, in 1911, she held the position for almost 40 years. Her greatest contributions to Salem history include the translation of the German diaries of Moravian churches in the area and the publication of *The Road to Salem*, for which she was awarded the Mayflower Cup in 1944 for best work of nonfiction by a North Carolina author. Adelaide is seen *c.* 1895 in a photograph taken by Sylvester E. Hough. (Collection of Old Salem Museums & Gardens.)

Elias A. Vogler was a man of many talents. Best known as a merchant, Elias also served Salem as an artist, justice of the peace, mayor, surveyor, and architect. He also served on various county committees and was active in the Moravian Church. In 1867, Elias built his new store on Main Street in Salem, where goods and wares of all kinds could be purchased. The store is seen in this *c.* 1870 photograph. (Collection of Old Salem Museums & Gardens.)

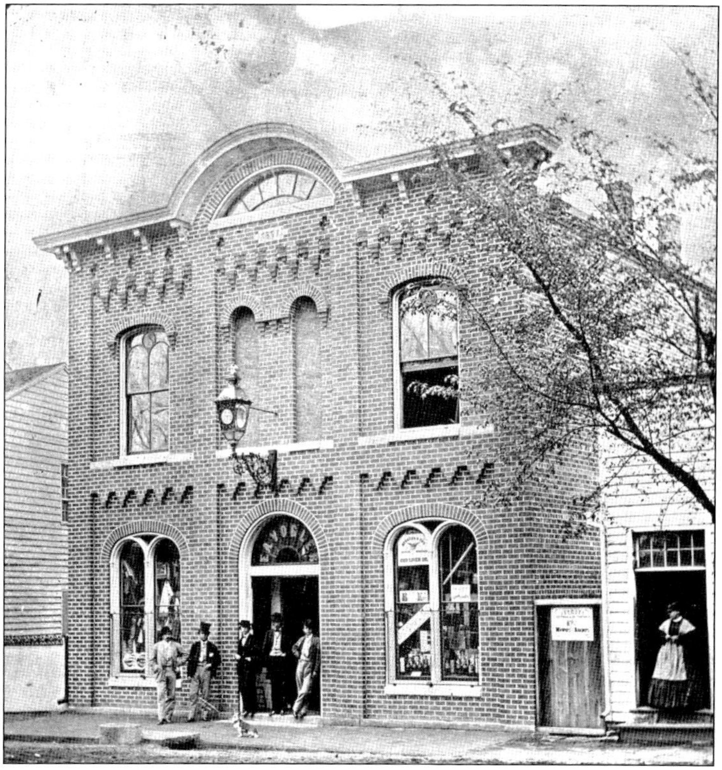

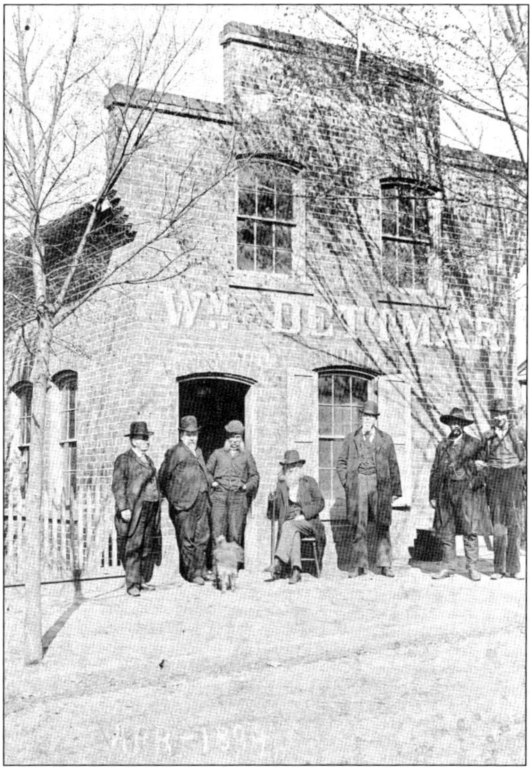

William Dettmar, a native of Germany, arrived in Salem in 1850. There he went to work with Timothy Vogler, where he became a skilled gunsmith. Eighteen years later, he built his own gunsmith shop, seen in this 1894 photograph, on the north end of Main Street in Salem. The men standing in front of the shop are, from left to right, William Dettmar, Dr. John F. Shaffner Sr., ? Lichtenthaler, three unidentified, and Thomas C. Hege. (Collection of Old Salem Museums & Gardens.)

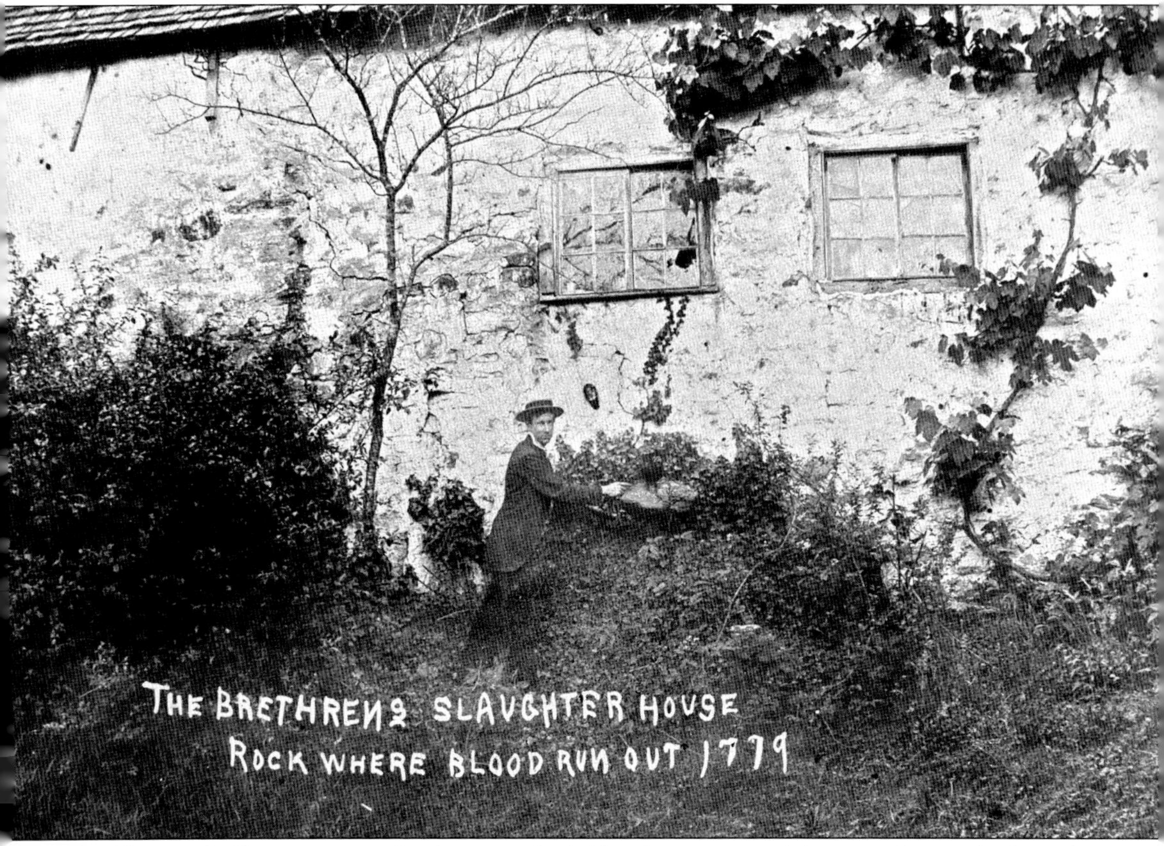

Thomas C. Hege points at the drain in which blood was removed, by way of a trough, from the interior of the slaughterhouse in Salem *c.* 1895. The slaughterhouse, built in 1784, was a major industrial building in Salem. The building was used for the slaughter of cattle until 1803. In 1816, Karsten Peterson converted the building for use as a furniture-making shop. His descendants continued that business until the 1890s. In 1897, part of the building collapsed, and in 1917, it was demolished. (Collection of the Wachovia Historical Society; Photograph courtesy of Old Salem Museums & Gardens.)

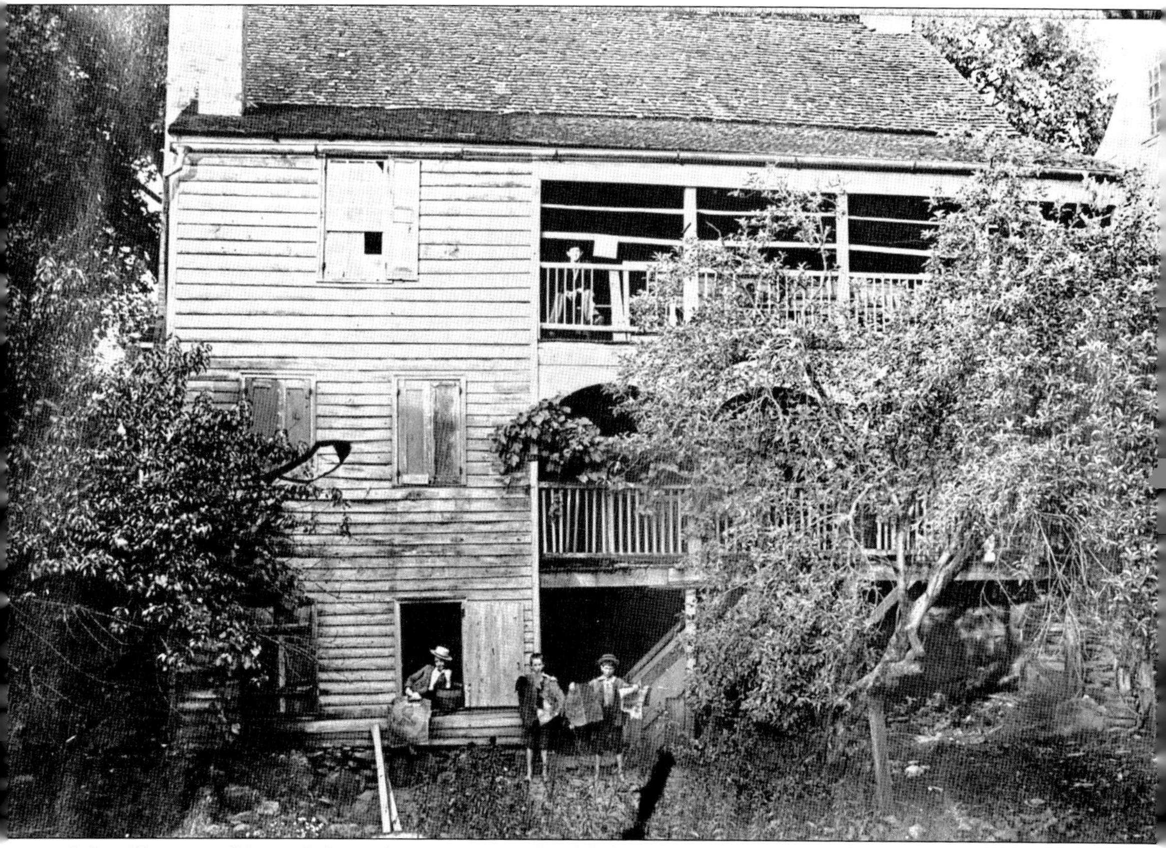

John Christian Blum, Salem's first printer and publisher, built this house in 1815 on Main Street in Salem. Financial difficulties, however, did not allow him to keep it. Levi Blum, John's son, purchased the house in 1854 and continued the printing business with his brother, Edward. The back of the Blum House is seen in this *c.* 1900 photograph where young boys appear to hold old newspapers. (Collection of the Moravian Archives, Winston-Salem, North Carolina; Photograph courtesy of Old Salem Museums & Gardens.)

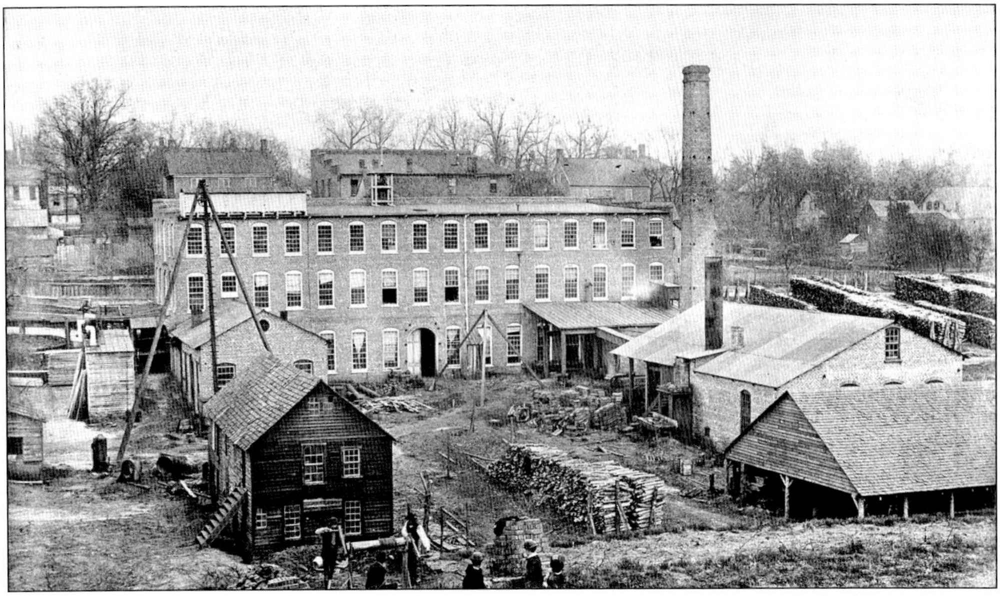

Around 1867, Constantine A. Hege began an iron works business in a small shed in Salem. By 1882, demand for his products, which included engines, wood planers, saw mills, and a general line of woodworking machinery, had increased so much that he found it necessary to expand and erected a three-story building on Salt Street at the cost of about $30,000. That building, the Salem Iron Works, is seen in this *c.* 1890 photograph. (Collection of Old Salem Museums & Gardens.)

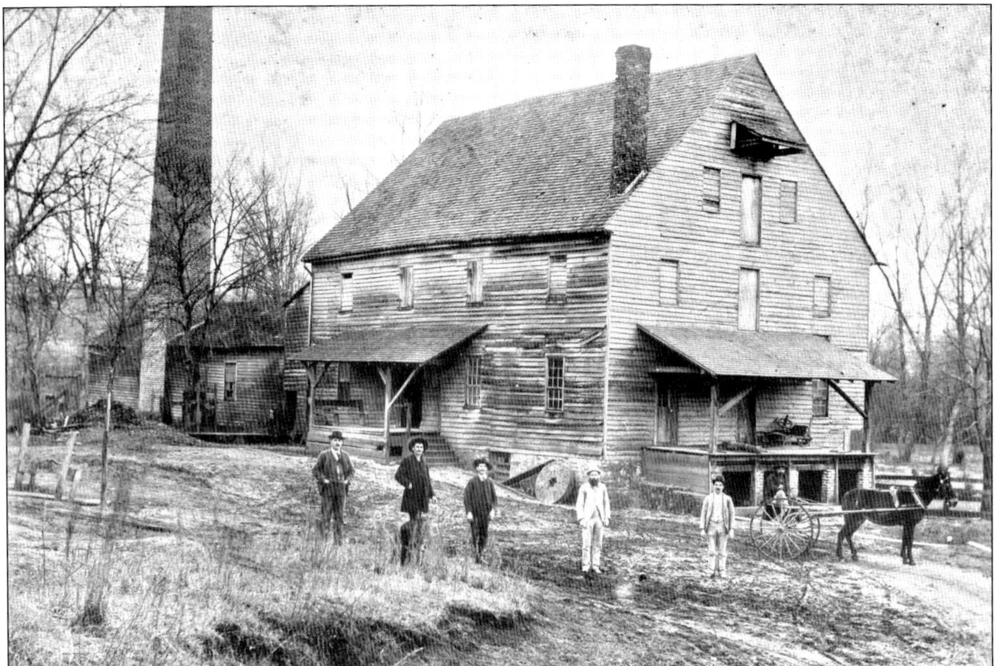

The photographer Frank E. Hege documented the Salem Mill, where corn and wheat were ground, only a few years prior to the 1902 fire. (Collection of Old Salem Museums & Gardens.)

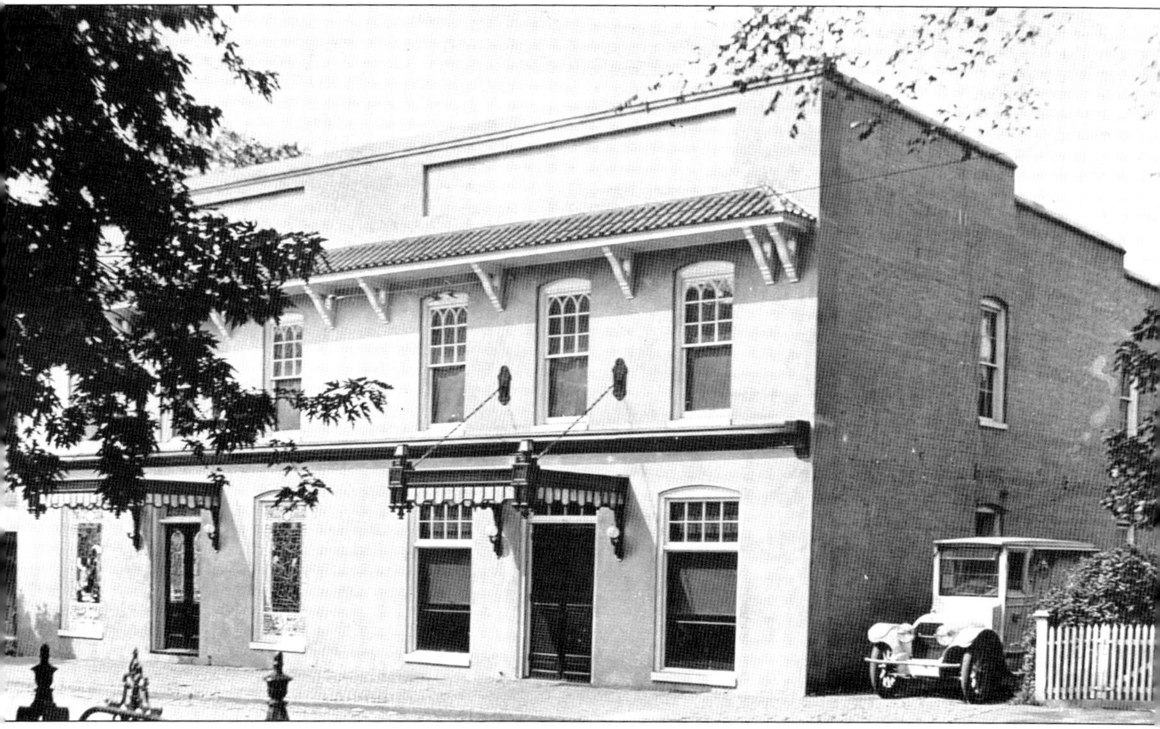

Frank Vogler became a partner in his father's undertaking and furniture business, A. C. Vogler and Son, in 1885. Years later, he graduated from the Clarke's School of Embalming in Cincinnati and held several positions in organizations relating to embalming and the funeral business. In 1907, the furniture line of the business was dropped, and by 1910, Frank's sons had joined the business. The name of the company was then changed to Frank Vogler and Sons. Their establishment, which still stands on South Main Street in Winston-Salem, is seen in this photograph taken by Irvin T. Rominger in 1918. (Collection of the Moravian Archives, Winston-Salem, North Carolina; Photograph courtesy of Old Salem Museums & Gardens.)

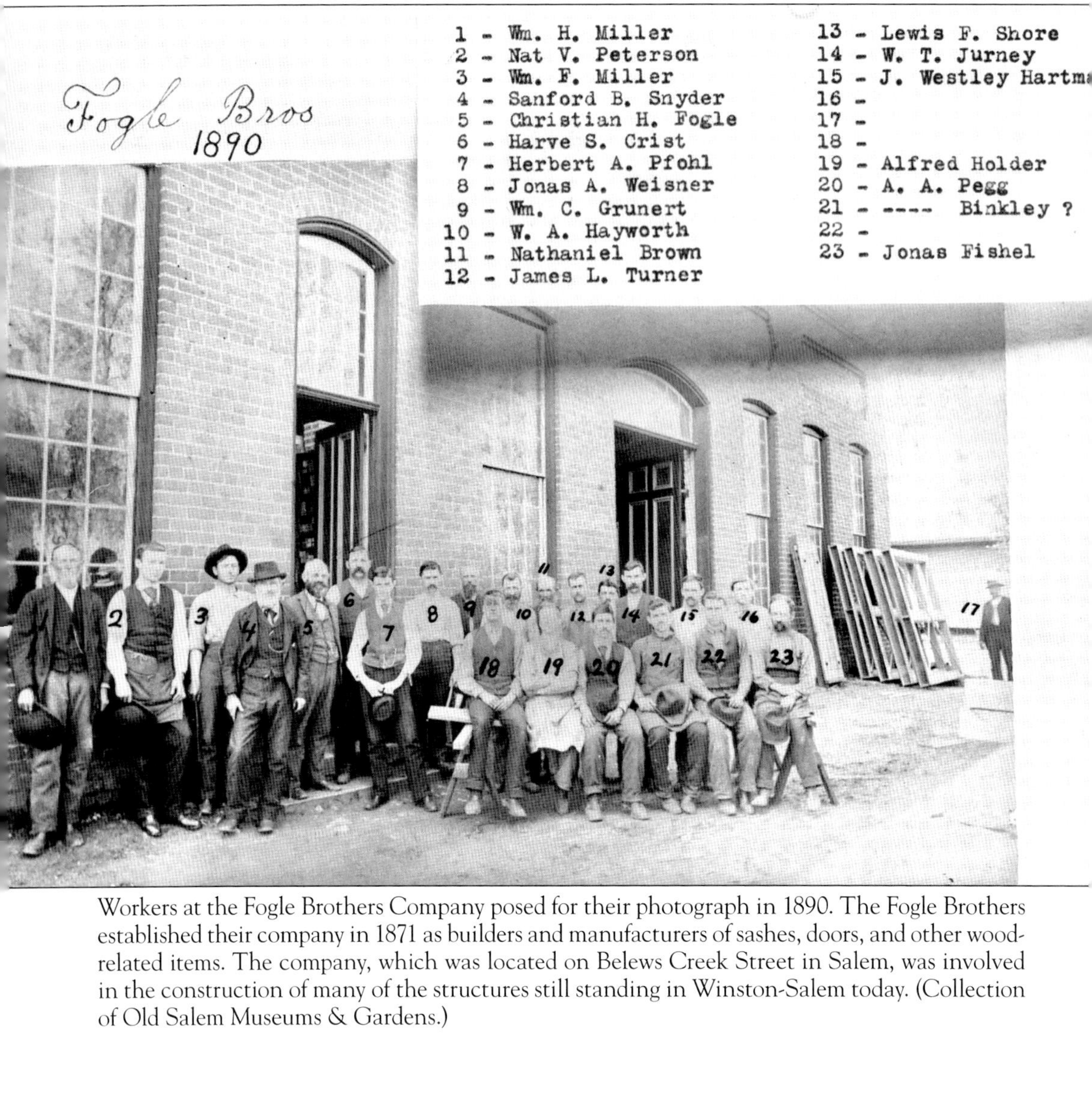

Workers at the Fogle Brothers Company posed for their photograph in 1890. The Fogle Brothers established their company in 1871 as builders and manufacturers of sashes, doors, and other wood-related items. The company, which was located on Belews Creek Street in Salem, was involved in the construction of many of the structures still standing in Winston-Salem today. (Collection of Old Salem Museums & Gardens.)

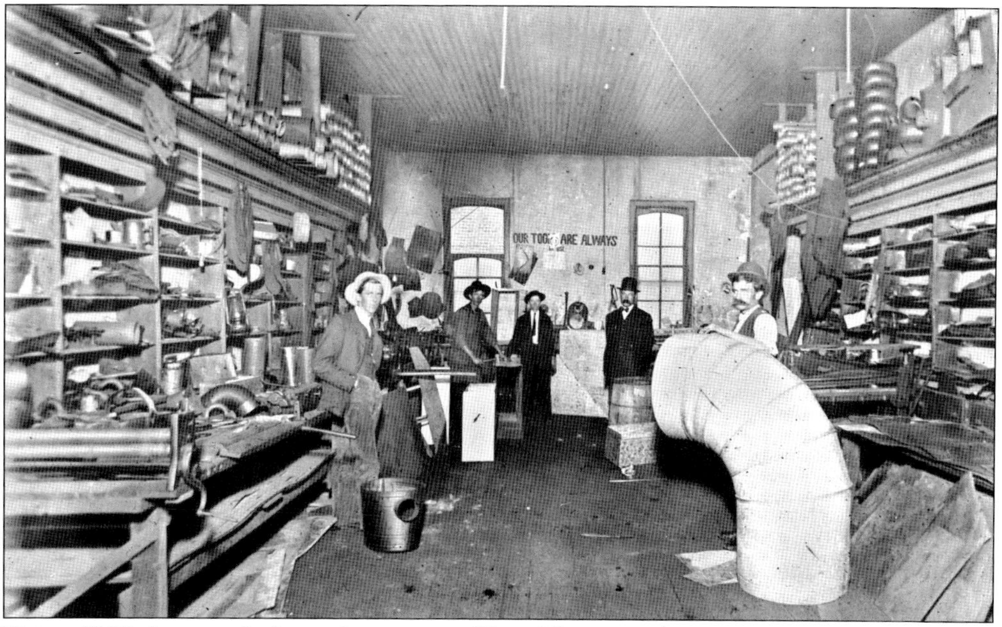

This c. 1900 photograph shows the interior of Peter Blum's tin shop in Winston. It is not known if this photograph was taken at his Liberty Street business or at his later Third Street shop. (Collection of the Wachovia Historical Society; Photograph courtesy of Old Salem Museums & Gardens.)

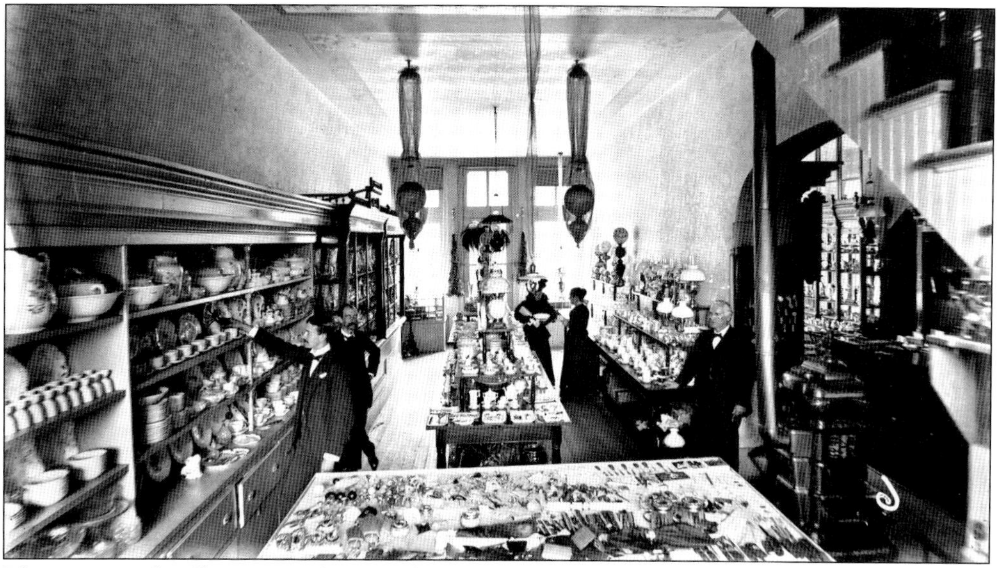

The interior of William T. Vogler's jewelry store, which was located on Main Street in Winston, is seen in this 1899 photograph. Vogler sold clocks, watches, jewelry, optical goods, and china and also offered engraving and repair services. Harry W. Peterson stands at left with his arm extended, Henry E. Vogler stands behind Peterson, and William T. Vogler stands at right. Harry Peterson began working as an errand boy at Vogler's store after finishing his studies at the Salem Boys' School. He later became an expert watch repairman. Harry worked at Vogler's store through three generations of the Vogler family. (Collection of the Wachovia Historical Society; Photograph courtesy of Old Salem Museums & Gardens.)

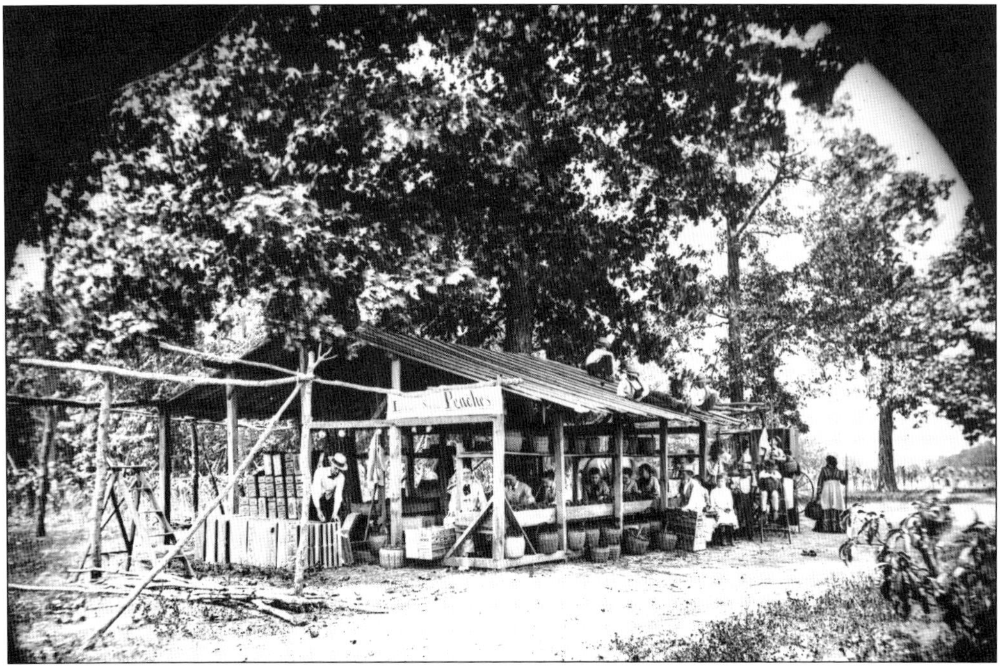

Henry Alexander Lineback, a photographer in Salem, documented this view of "Lineback's Selected Peaches," c. 1885. The exact location of the peach stand is unknown. (Collection of Old Salem Museums & Gardens.)

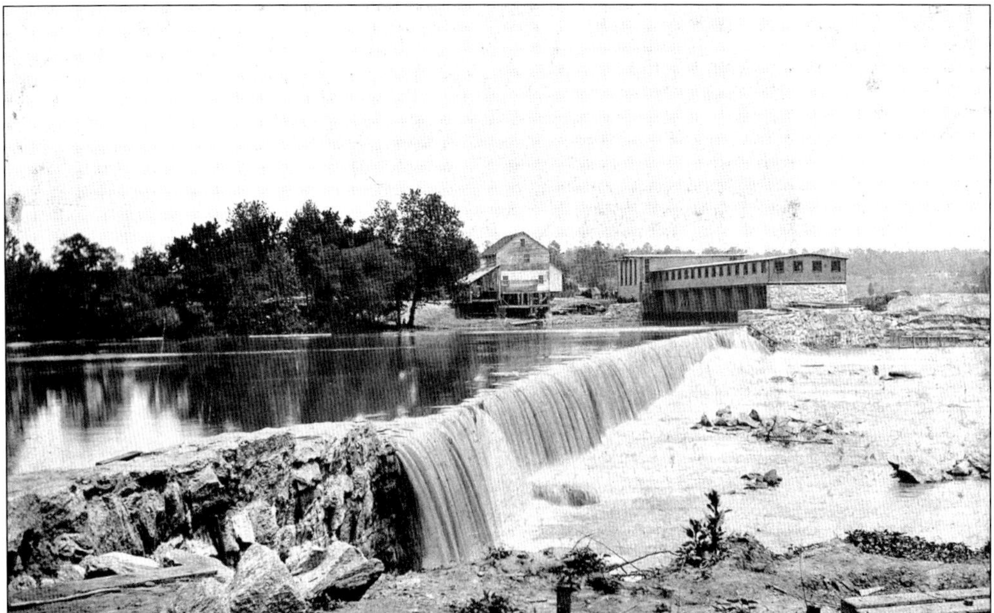

Idol's hydroelectric generation station was begun by Henry Elias Fries and put into operation by the Fries Manufacturing and Power Company in 1898. The station, located on the Yadkin River in Forsyth County, supplied the towns of Salem and Winston with power for their mills, factories, street lighting, and electric railway. The station is seen in this photograph taken c. 1900. (Collection of Old Salem Museums & Gardens.)

Four

At Play

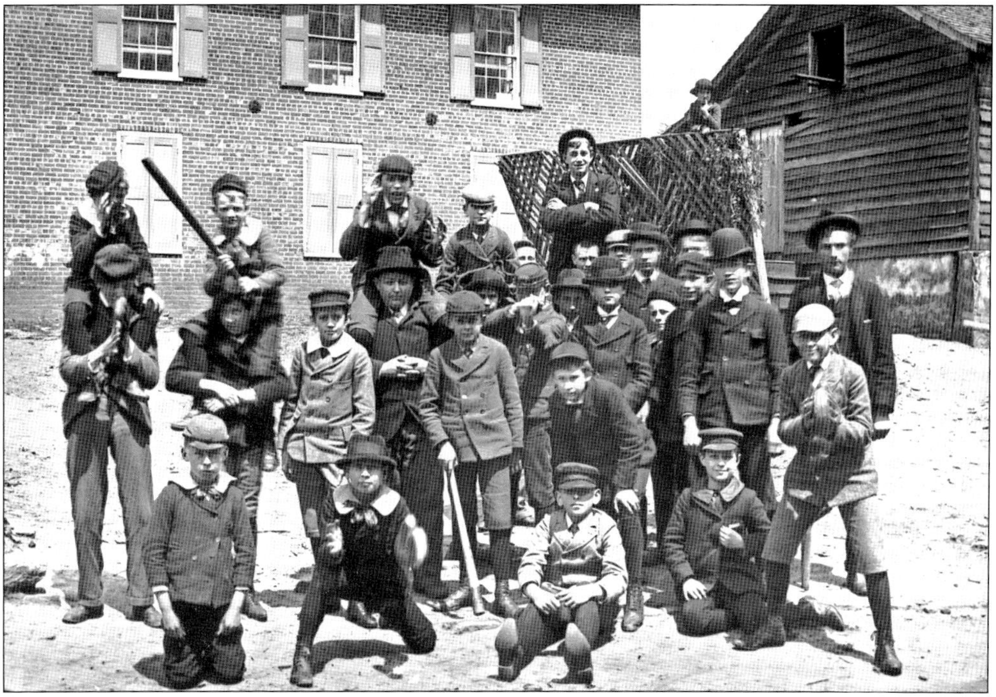

Salem Boys' School students playfully posed for their photograph in the rear yard of their school building c. 1895. (Collection of the Wachovia Historical Society; Photograph courtesy of Old Salem Museums & Gardens.)

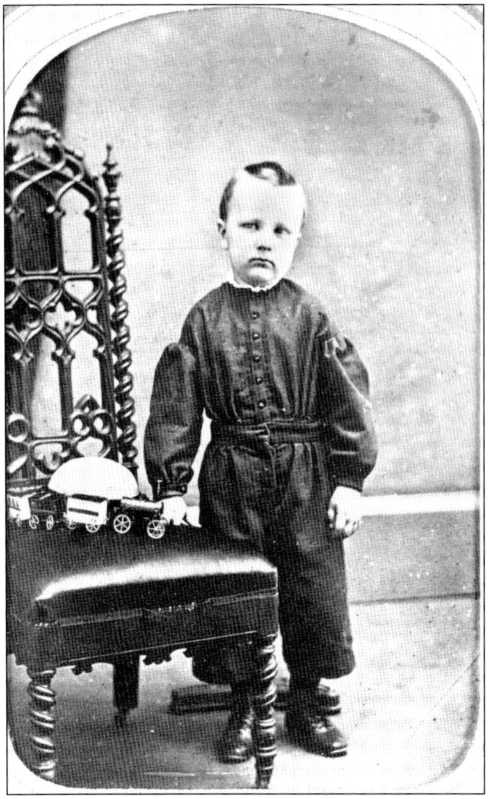

Emil de Schweinitz (top) and his sister Anna Paulina (bottom) were photographed, along with their toys, in the Salem studio of Henry Alexander Lineback, *c.* 1868. (Collection of Old Salem Museums & Gardens.)

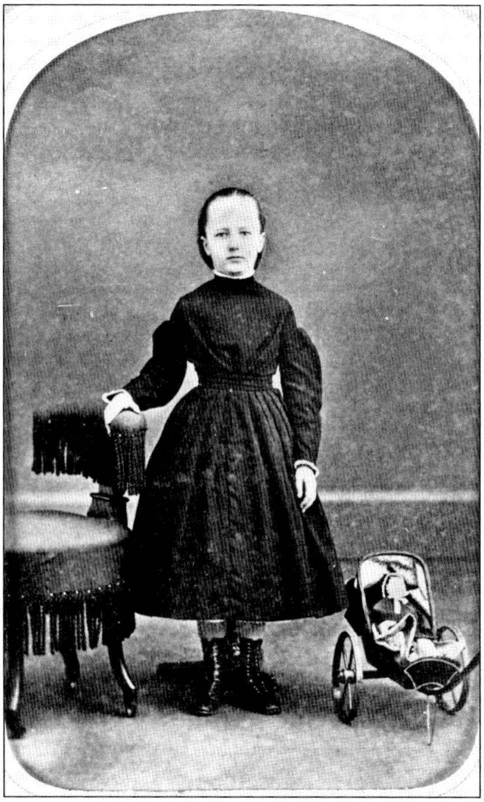

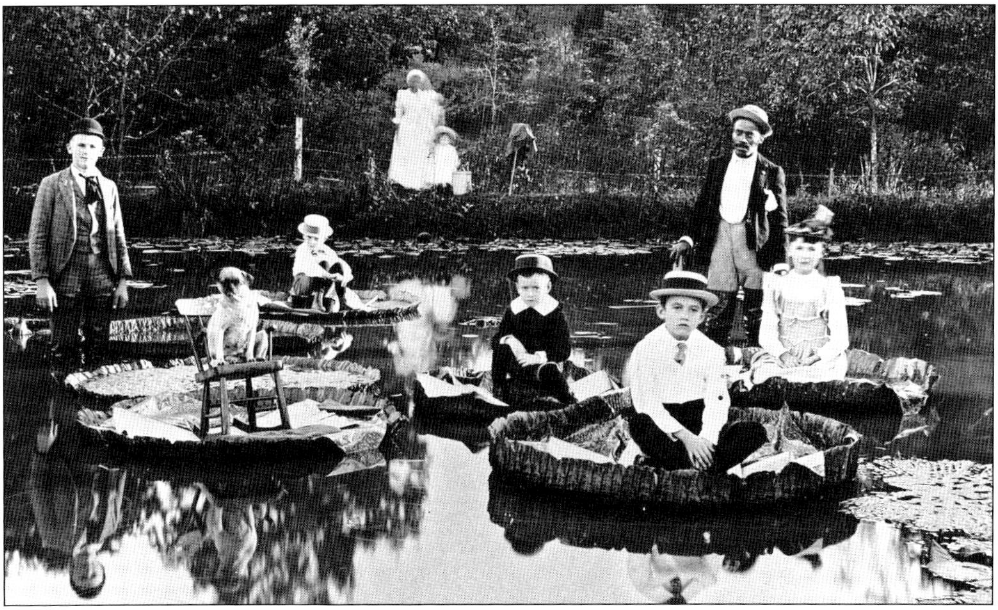

Four children, and a dog in a rocking chair, are seen testing the weight limits of Dr. Henry T. Bahnson's giant lily pads. Dr. Bahnson grew these remarkable specimens in a pond behind his house, located on Church Street in Salem. Thomas S. Wright, the African American man standing to the right, and his wife, Isabella, seen standing on the bank, were both employees of Dr. Bahnson. Sylvester E. Hough took this photograph *c.* 1890. (Collection of Old Salem Museums & Gardens.)

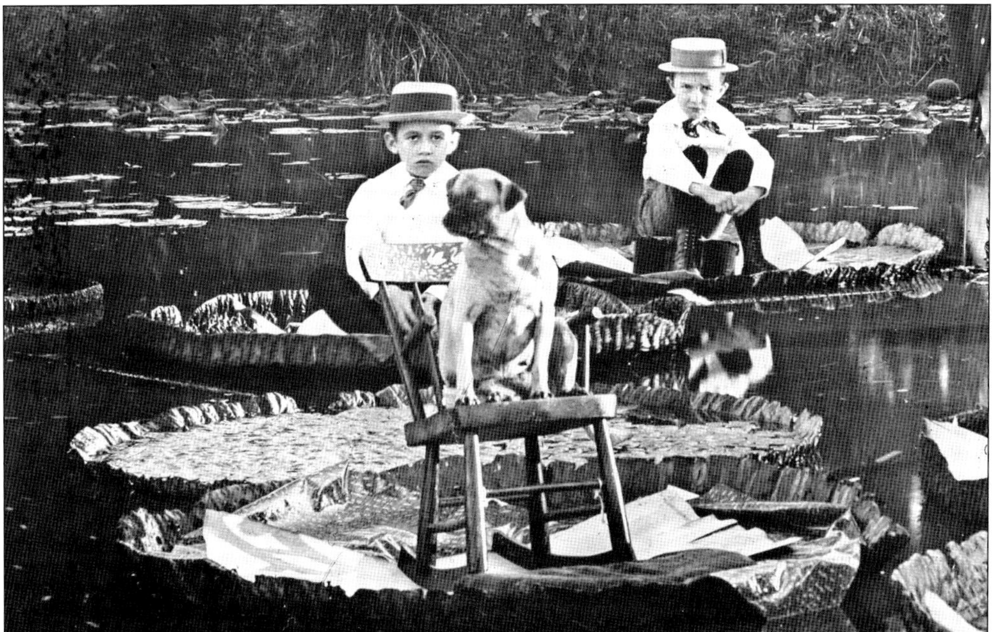

Another photograph of Dr. Bahnson's lily pond, taken on the same day as the above view, shows a detailed look at the boys and the dog in a different seating arrangement. (Collection of the Wachovia Historical Society; Photograph courtesy of Old Salem Museums & Gardens.)

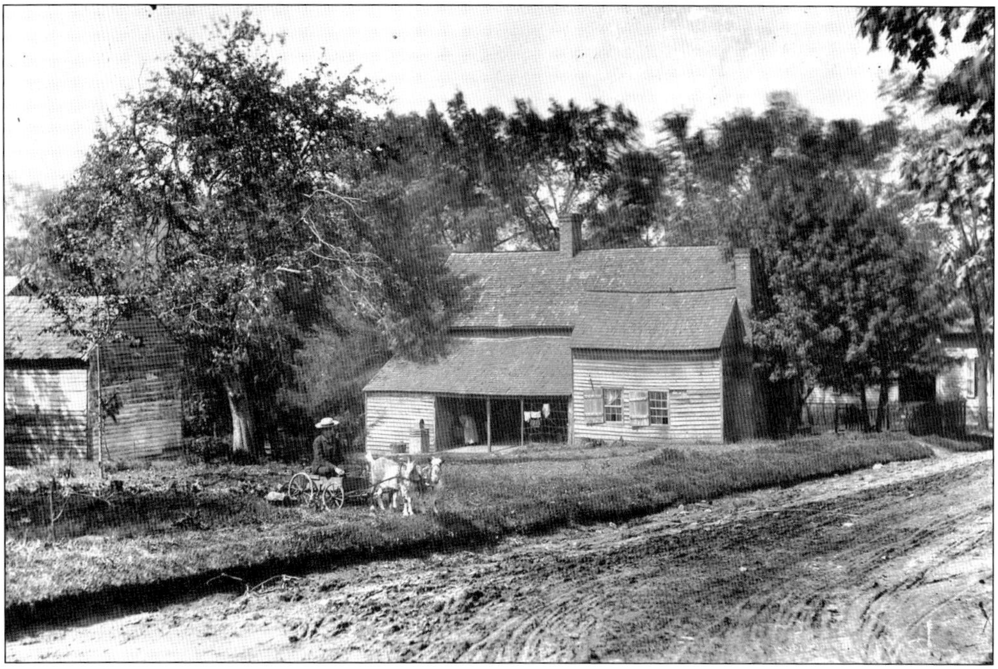

Goats Nellie and Tony took William "Willie" Cooper for a ride *c.* 1885 behind the Hauser House, which was located on the corner of Main and Cemetery Streets in Salem. (Collection of the Wachovia Historical Society; Photograph courtesy of Old Salem Museums & Gardens.)

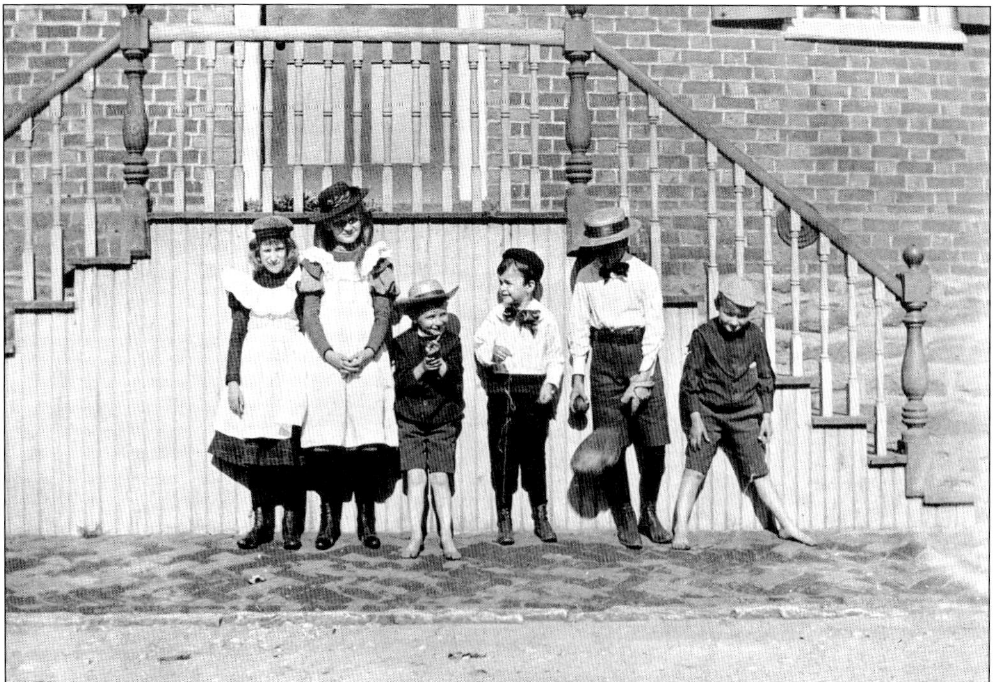

A group of children, seen standing in front of the Vierling House in Salem, were photographed in the early 20th century. (Collection of Old Salem Museums & Gardens.)

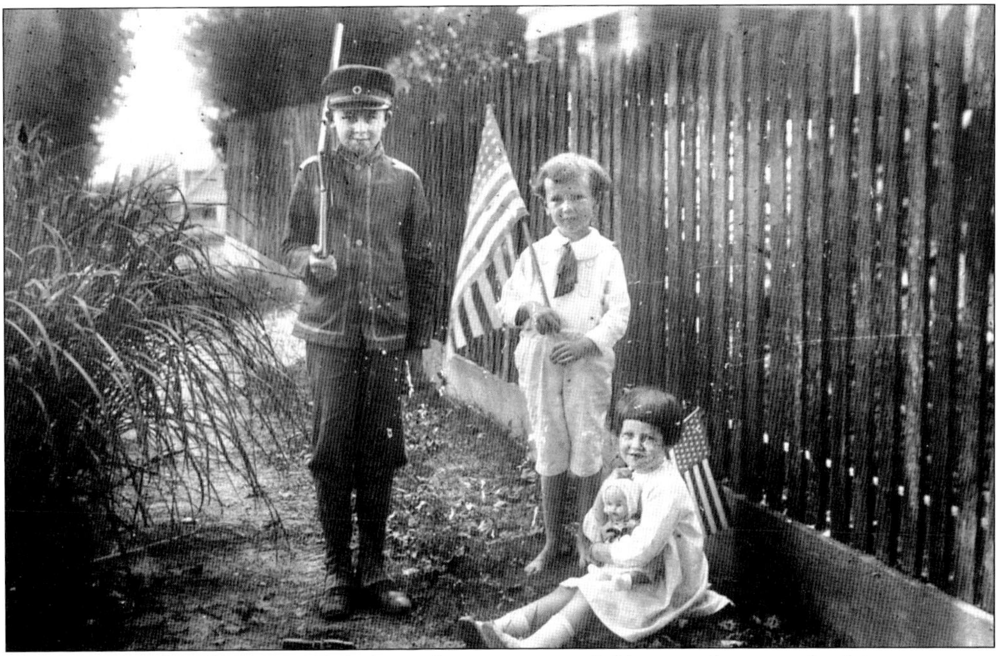

This photograph, taken 1918–1919 shows three patriotic children on the grounds of the parsonage at Clemmons Moravian Church. The children are, from left to right, Harry Edward Peterson, Wilson Lamb, and Josephine Henrietta Peterson. (Collection of the Wachovia Historical Society; Photograph courtesy of Old Salem Museums & Gardens.)

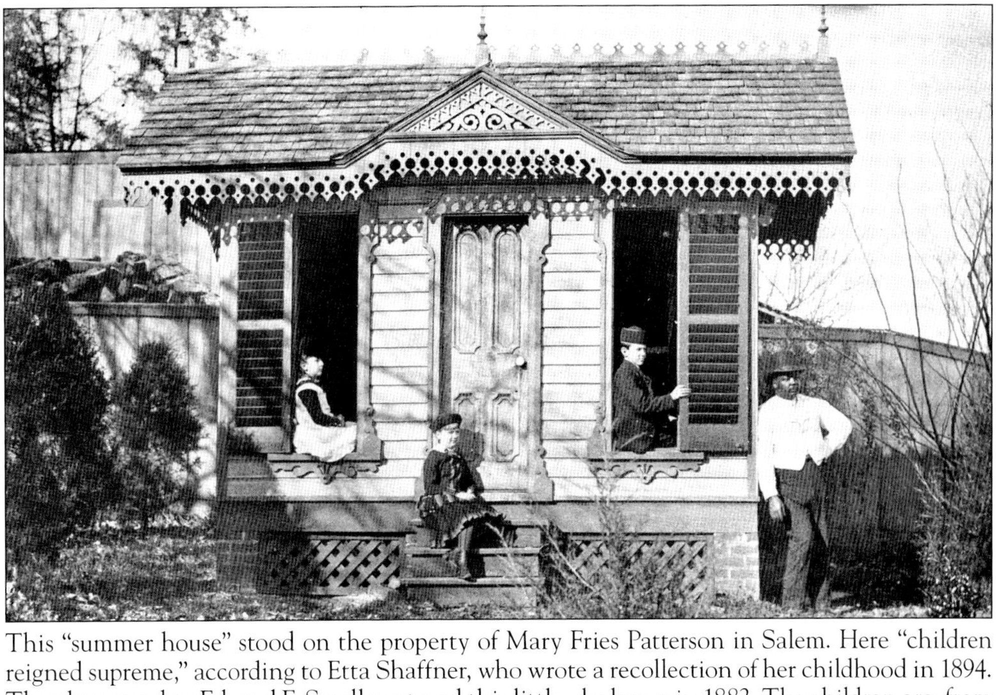

This "summer house" stood on the property of Mary Fries Patterson in Salem. Here "children reigned supreme," according to Etta Shaffner, who wrote a recollection of her childhood in 1894. The photographer Edward F. Small captured this little playhouse in 1882. The children are, from left to right, Mary Elizabeth Fries, Adelaide Fries, and Drew Patterson. (Collection of Old Salem Museums & Gardens.)

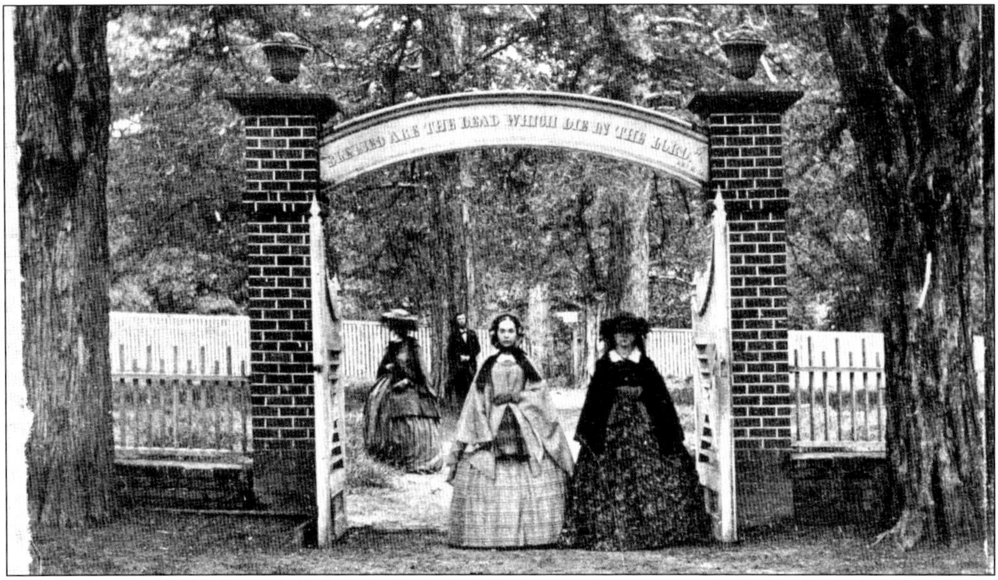

This photograph, taken *c.* 1865, shows an entrance to God's Acre at Salem. The cemetery was, and continues to be, a popular spot for the taking of photographs and leisurely walks. (Collection of Old Salem Museums & Gardens.)

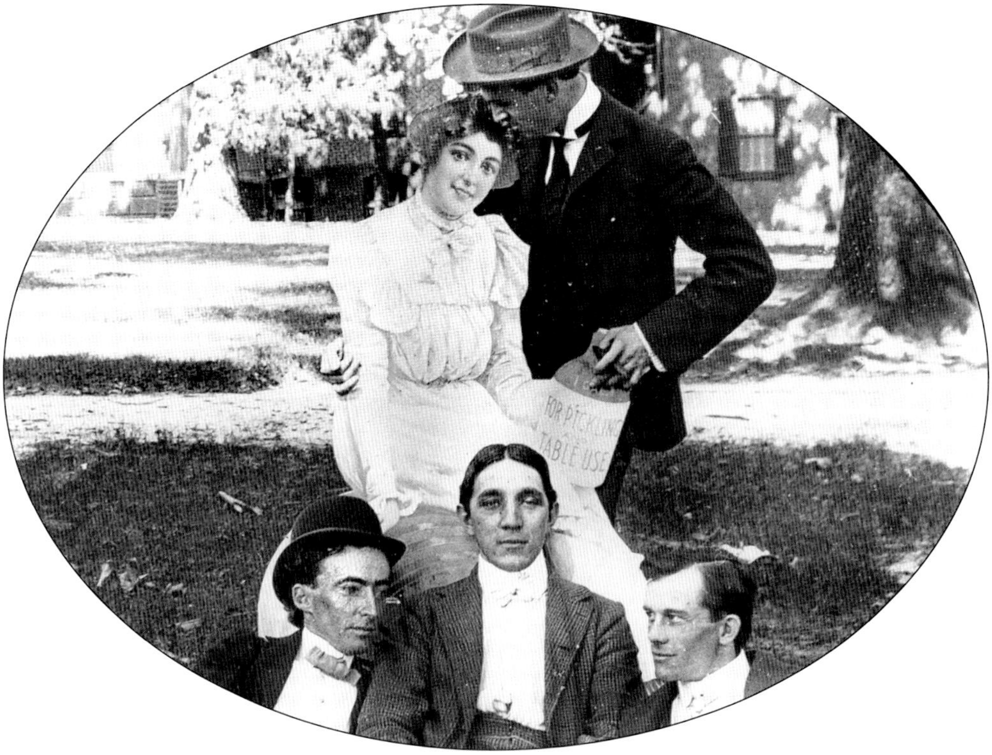

On July 4, 1901, these four young men relaxed in the Salem Square along with "one girl." Look closely and you will notice that the girl, along with her jug of "pickling," is made of cardboard. (Collection of the Wachovia Historical Society; Photograph courtesy of Old Salem Museums & Gardens.)

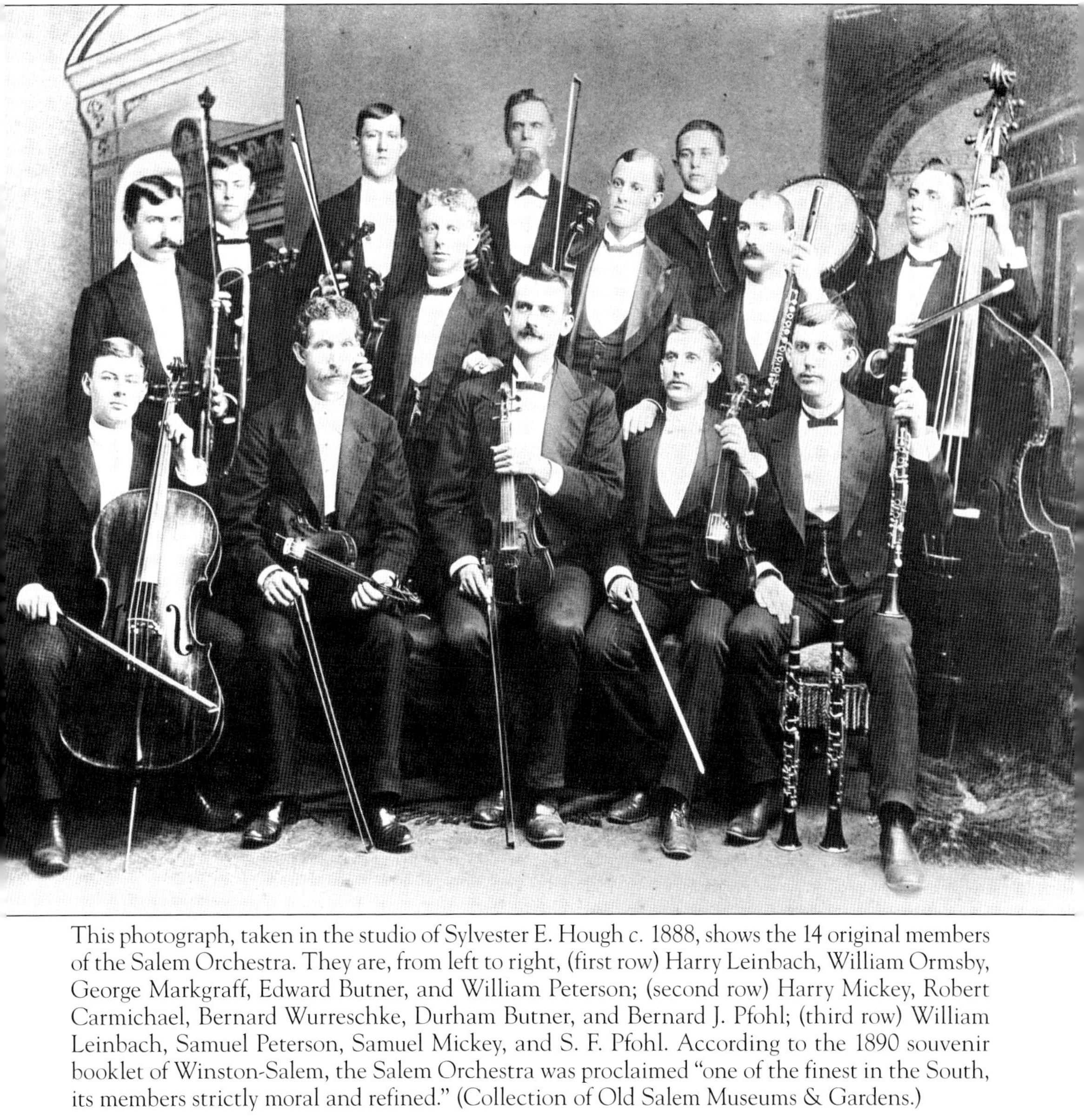

This photograph, taken in the studio of Sylvester E. Hough *c.* 1888, shows the 14 original members of the Salem Orchestra. They are, from left to right, (first row) Harry Leinbach, William Ormsby, George Markgraff, Edward Butner, and William Peterson; (second row) Harry Mickey, Robert Carmichael, Bernard Wurreschke, Durham Butner, and Bernard J. Pfohl; (third row) William Leinbach, Samuel Peterson, Samuel Mickey, and S. F. Pfohl. According to the 1890 souvenir booklet of Winston-Salem, the Salem Orchestra was proclaimed "one of the finest in the South, its members strictly moral and refined." (Collection of Old Salem Museums & Gardens.)

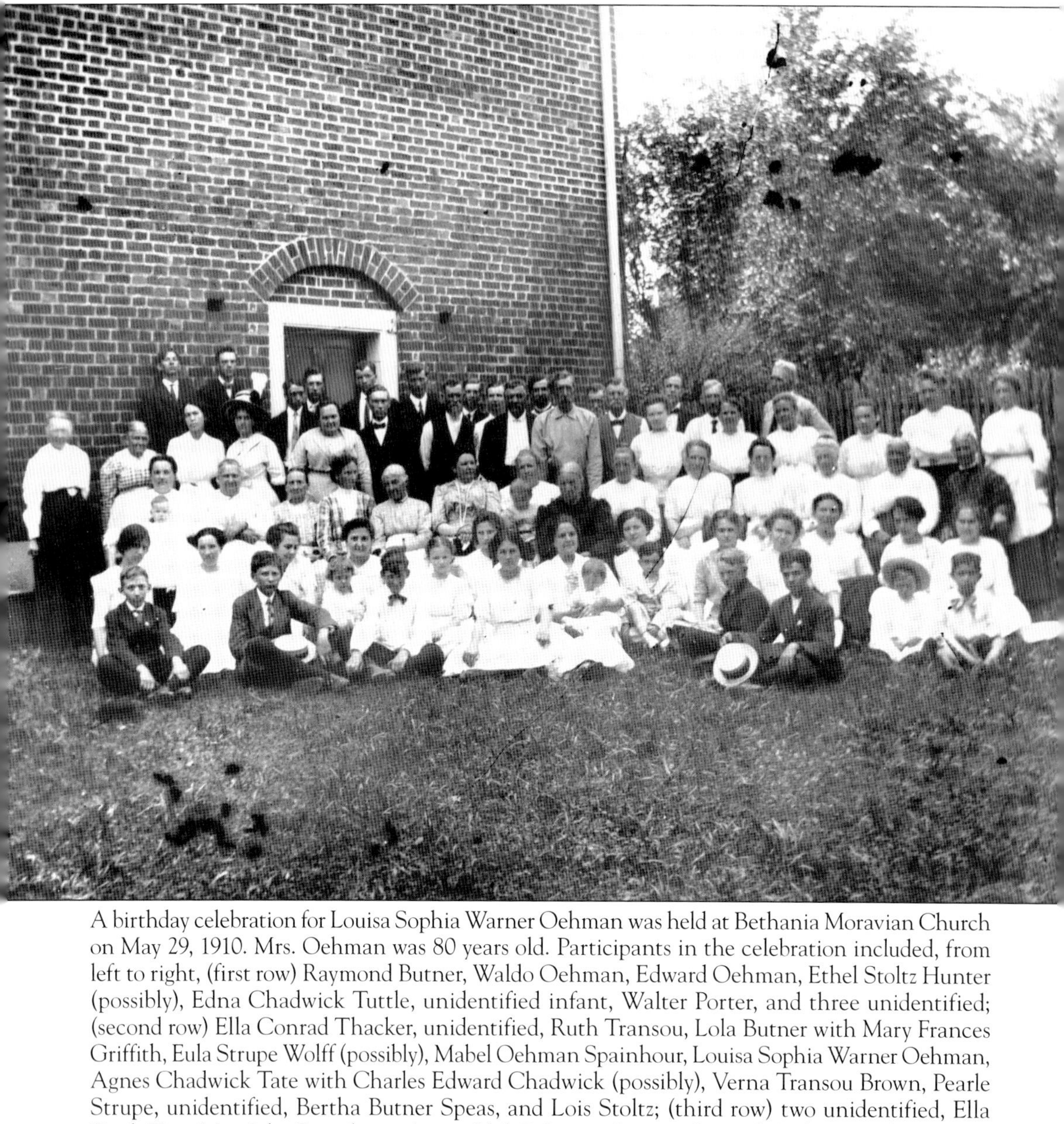

A birthday celebration for Louisa Sophia Warner Oehman was held at Bethania Moravian Church on May 29, 1910. Mrs. Oehman was 80 years old. Participants in the celebration included, from left to right, (first row) Raymond Butner, Waldo Oehman, Edward Oehman, Ethel Stoltz Hunter (possibly), Edna Chadwick Tuttle, unidentified infant, Walter Porter, and three unidentified; (second row) Ella Conrad Thacker, unidentified, Ruth Transou, Lola Butner with Mary Frances Griffith, Eula Strupe Wolff (possibly), Mabel Oehman Spainhour, Louisa Sophia Warner Oehman, Agnes Chadwick Tate with Charles Edward Chadwick (possibly), Verna Transou Brown, Pearle Strupe, unidentified, Bertha Butner Speas, and Lois Stoltz; (third row) two unidentified, Ella Doub Tise, Mrs. Jake Spainhour, Annie Idol Oehman, Joanna Conrad Grabs, ? Mickey, Luella Oehman Chadwick with unidentified, Alice Oehman Porter, Nora Livengood Flynt (possibly), unidentified, Dora Stoltz, Sarah Stoltz Butner, and Frances Grabs Transou (possibly); (fourth row) Martha Butner Sides, unidentified, Lessie Walker, Fannie Tise Nifong, Maude Stauber Stoltz, F. Walter Grabs, Jake Spainhour, John Chadwick, Augustus Oehman, George Porter, May Strupe Chadwick, Annie Moser Butner, Emma Greider Lehman, Minnie Grabs Strupe, Minnie Dull Conrad, and Rosa Conrad Grabs; (fifth row) Emory Cline, Lee Grubbs, Harold Butner, Ralph Oehman, Eugene Chadwick, Numa Spainhour, Roy Spainhour, Walter Strupe, Edwin T. Strupe, unidentified, Charles O. Chadwick, Robert O. Butner, and Egbert T. Lehman. (Private collection; Photograph courtesy of Old Salem Museums & Gardens.)

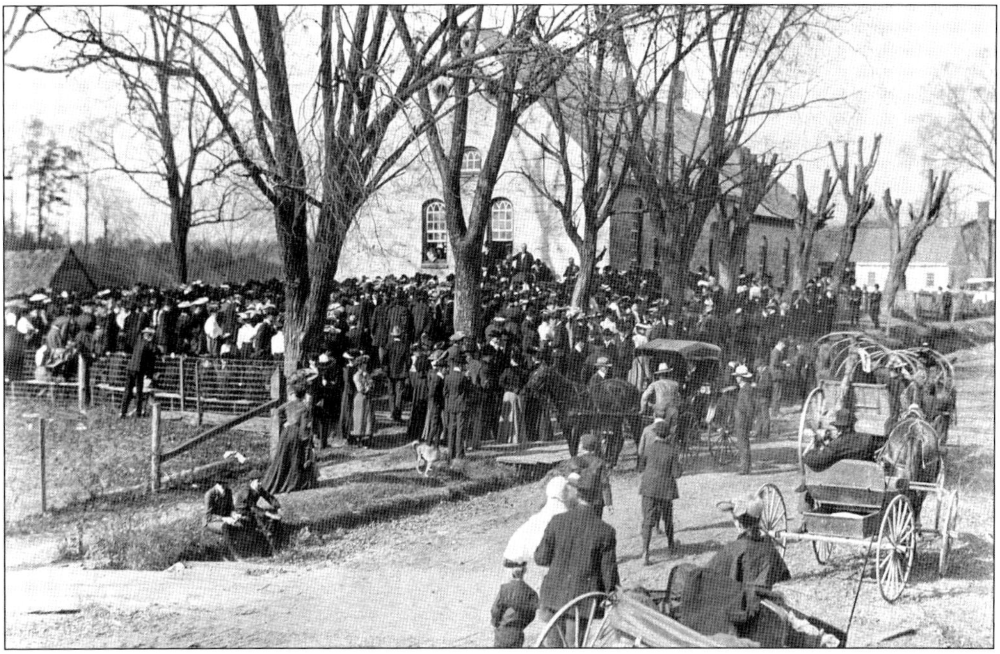

On November 17, 1903, several thousand people gathered at Bethabara, the oldest settlement in the Wachovia tract, to celebrate the sesquicentennial of the founding of Wachovia. The day was celebrated with the unveiling of monuments, the reading of papers, and the singing of hymns. (Collection of Old Salem Museums & Gardens.)

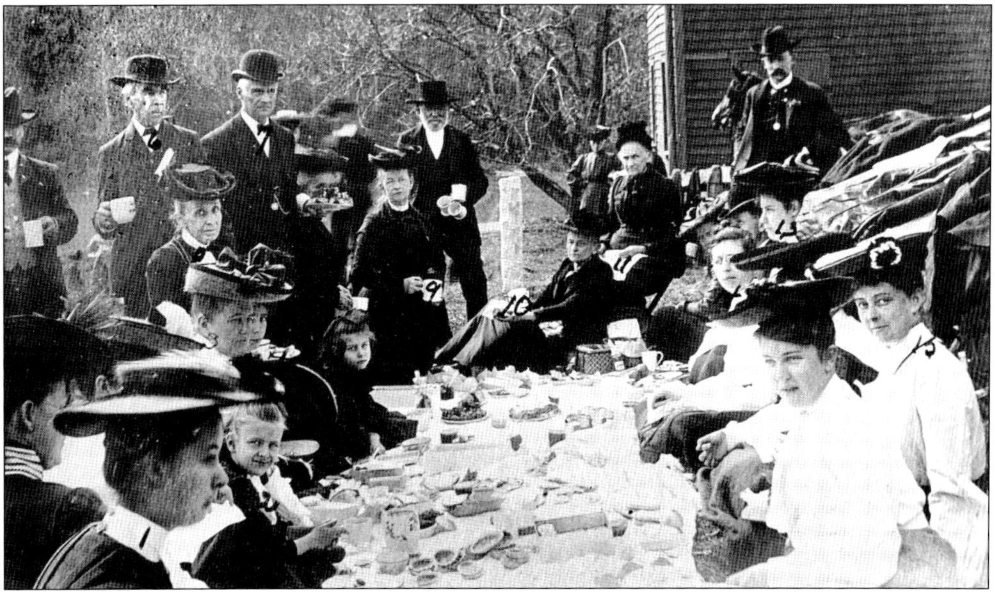

This photograph shows a picnic that occurred at Bethabara on the day of the sesquicentennial celebration in 1903. Picnickers are, in correspondence with the numbers, (1) ? Siddall, (2) Gertrude Vogler, (3) Amanda W. Spach, (4) May ?, (5) ? Goslen, (6) Allen A. Spach, (7) William T. Vogler, (8) Helen Vogler, (9) Mary Horton, (10) Maria Vogler, (11) Martha Peterson, (12) James Peterson, (13) Emma Vogler, (14) unidentified, and (15) Annie Wheeler. (Private collection; Photograph courtesy of Old Salem Museums & Gardens.)

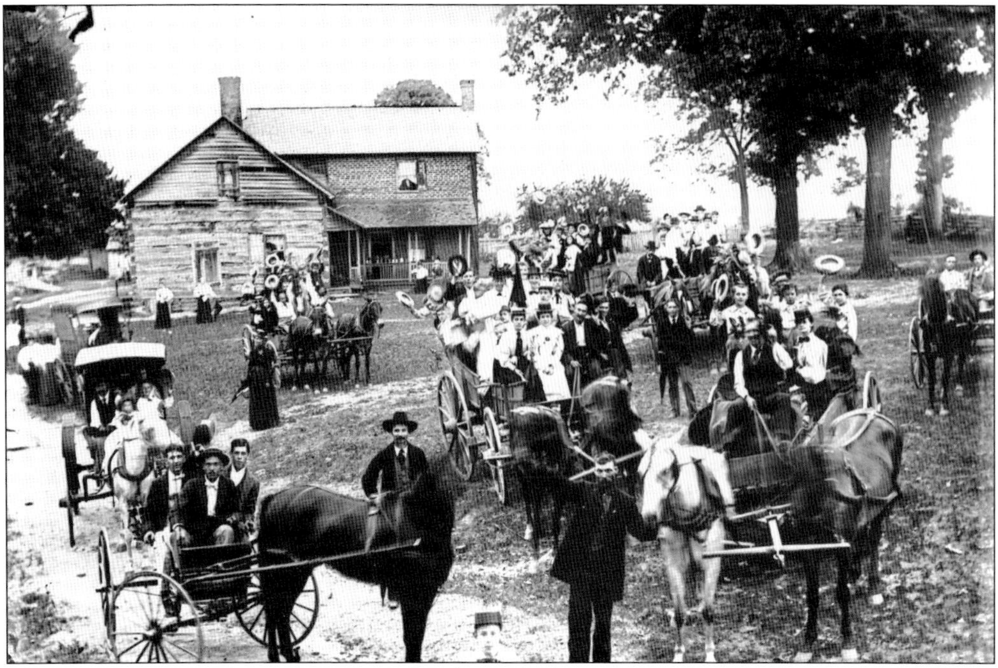

Harrison Reid's farm, located near Friedland, was the location for many Moravian Sunday school picnics. Picnics on the property apparently continued after Reid's death in 1887, as this group was photographed *c.* 1895. (Collection of the Wachovia Historical Society; Photograph courtesy of Old Salem Museums & Gardens.)

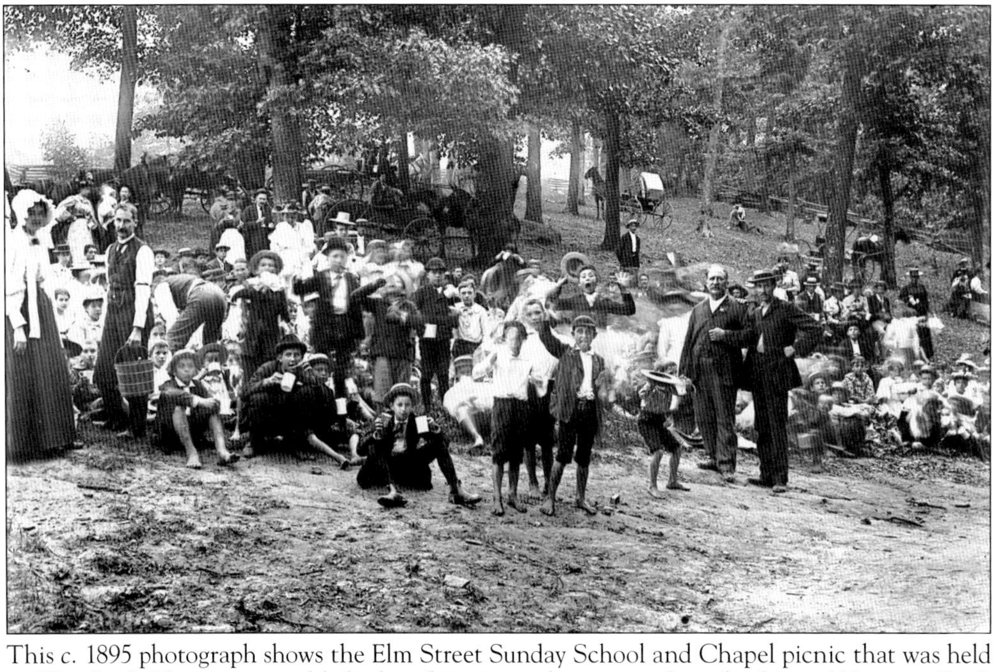

This *c.* 1895 photograph shows the Elm Street Sunday School and Chapel picnic that was held in "Southside;" however, it is likely that this picnic also occurred on the farm of Harrison Reid. Thomas C. Hege can be seen standing at right with hand on hip and hat on head. (Collection of the Wachovia Historical Society; Photograph courtesy of Old Salem Museums & Gardens.)

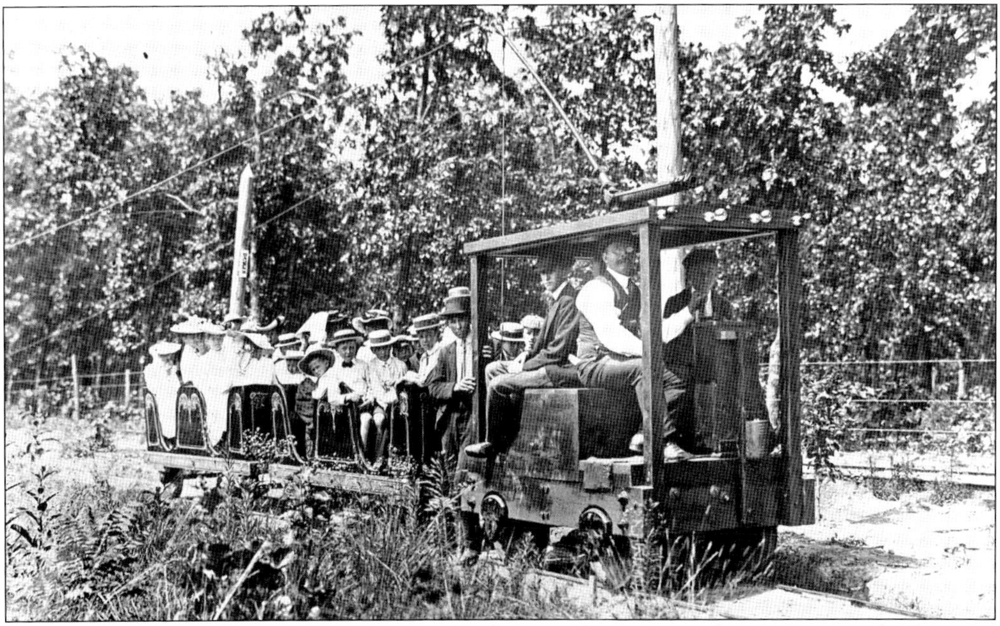

Nissen Park, which was located in the Southside area of Winston-Salem, was a popular location for Moravian Sunday school picnics. These children were photographed taking a ride on the park's miniature railroad in 1903. (Collection of Old Salem Museums & Gardens.)

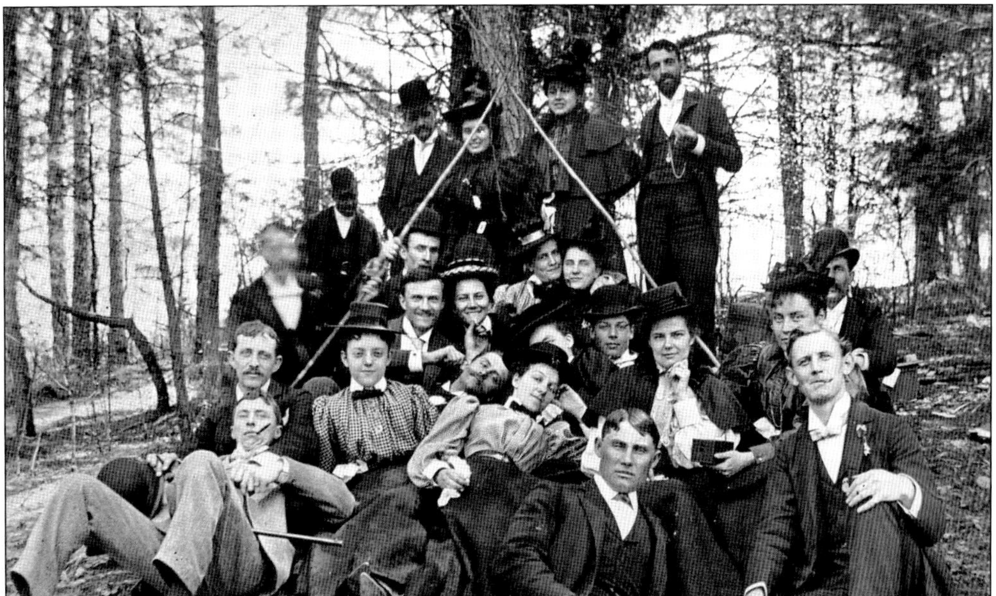

Harry W. Peterson captured this view of a picnic that occurred near Mayodan, North Carolina, c. 1895. Edna Fischer can be seen second from left (wearing a checkered blouse and hat), Nathaniel Peterson is the second man behind Edna (wearing the derby and holding a pole), and Walter J. Hege can be seen directly to the right of Edna (with his head lying on a woman's shoulder). Look closely and you will notice that the crossed sticks appear to be fishing poles, the lady to the far right holds a camera, and the man at the bottom left has a rifle lying across his lap. (Collection of the Wachovia Historical Society; Photograph courtesy of Old Salem Museums & Gardens.)

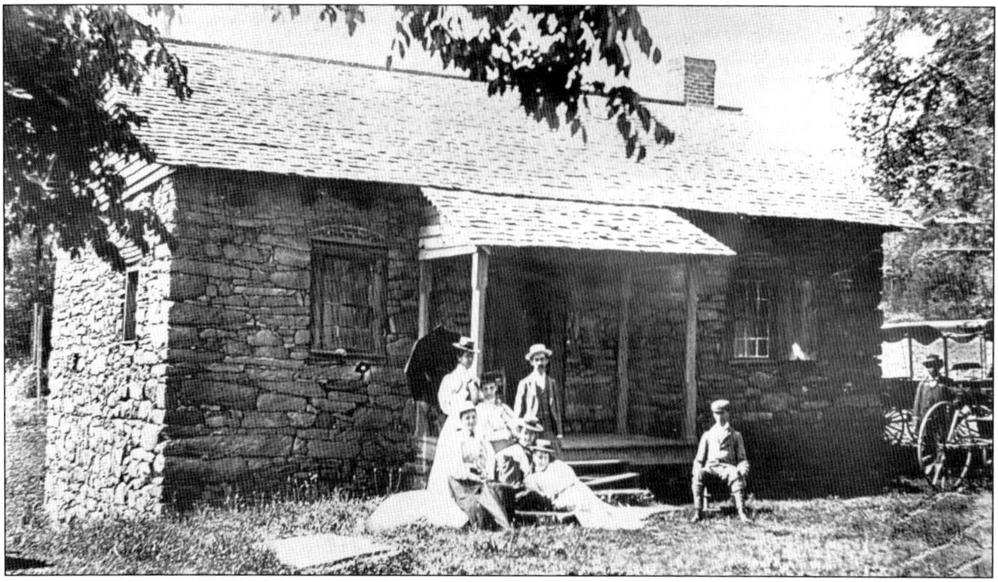

Adam Spach's Rock House, located in Friedberg and seen in this c. 1915 photograph, was a popular destination for many Moravian outings and picnics. The house, built in 1774, is now in ruins, but the site was listed on the National Register of Historic Places in 2002. (Collection of Old Salem Museums & Gardens.)

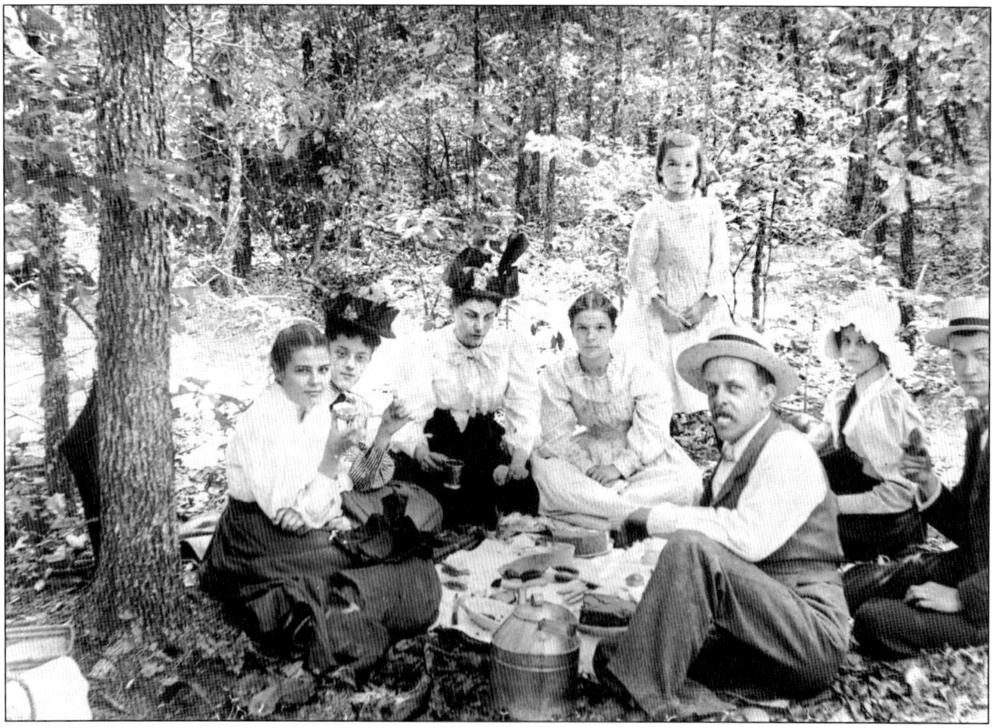

This photograph shows a picnic that was held on the grounds of Oak Grove Moravian Church c. 1895. Edna Fischer can be seen second from left, while Harry W. Peterson can be seen far right holding a cookie or biscuit. (Collection of the Wachovia Historical Society; Photograph courtesy of Old Salem Museums & Gardens.)

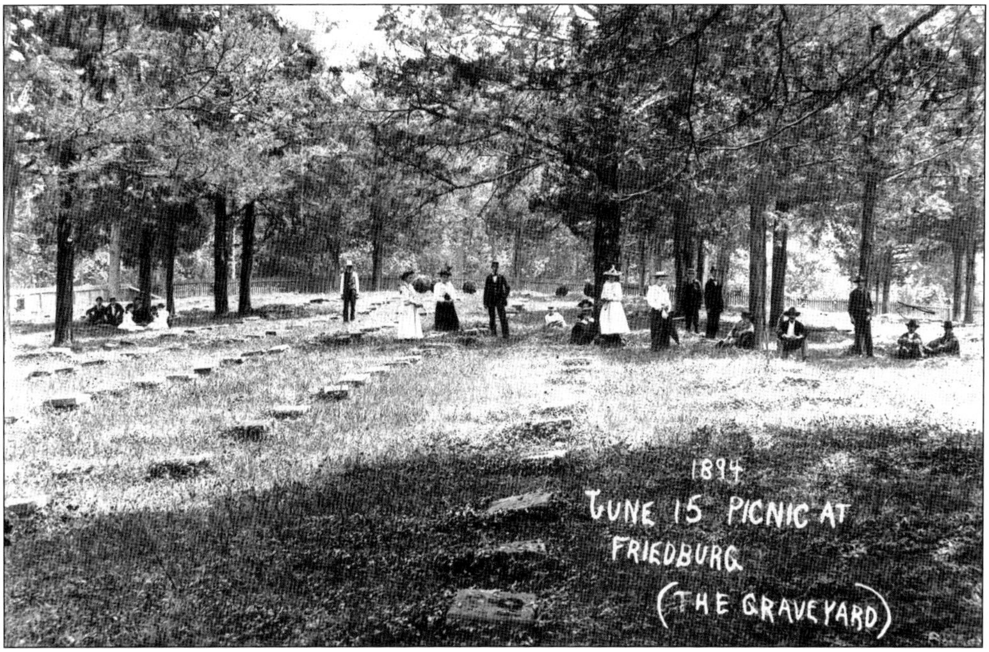

Thomas C. Hege photographed a group of people as they visited God's Acre at Friedberg on the day of a picnic in 1894. (Collection of the Wachovia Historical Society; Photograph courtesy of Old Salem Museums & Gardens.)

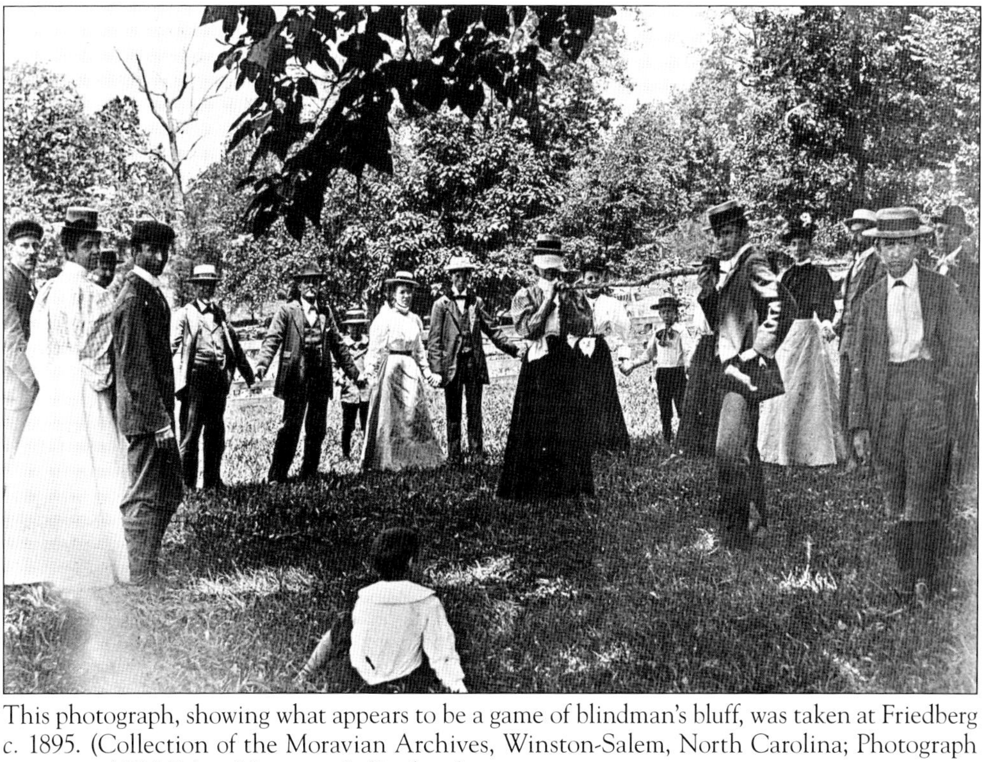

This photograph, showing what appears to be a game of blindman's bluff, was taken at Friedberg c. 1895. (Collection of the Moravian Archives, Winston-Salem, North Carolina; Photograph courtesy of Old Salem Museums & Gardens.)

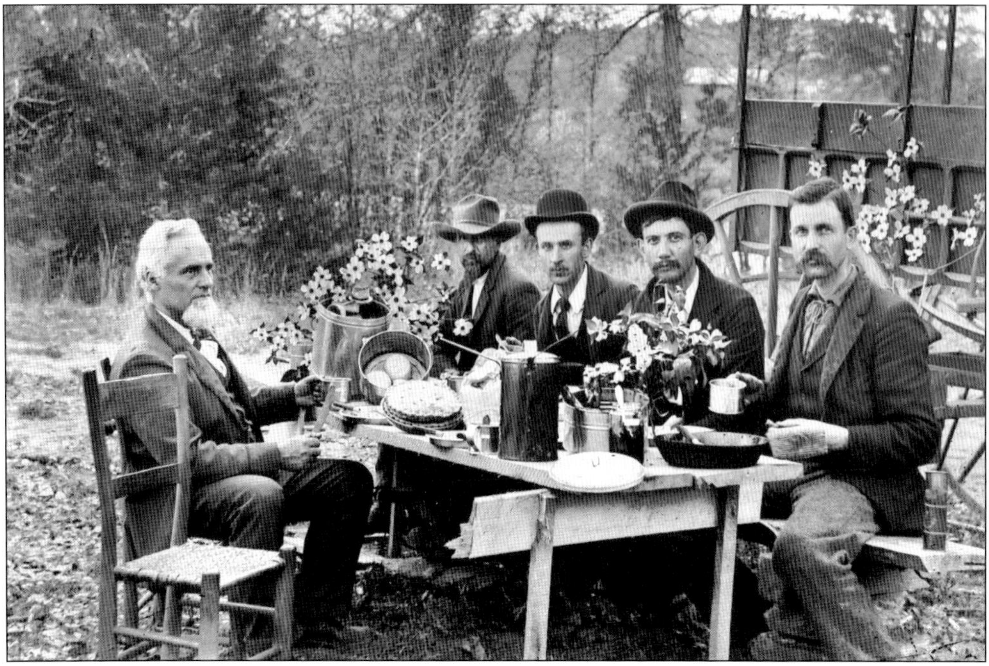

In 1896, this group of men took a fishing trip to Fries Mill. It is most likely that their camping spot was located near the Fries-owned mill in Mayodan. The men are, from left to right, William T. Vogler, unidentified, Nathaniel Peterson, unidentified, and Shirley Rogers. (Collection of the Wachovia Historical Society; Photograph courtesy of Old Salem Museums & Gardens.)

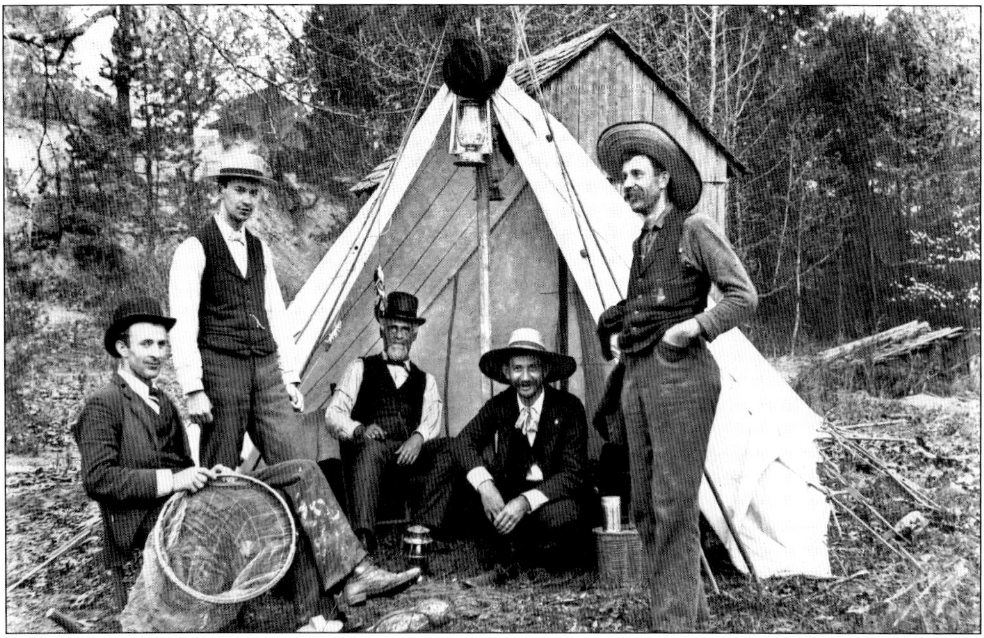

This photograph shows the campsite of the men at Fries Mill in 1896. The men are, from left to right, Nathaniel Peterson, Harry W. Peterson, William T. Vogler, unidentified, and Shirley Rogers. (Collection of the Wachovia Historical Society; Photograph courtesy of Old Salem Museums & Gardens.)

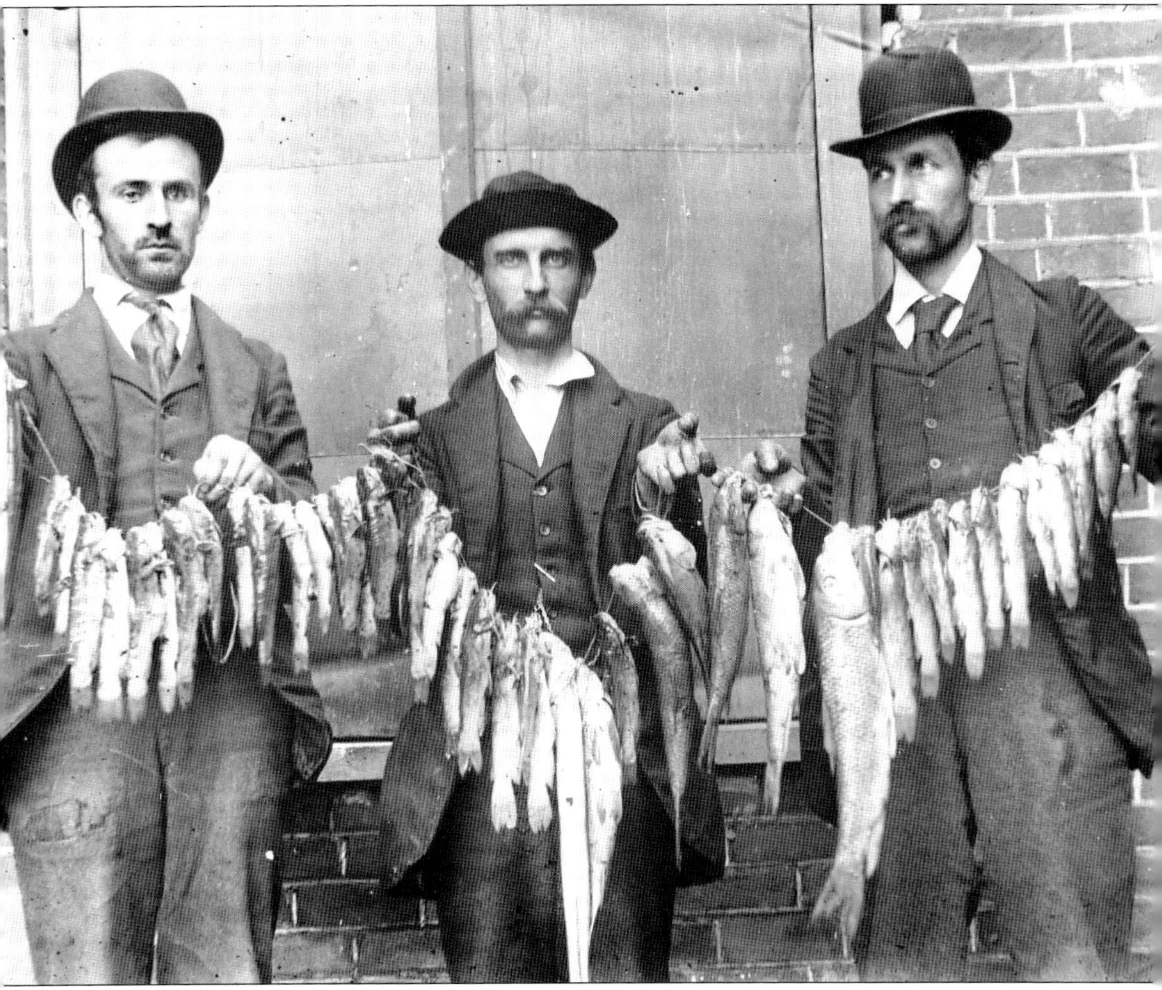

These three fisherman are seen displaying their catch *c.* 1896. It is likely this photograph was taken during the 1896 Fries Mill fishing trip. The men are, from left to right, Nathaniel Peterson, unidentified, and Shirley Rogers. Note Nathaniel Peterson's left eye, which was glass. Peterson, who was a carpenter, lost his eye in a work-related accident. (Collection of the Wachovia Historical Society; Photograph courtesy of Old Salem Museums & Gardens.)

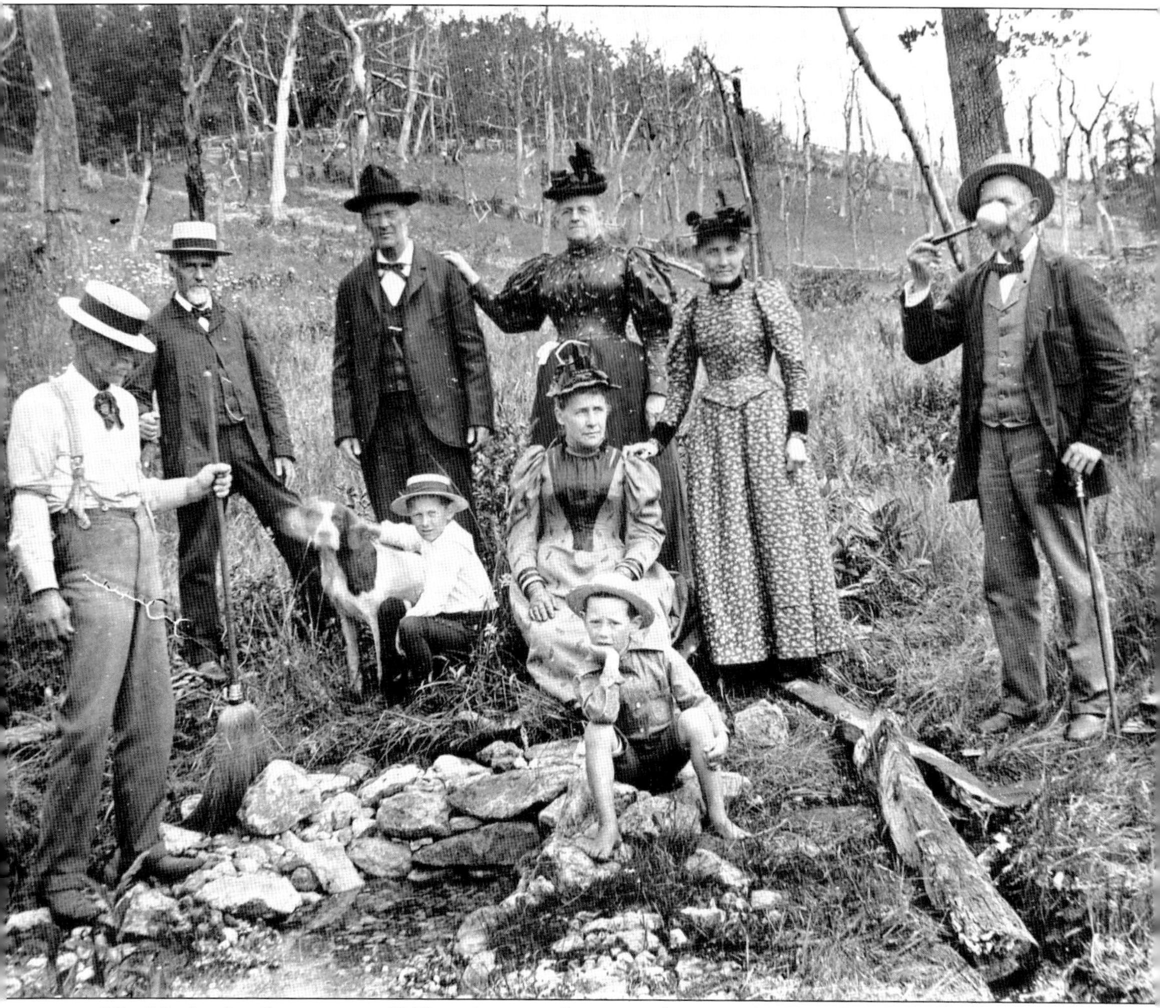

The Vogler family is seen *c.* 1895 at the site of a mineral spring that was located in Roaring Gap. In 1909, William T. Vogler built a cottage in the area for his daughter, Emma, who suffered from allergies. The adults are, from left to right, (standing) unidentified, William T. Vogler, Alexander C. Vogler, Antoinette Hauser Vogler, Johanna Mack Vogler, and unidentified; (seated) Regina Vogler; the children are unidentified. (Collection of the Wachovia Historical Society; Photograph courtesy of Old Salem Museums & Gardens.)

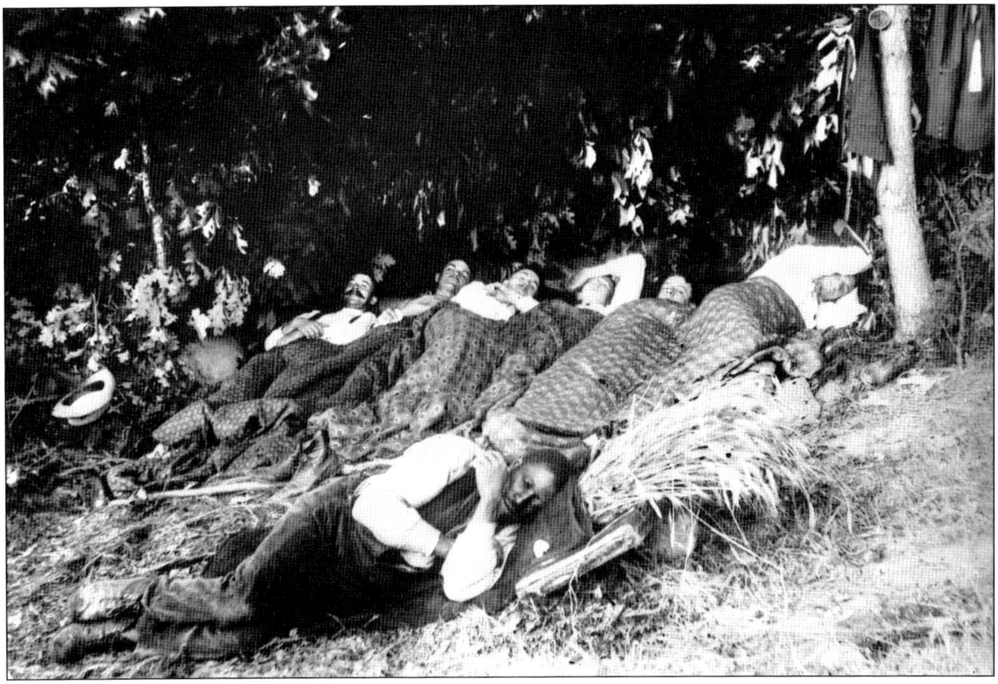

This photograph, taken in 1899 during a camping trip at Pilot Mountain, is titled, "just before rising." Harry W. Peterson can be seen far left with mustache. (Collection of the Wachovia Historical Society; Photograph courtesy of Old Salem Museums & Gardens.)

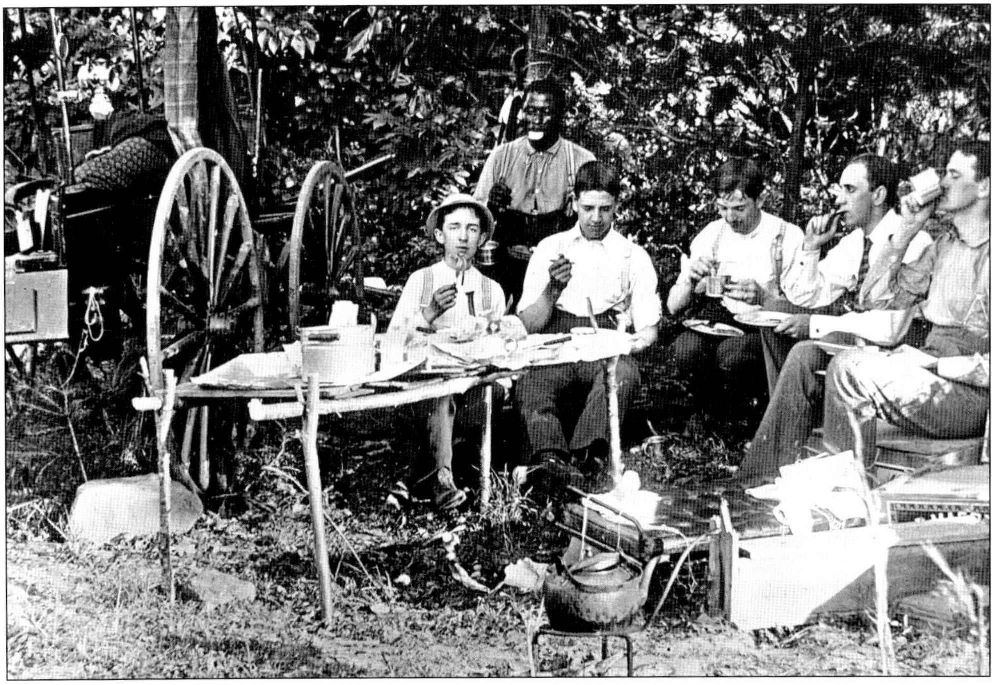

A group of young men set up camp at Pilot Mountain in 1899. Harry W. Peterson, not seen in this photograph but who likely took the image, titled this view "refreshing the inner man." (Collection of the Wachovia Historical Society; Photograph courtesy of Old Salem Museums & Gardens.)

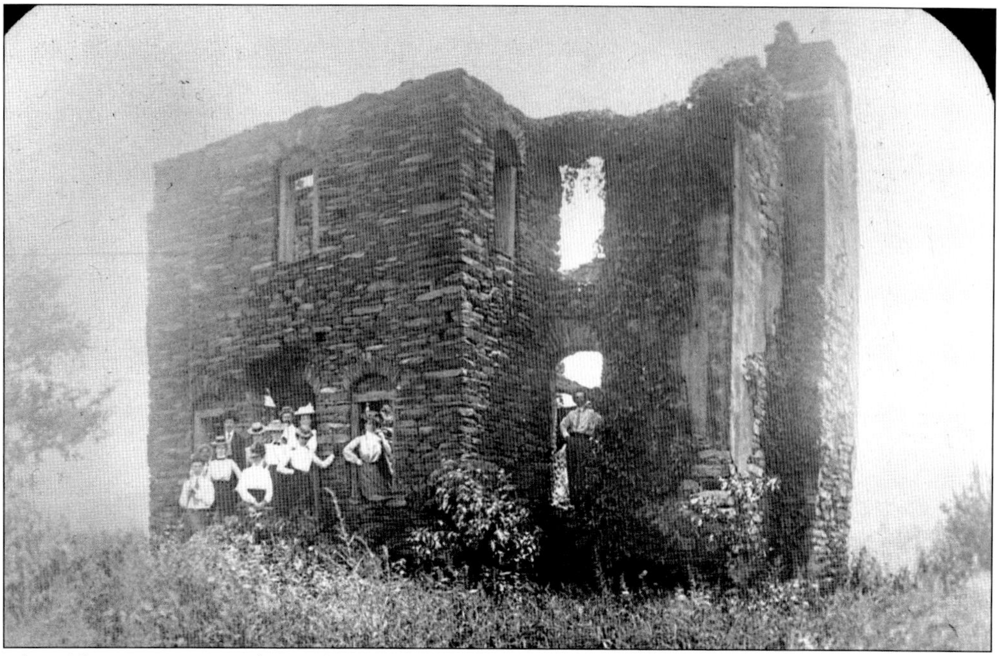

The old Martin House, located in Stokes County, was a popular site for group outings. Harry W. Peterson can be seen standing in the back of the doorway in this photograph taken c. 1900. (Collection of the Wachovia Historical Society; Photograph courtesy of Old Salem Museums & Gardens.)

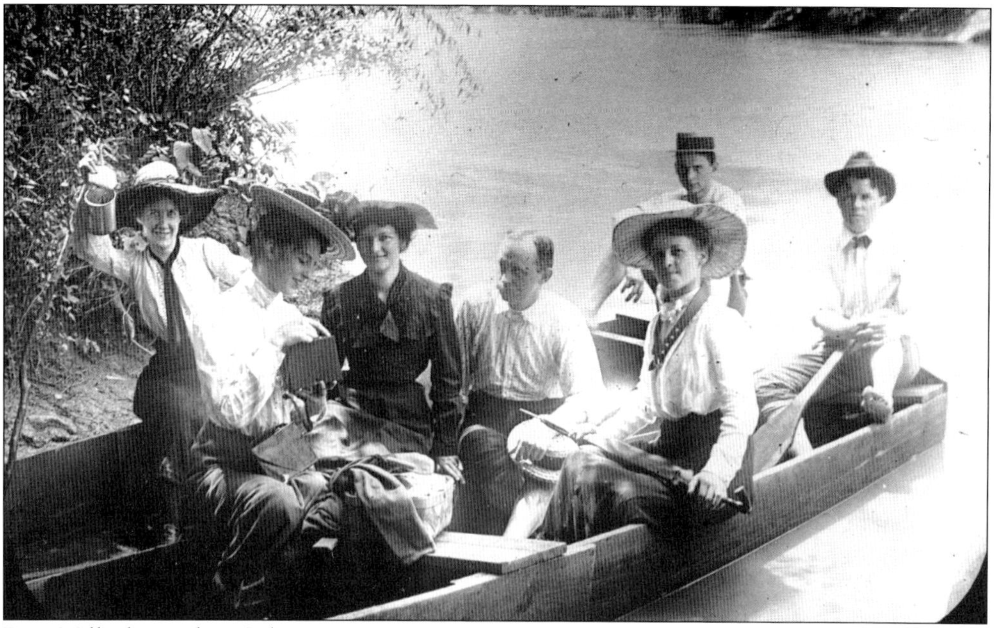

Bost Mills, located in Cabarrus County, was a popular destination for Salem residents. This photograph is one of a series taken at a "house party" that occurred in 1902. Notice the woman sitting in front of the boat holding a camera in the direction of Walter J. Hege, who sits in the center. (Collection of the Wachovia Historical Society; Photograph courtesy of Old Salem Museums & Gardens.)

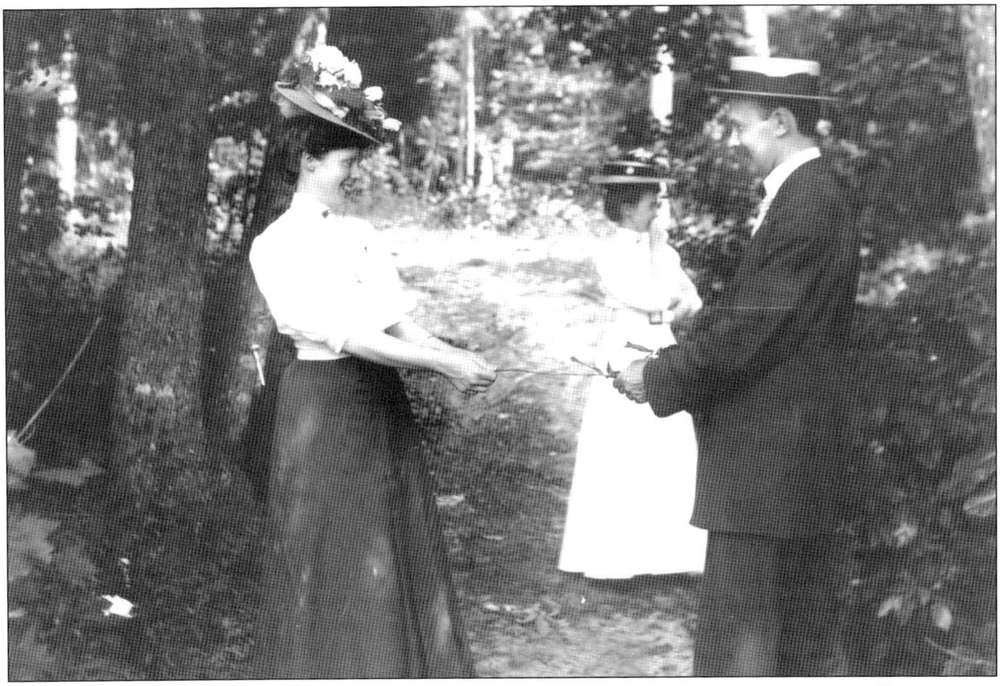

Bertha Josephine Hall and Harry Walter Peterson are seen "courting in Kernersville" *c.* 1905. The two were married on November 23, 1907. (Collection of the Wachovia Historical Society; Photograph courtesy of Old Salem Museums & Gardens.)

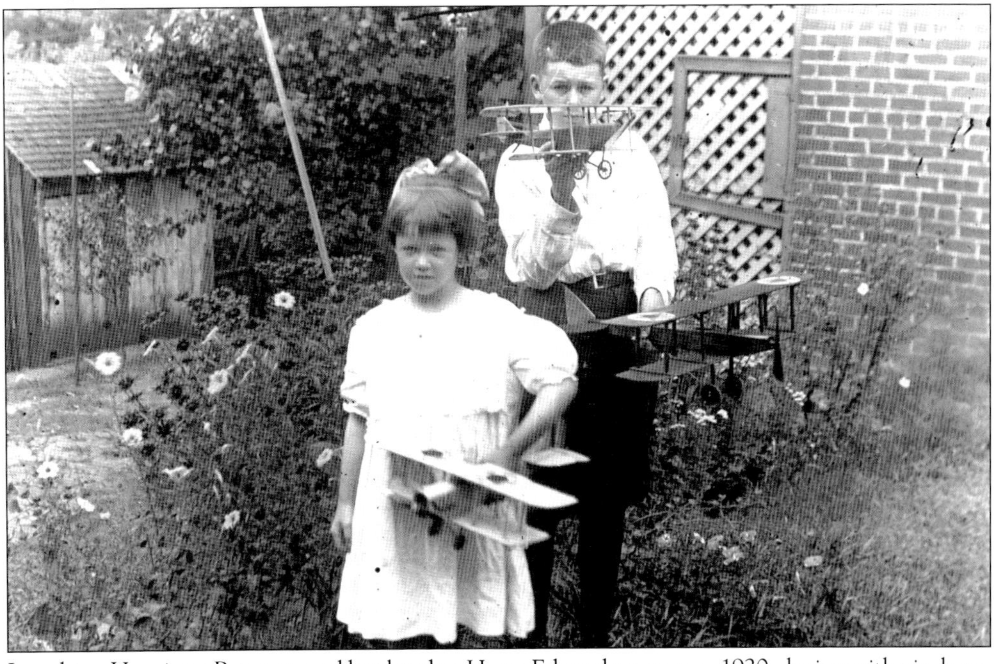

Josephine Henrietta Peterson and her brother Harry Edward are seen *c.* 1920 playing with airplanes that were made by their father, Harry W. Peterson. The photograph was likely taken in the yard of their home, located on Poplar Street in Winston-Salem. (Collection of the Wachovia Historical Society; Photograph courtesy of Old Salem Museums & Gardens.)

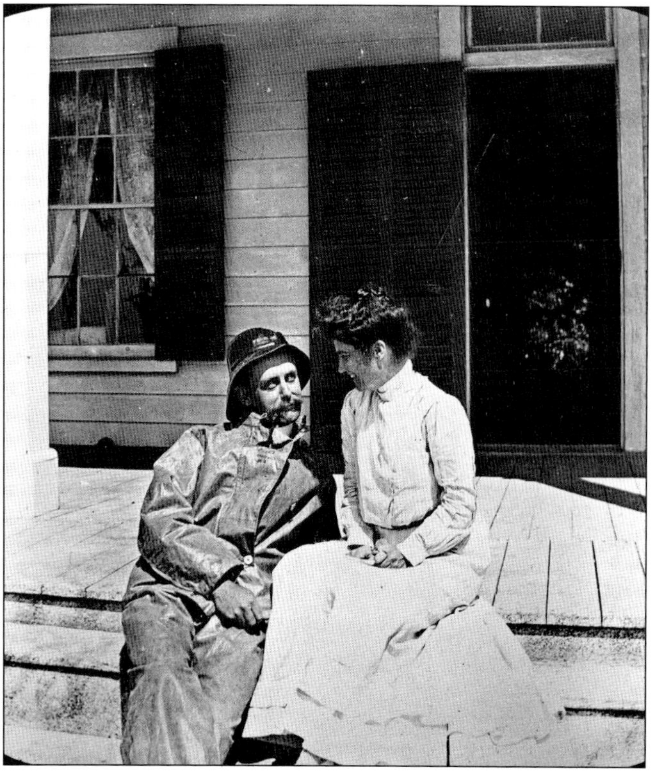

Walter J. Hege and an unidentified woman were photographed on a visit to Beaufort in September 1904. (Collection of the Wachovia Historical Society; Photograph courtesy of Old Salem Museums & Gardens.)

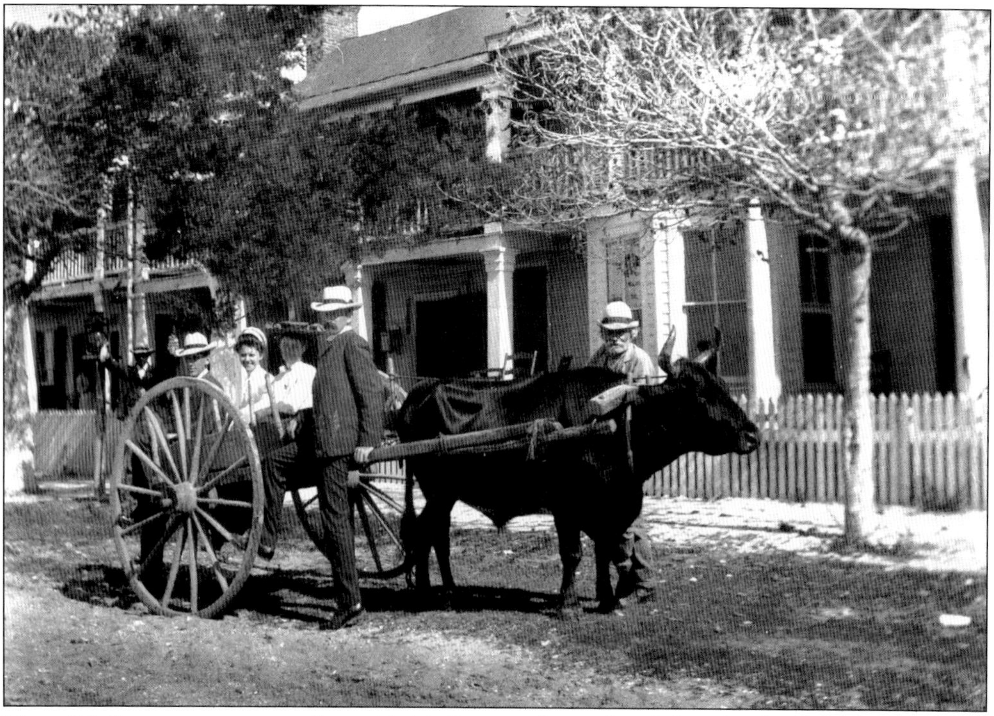

Harry W. Peterson, seen standing with his foot on the spoke of the wheel, vacationed with his friends in Beaufort in September 1904. (Collection of Old Salem Museums & Gardens.)

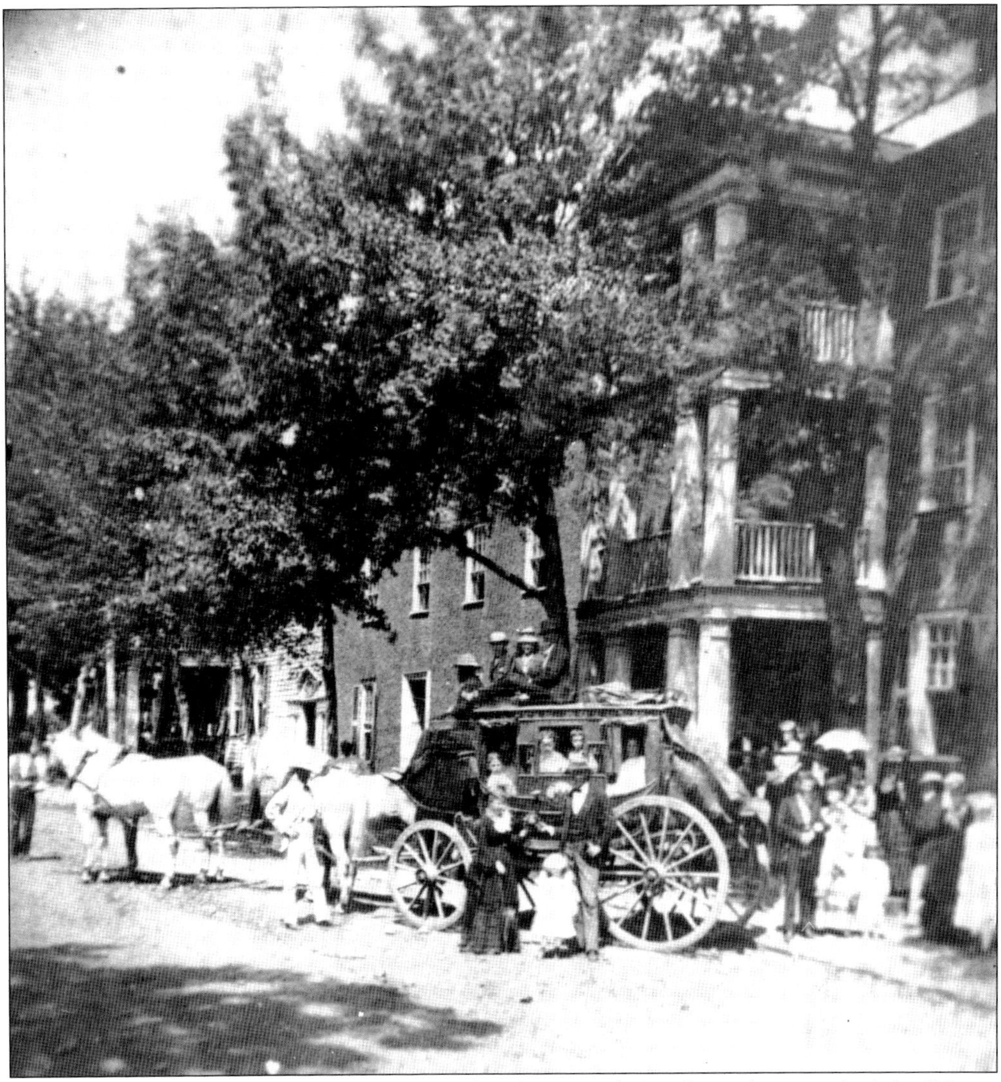

Rufus Morgan, a nationally known photographer from North Carolina, photographed the "Hattie Butner" stagecoach in front of the Eagle Hotel in Asheville during 1872. The stagecoach was a nine-passenger Concord coach that was built for Edwin T. Clemmons that same year. The stagecoach was named "Hattie Butner" in honor of Clemmons's wife. Asheville was a popular destination for Salem residents. (Collection of the Wachovia Historical Society; Photograph courtesy of Old Salem Museums & Gardens.)

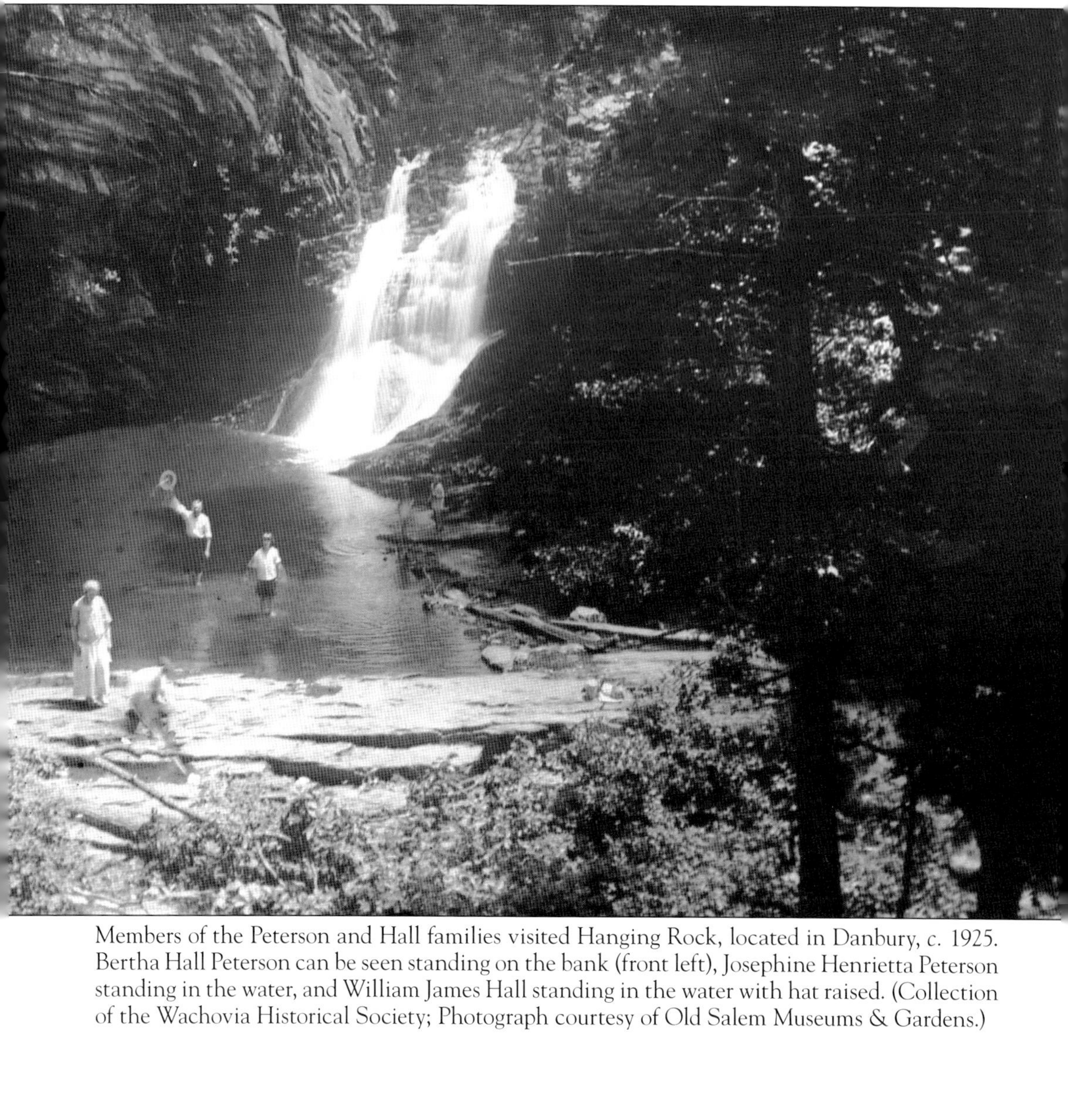

Members of the Peterson and Hall families visited Hanging Rock, located in Danbury, c. 1925. Bertha Hall Peterson can be seen standing on the bank (front left), Josephine Henrietta Peterson standing in the water, and William James Hall standing in the water with hat raised. (Collection of the Wachovia Historical Society; Photograph courtesy of Old Salem Museums & Gardens.)

Five

At Worship

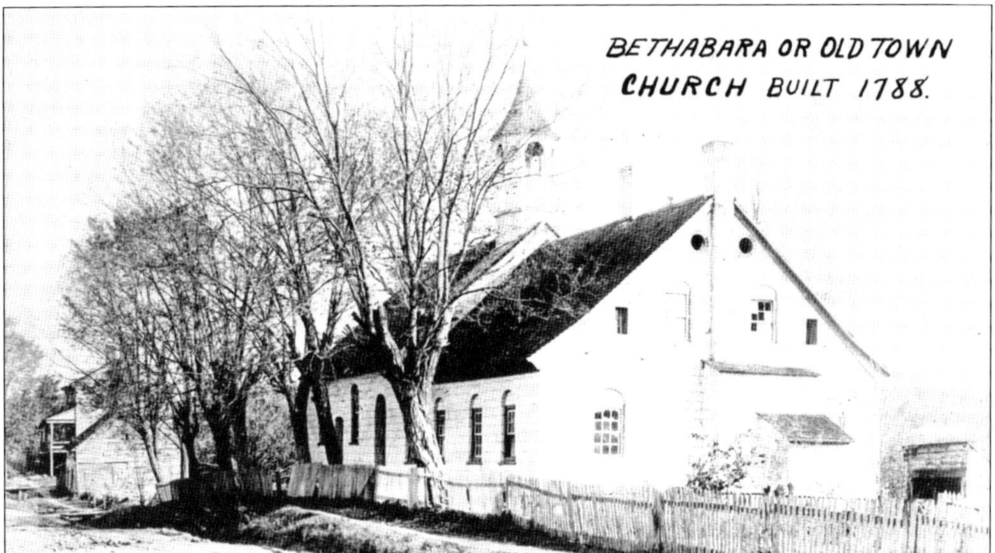

This photograph, taken *c.* 1900, shows the 1788 Gemein Haus at Bethabara. (Collection of Old Salem Museums & Gardens.)

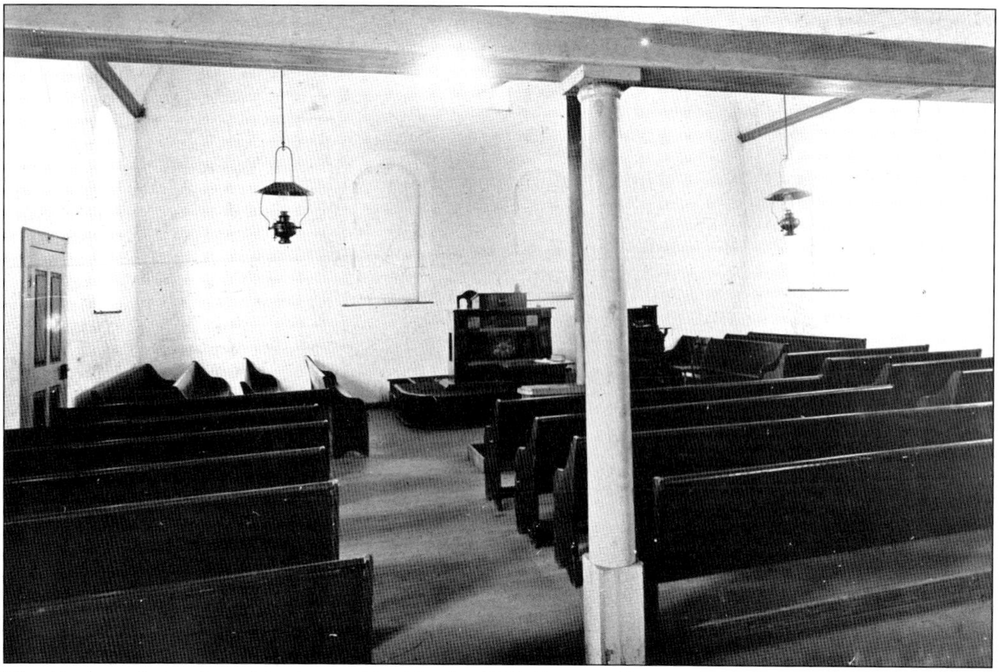

The *Saal*, or place of worship, located inside the 1788 Gemein Haus at Bethabara, was photographed c. 1900. (Collection of the Wachovia Historical Society; Photograph courtesy of Old Salem Museums & Gardens.)

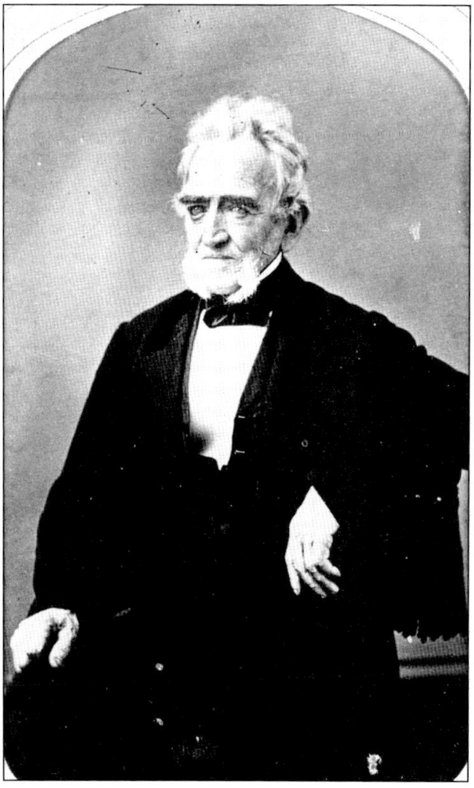

Bishop Johann Christian Jacobson, seen in this 1864–1866 photograph, was the pastor of Bethabara Moravian Church from 1828 to 1832 and Bethania Moravian Church from 1826 to 1834. In addition, Bishop Jacobson also held many other positions within the Moravian Church. (Collection of Old Salem Museums & Gardens.)

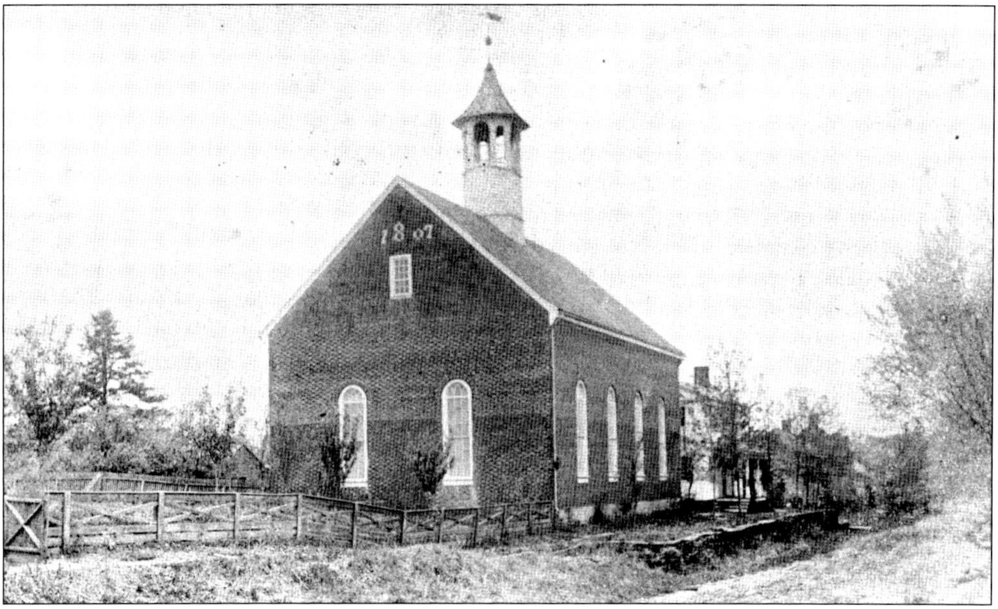

Bethania Moravian Church and parsonage (located to the right of the church) are seen in this *c.* 1900 photograph. (Private collection; Photograph courtesy of Old Salem Museums & Gardens.)

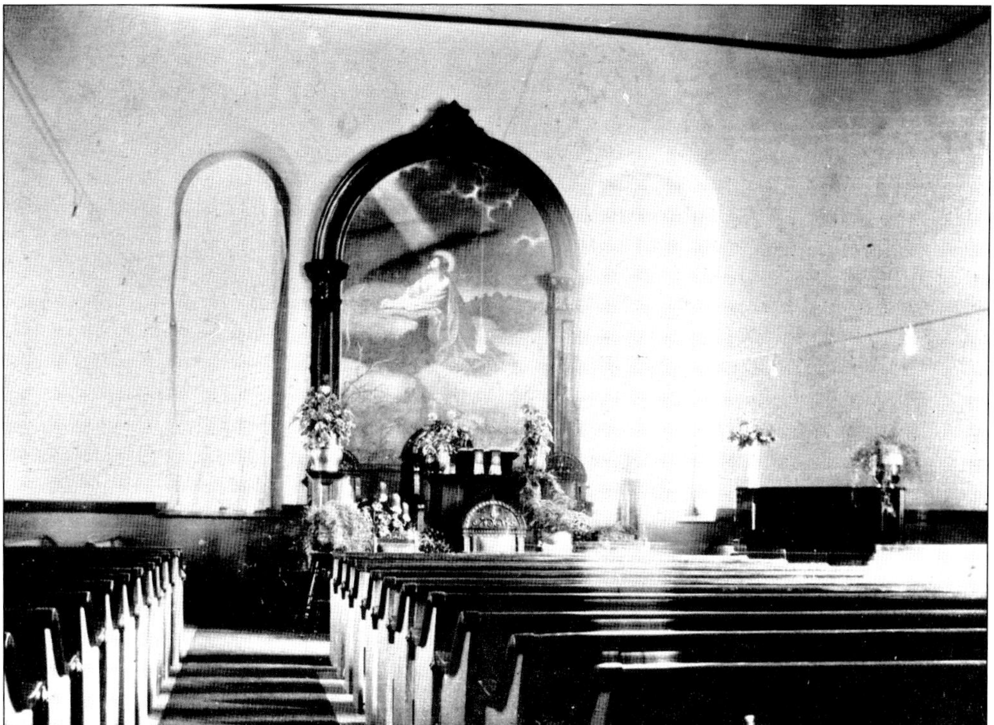
This photograph shows the interior of Bethania Moravian Church prior to the 1942 fire. (Private collection; Photograph courtesy of Old Salem Museums & Gardens.)

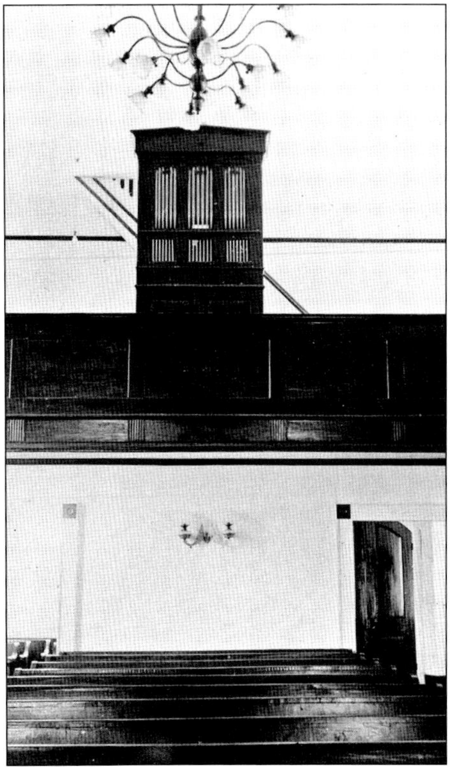

An interior view of Bethania Moravian Church, photographed in the early 20th century, shows the 1773 organ built by Joseph F. Bullitscheck. The organ was completely destroyed in the 1942 fire. (Collection of the Moravian Archives, Winston-Salem, North Carolina; Photograph courtesy of Old Salem Museums & Gardens.)

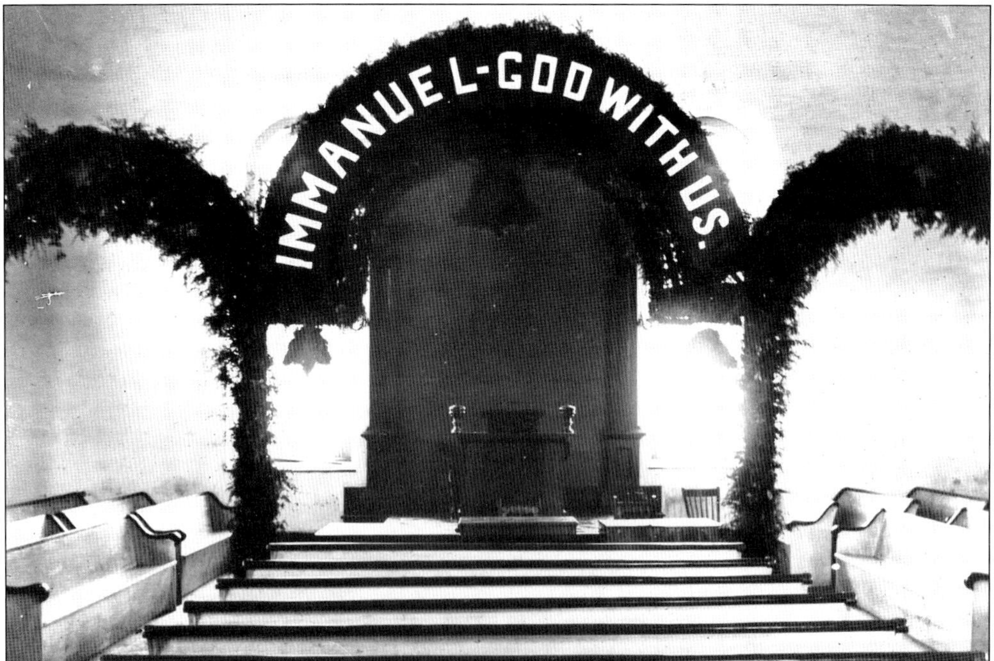

The pulpit at Bethania Moravian Church, decorated for Christmas, was photographed *c.* 1900. (Collection of the Wachovia Historical Society; Photograph courtesy of Old Salem Museums & Gardens.)

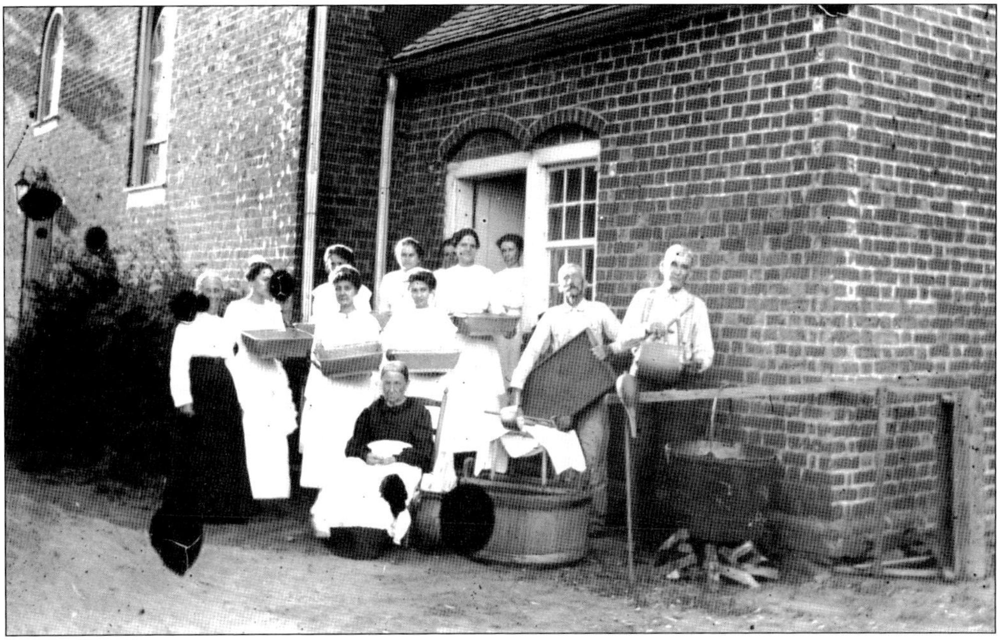

The Moravian lovefeast, served at special occasions in the church, most often consists of a sweetened bun and coffee. Those who serve this simple meal are called *Dieners*, which is the German word for "servers." Dieners (those in the all-white dresses) and other members of Bethania Moravian Church were photographed outside the church kitchen in 1909. Members are, from left to right, (center, seated) Louisa Oehman; (first row) Martha Sides, Lessie Walker, Lola Butner, Ruth Transou, R. O. Butner, and Egbert Lehman; (second row) Bertha Butner Speas, Lois Stoltz, and Edna Chadwick Tuttle; (third row) Emma Grieder Lehman and Rosa Conrad Grabs. (Collection of the Wachovia Historical Society; Photograph courtesy of Old Salem Museums & Gardens.)

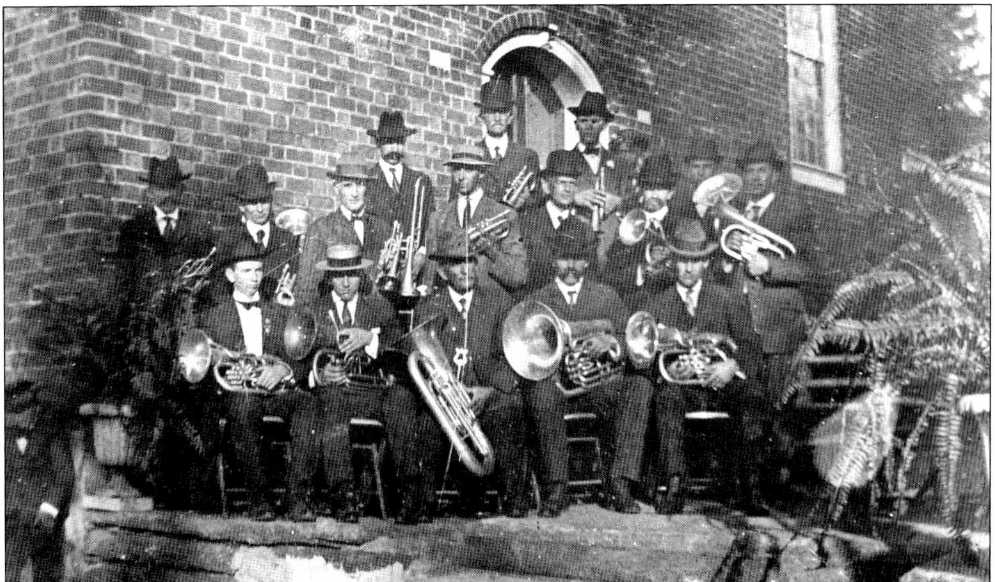

The Bethania Moravian Church Band was photographed outside their church in 1909. (Private collection; Photograph courtesy of Old Salem Museums & Gardens.)

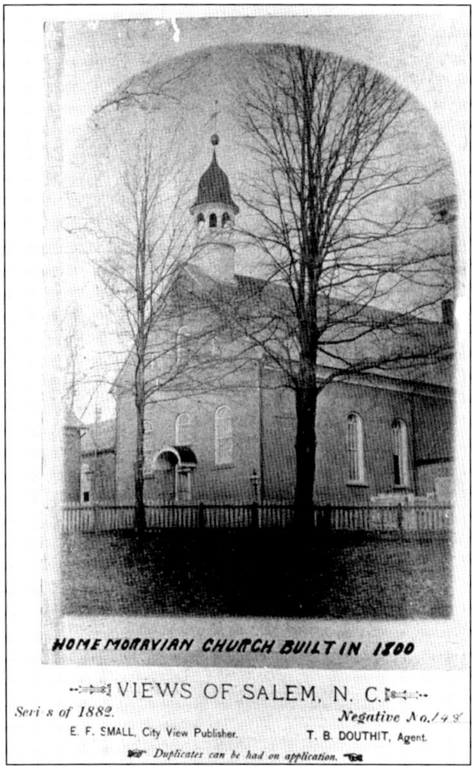

Home Moravian Church, located in Salem, was photographed by Edward F. Small in 1882. (Collection of Old Salem Museums & Gardens.)

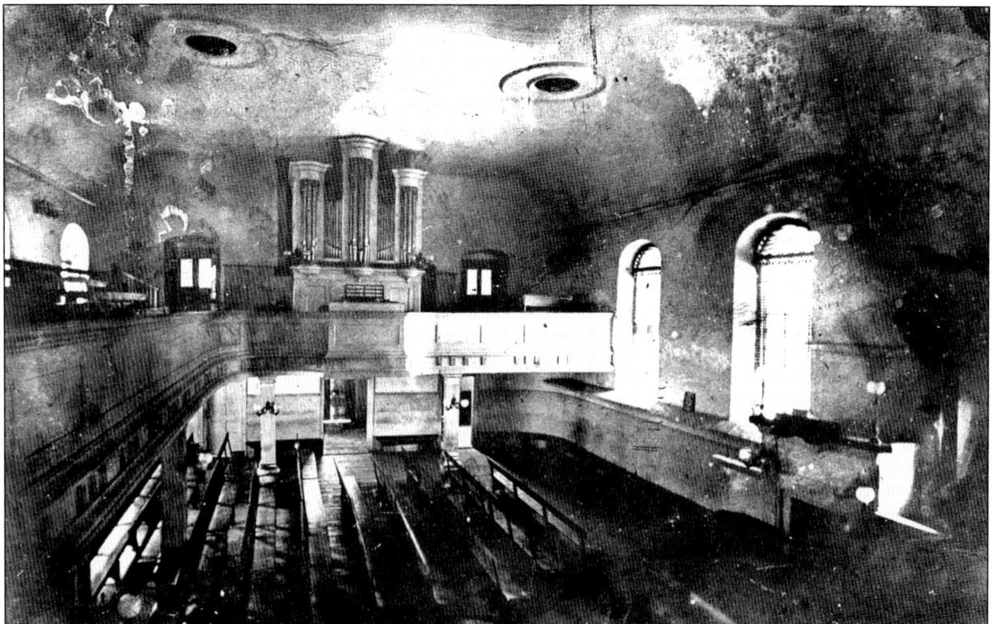

The interior of Home Moravian Church was photographed *c.* 1860 and shows the earliest known view of the 1799/1800 Tannenberg organ. The organ, now restored, can be seen, and heard, in the James A. Gray Auditorium located in the Old Salem Visitor Center. (Collection of the Wachovia Historical Society; Photograph courtesy of Old Salem Museums & Gardens.)

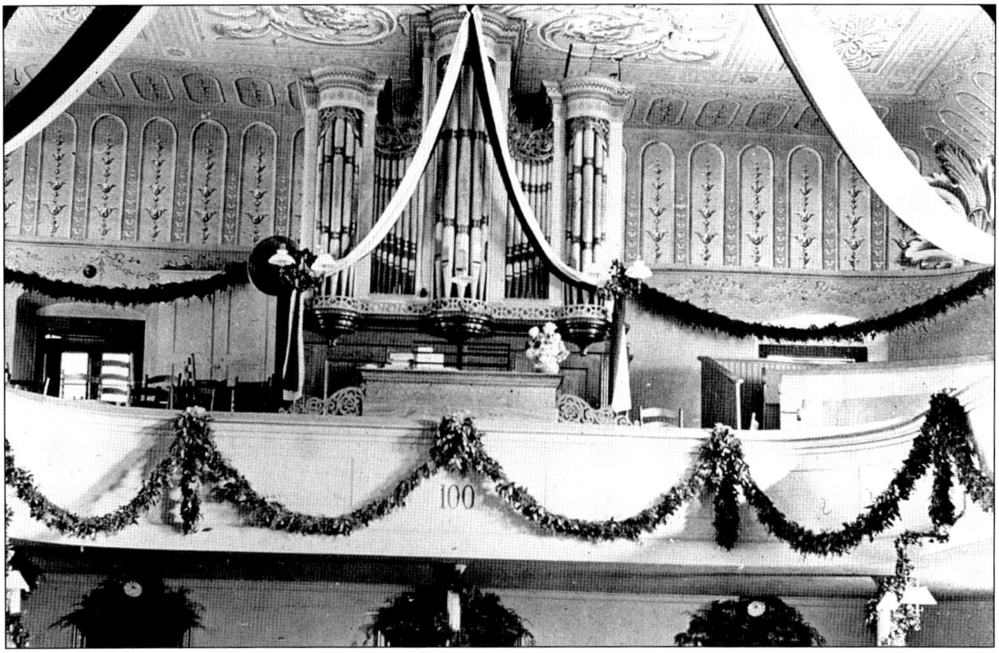

According to the church memorabilia of 1900, at the stroke of 9:00 a.m. on Friday November 9, exactly 100 years had elapsed since the consecration of Home Moravian Church. This photograph, attributed to Harry W. Peterson, shows the church decorated for that joyous occasion. (Collection of the Wachovia Historical Society; Photograph courtesy of Old Salem Museums & Gardens.)

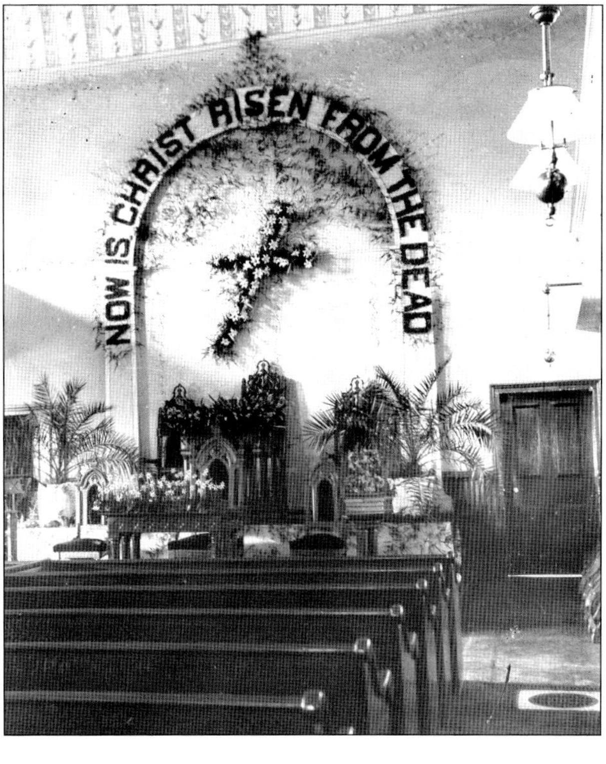

The pulpit of Home Moravian Church, decorated for Easter, was photographed in 1906. (Collection of the Wachovia Historical Society; Photograph courtesy of Old Salem Museums & Gardens.)

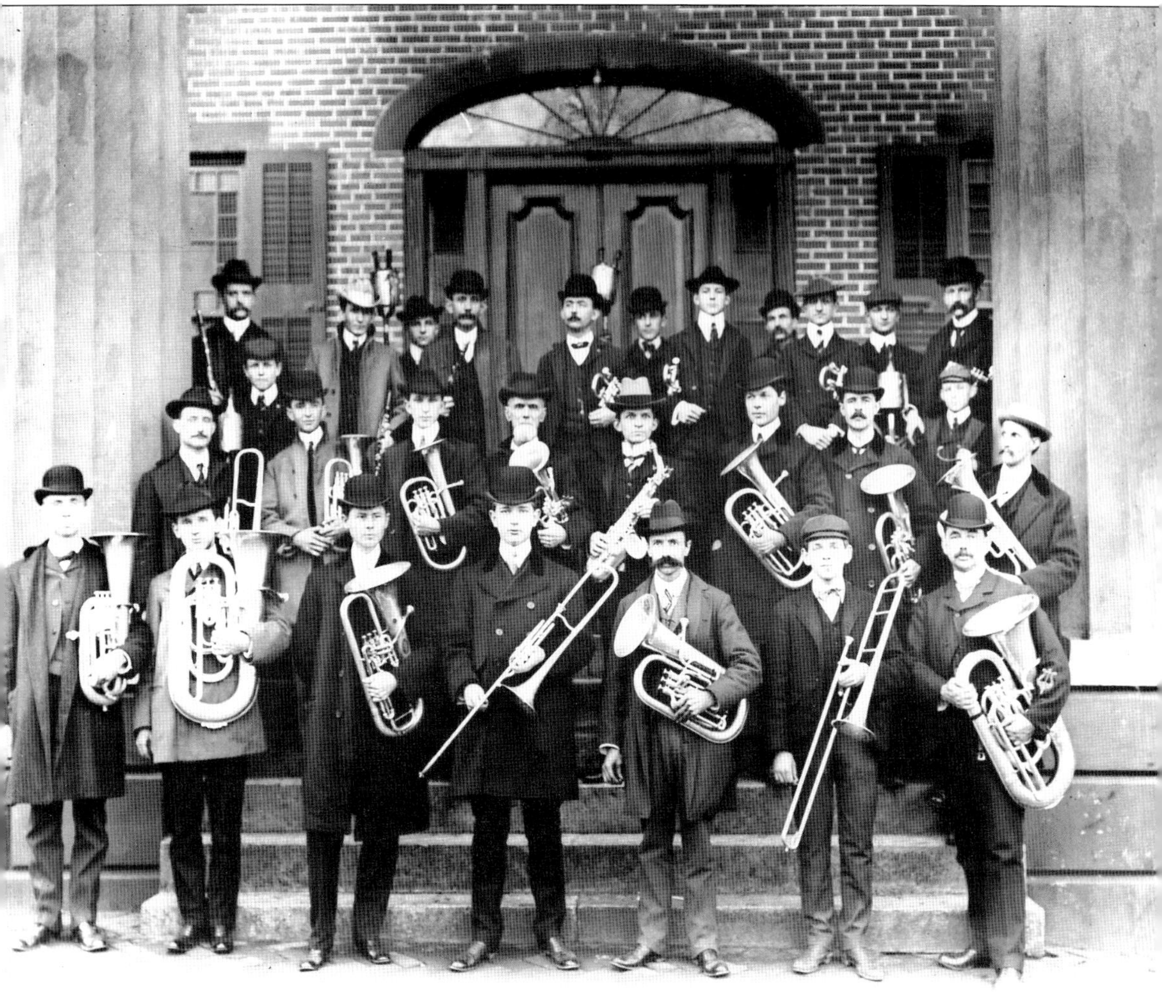

The Home Moravian Church Band was photographed on Easter 1903 in front of the Main Hall building at Salem Academy and College. The band members are, from left to right, (first row) Bernard J. Pfohl, Ralph Siewers, Franz Lawson, Agnew Bahnson, Harry Mickey, Fred Fogle, and Rufus Shultz; (second row) Hope Holland, Henry Foy, Charles Johnson, Samuel T. Mickey, James Kapp, Edward T. Mickey, Samuel Pfohl, and Bernhard Wurreschke; (third row) Walter Hege, Charles Woollen, William Peterson, Ernest Stockton, Clyde Rights, Junius Goslen, Paul Fogle, and James Peterson; (torch bearers) Horace Vance, Samuel Welfare, Charles Vogler, Shirley Rogers, and Clarence Leinbach. (Collection of the Wachovia Historical Society; Photograph courtesy of Old Salem Museums & Gardens.)

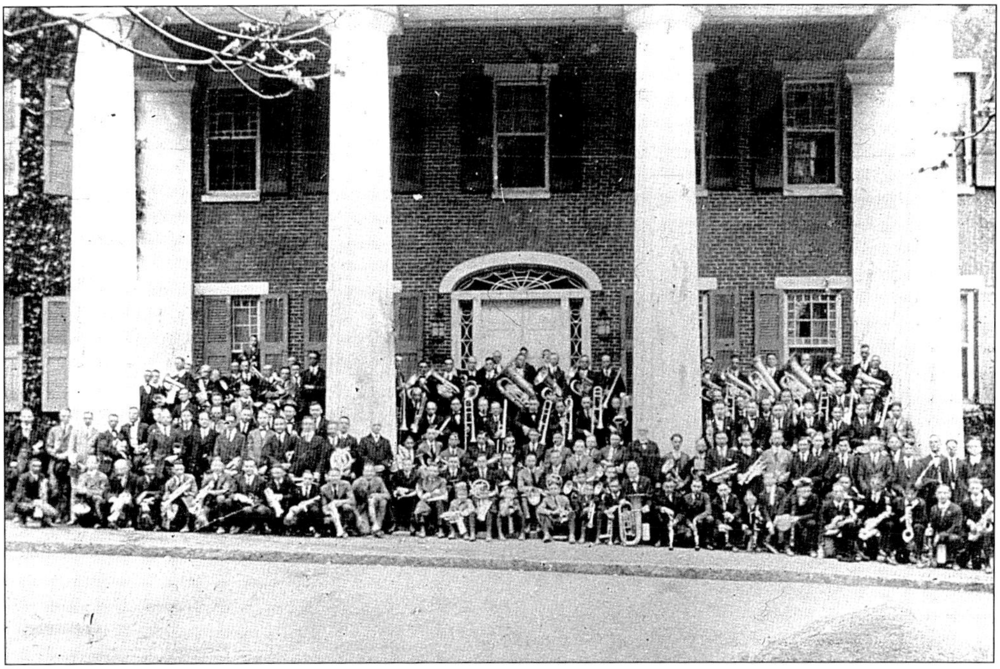

This photograph shows the Home Moravian Church Band gathered in front of Salem Academy and College's Main Hall building for Easter in 1922. (Collection of the Wachovia Historical Society; Photograph courtesy of Old Salem Museums & Gardens.)

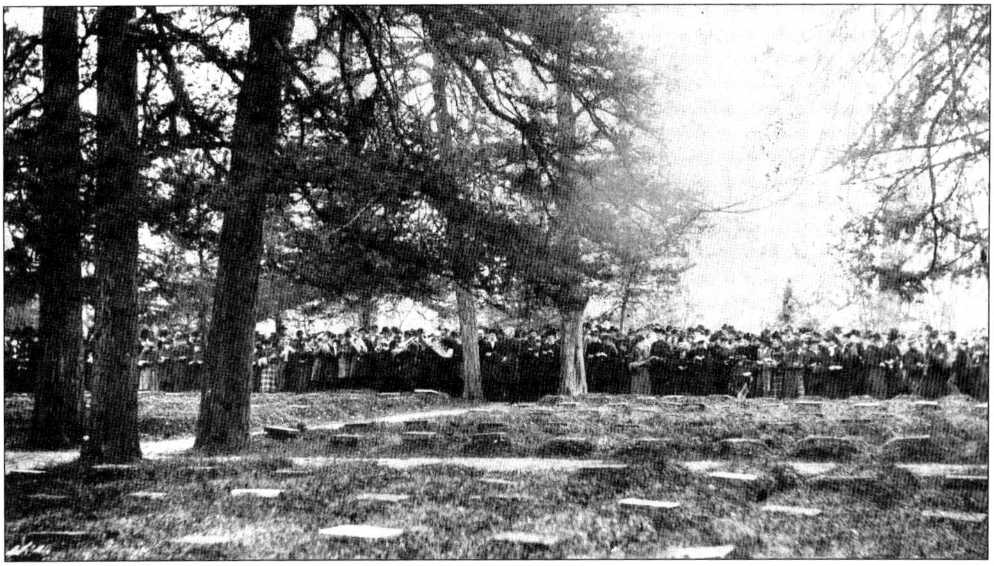

The Easter sunrise service begins before dawn on Easter Sunday. In Salem, it begins in front of Home Moravian Church. There a minister proclaims, "The Lord is risen!" and the worshippers respond, "The Lord is risen indeed." During the service, the worshippers walk to God's Acre as the Moravian bands play familiar hymns. As the sun begins to shine, the service comes to an end. The first Easter sunrise service in Salem occurred in 1772, and the tradition continues today. This photograph shows a service that occurred in 1885. (Collection of Old Salem Museums & Gardens.)

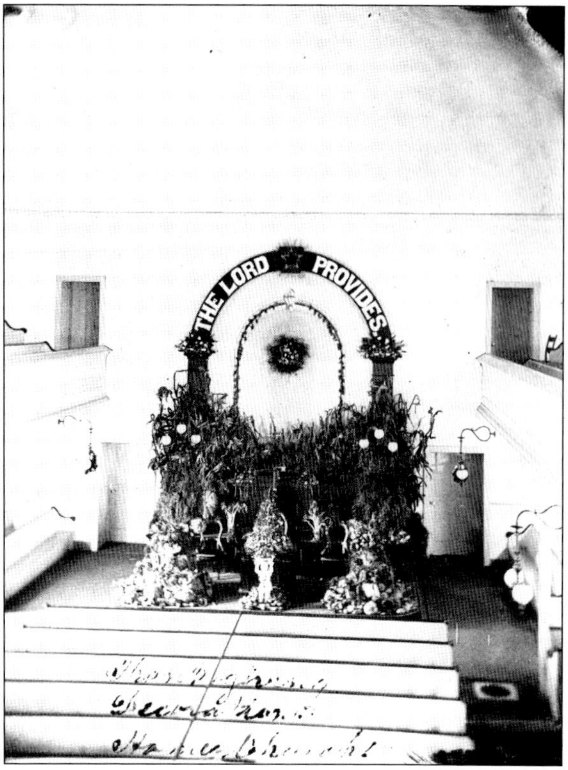

The pulpit of Home Moravian Church is seen decorated for Thanksgiving in these *c.* 1890 (top) and early-20th-century (bottom) photographs. (Top: Collection of Old Salem Museums & Gardens; Bottom: Collection of the Moravian Archives, Winston-Salem, North Carolina; Photograph courtesy of Old Salem Museums & Gardens.)

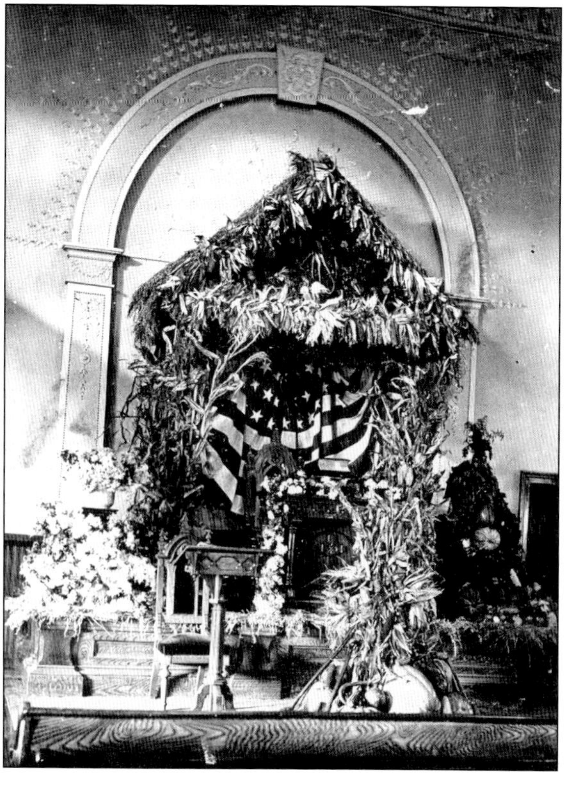

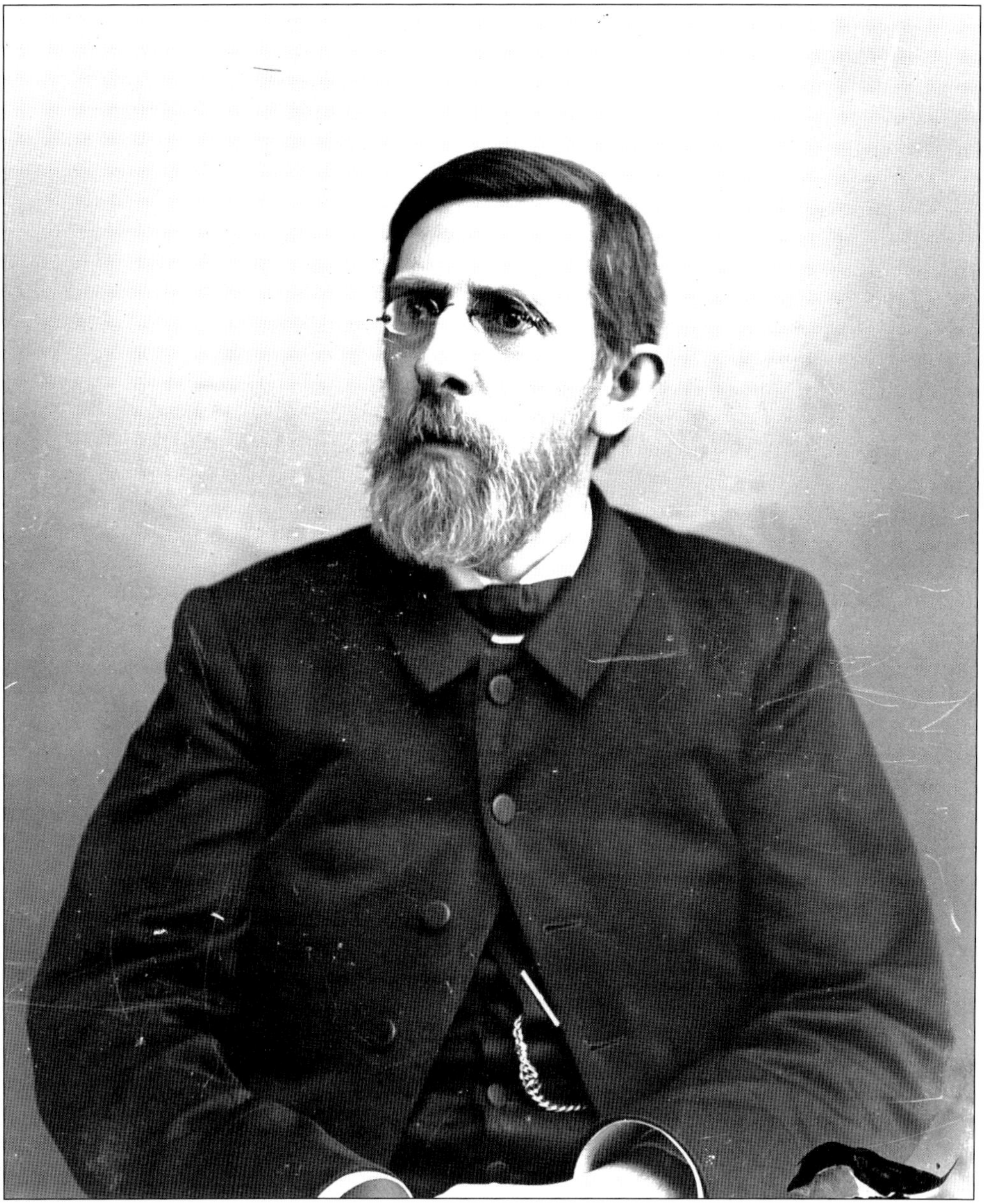

Bishop Edward Rondthaler, seen in this *c.* 1890 photograph, was the pastor of Home Moravian Church from 1877 to 1908. He also held many other positions and pastorates within the Moravian Church, including president of the Provincial Elders Conference of the Southern Province from 1890 to 1929. (Collection of the Wachovia Historical Society; Photograph courtesy of Old Salem Museums & Gardens.)

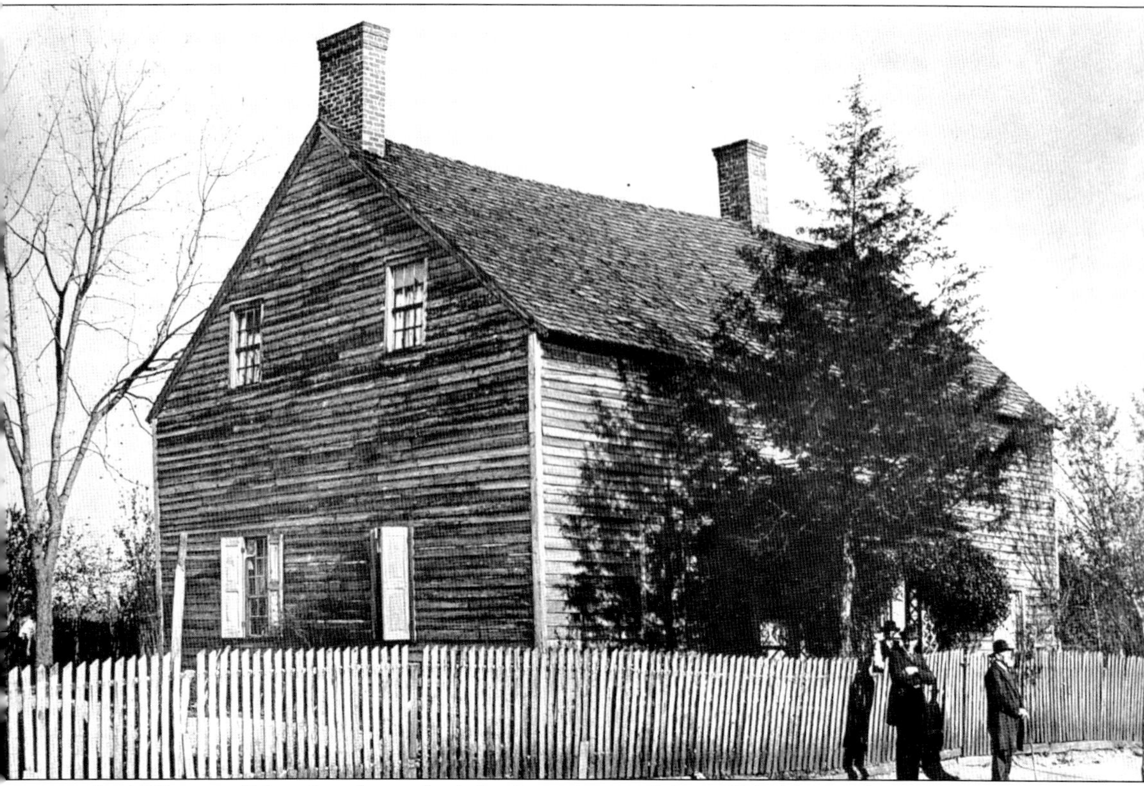

In 1823, a small log church was built by the volunteer labor of 30 African Americans in Salem. Located in the south end of town, next to the African American and Strangers' Graveyard, this church was originally called the "Negro" or "African" church. By 1860, more space was needed to accommodate increasing attendance, and in 1861, the log church was abandoned for a larger brick church. After the Civil War, the log church was used for a short while as the freedman's hospital and later as a residence. It was demolished in the early 20th century. The log church is seen, *c.* 1890, with clapboard. The men are, from left to right, Jefferson Fisher (behind fence), Thomas C. Hege, and Traugott Crist. (Collection of the Wachovia Historical Society; Photograph courtesy of Old Salem Museums & Gardens.)

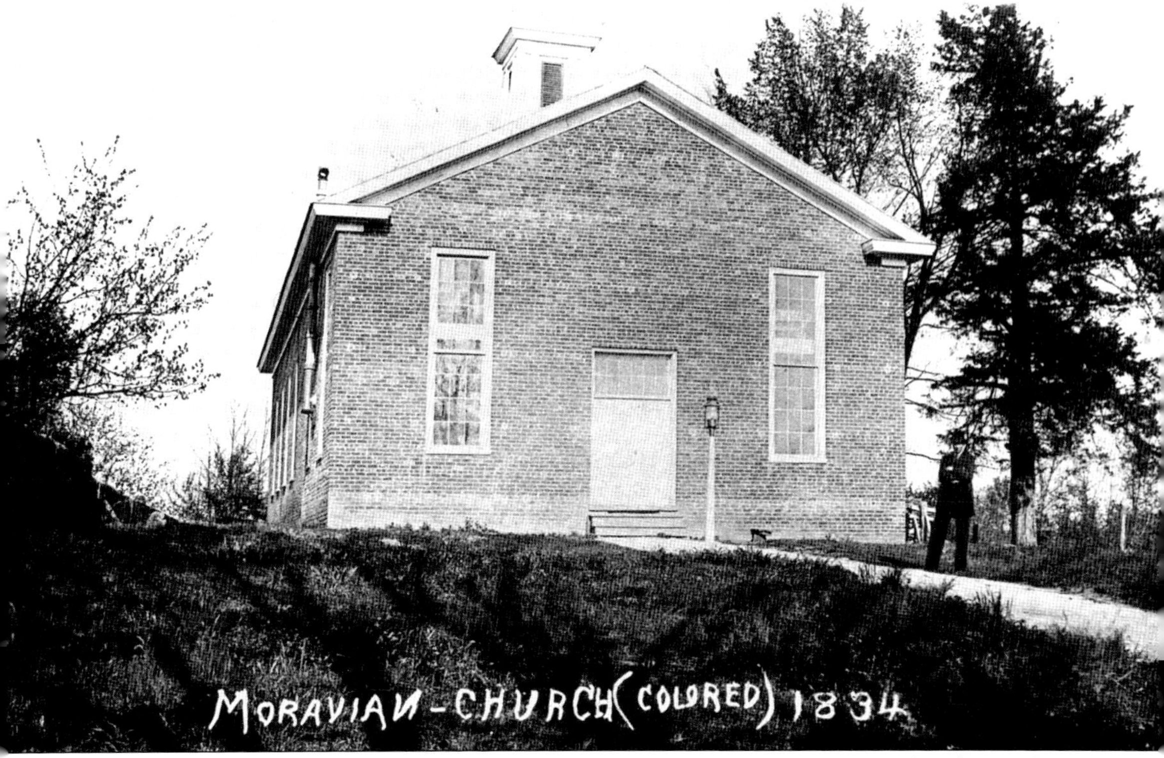

Thomas C. Hege is seen standing to the right of the 1861 African American church in Salem c. 1890. Here on May 21, 1865, the chaplain of the 10th Ohio Calvary Regiment, then passing through Salem, read the Emancipation Proclamation and announced that the Civil War was over and all slaves were free. In 1890, the church was enlarged and, after 1914, became known as St. Philip's. In 1952, the congregation moved to Happy Hill where a new church had been built. The St. Philip's congregation continues today in their fourth location, on Bon Air Avenue, in northern Winston-Salem. (Collection of Old Salem Museums & Gardens.)

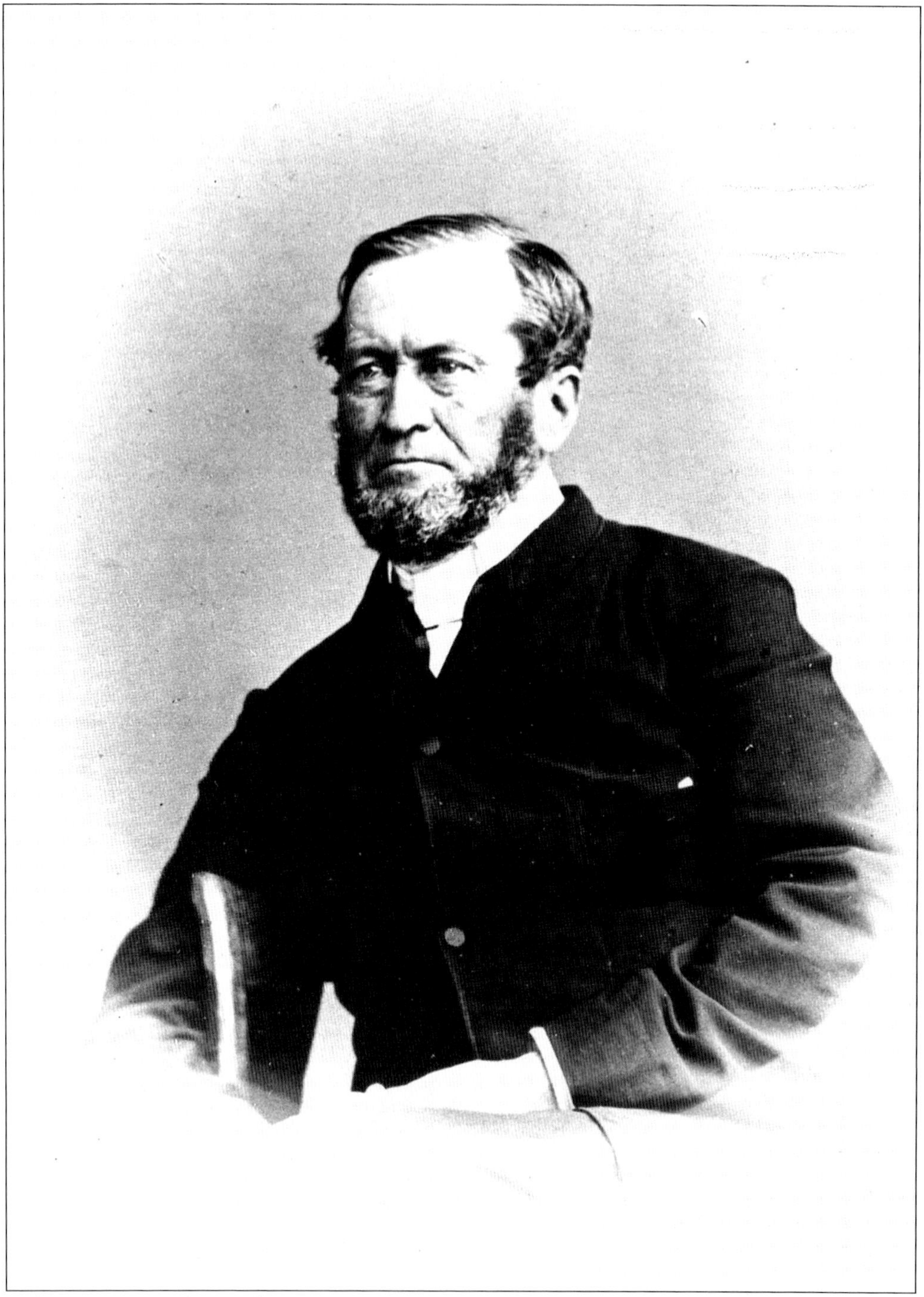

Bishop George Frederic Bahnson, seen in this *c.* 1865 photograph, served as pastor of the African American church in Salem from 1857 to 1859. Additionally he was the pastor of Home Moravian Church from 1849 to 1858 and from 1863 to 1869. Bishop Bahnson also served many other pastorates within the Moravian Church and was president of the Provincial Elders Conference of the Southern Province from 1858 to 1869. (Collection of Old Salem Museums & Gardens.)

The Elm Street Sunday School and Chapel was located in Salem on the corner of Academy Street and what is now Factory Row. Organized in 1867 under the direction of the Home Moravian Church congregation, the building was in constant use until 1912, when the Winston-Salem Southbound Railway purchased the property. The building is seen in this *c.* 1890 photograph. (Collection of Old Salem Museums & Gardens.)

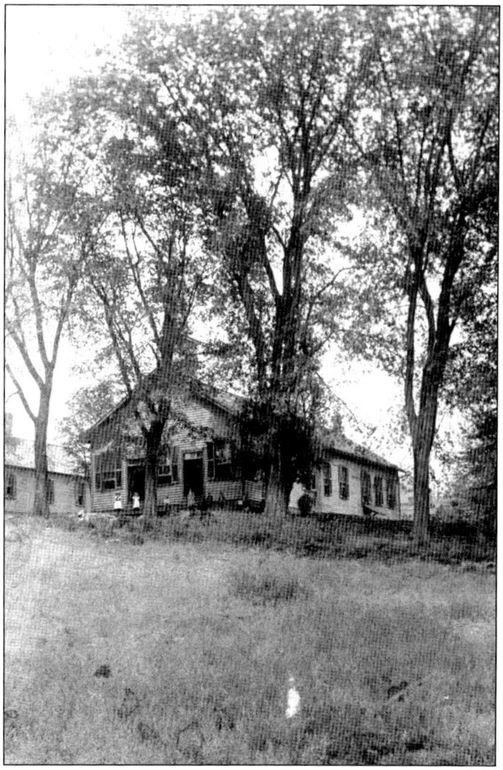

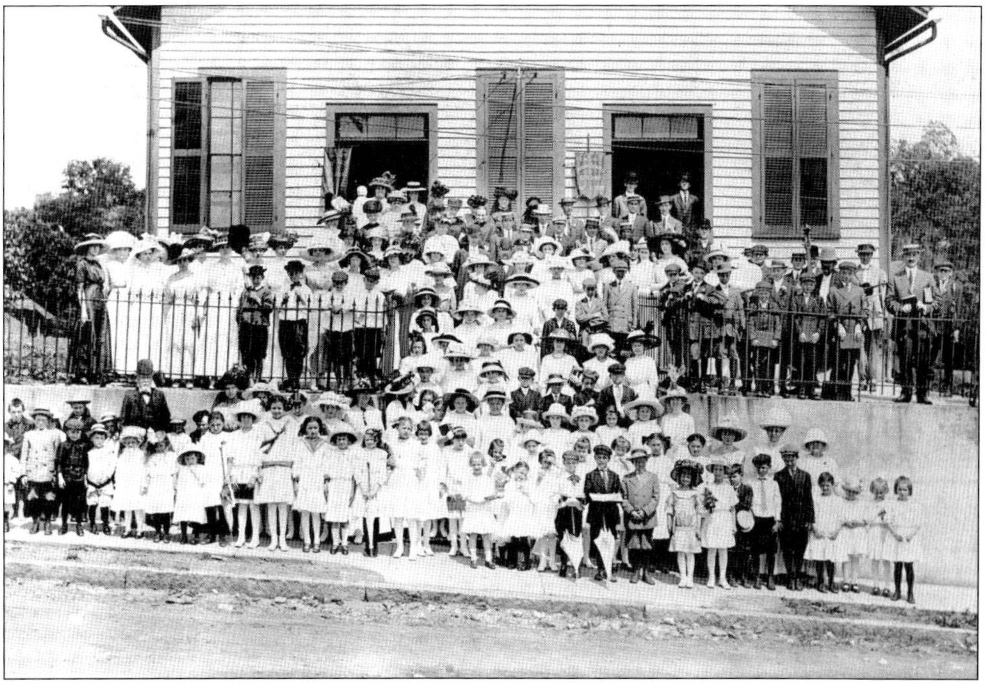

On April 14, 1907, members of the Elm Street Sunday School and Chapel celebrated their 40th anniversary. (Collection of the Moravian Archives, Winston-Salem, North Carolina; Photograph courtesy of Old Salem Museums & Gardens.)

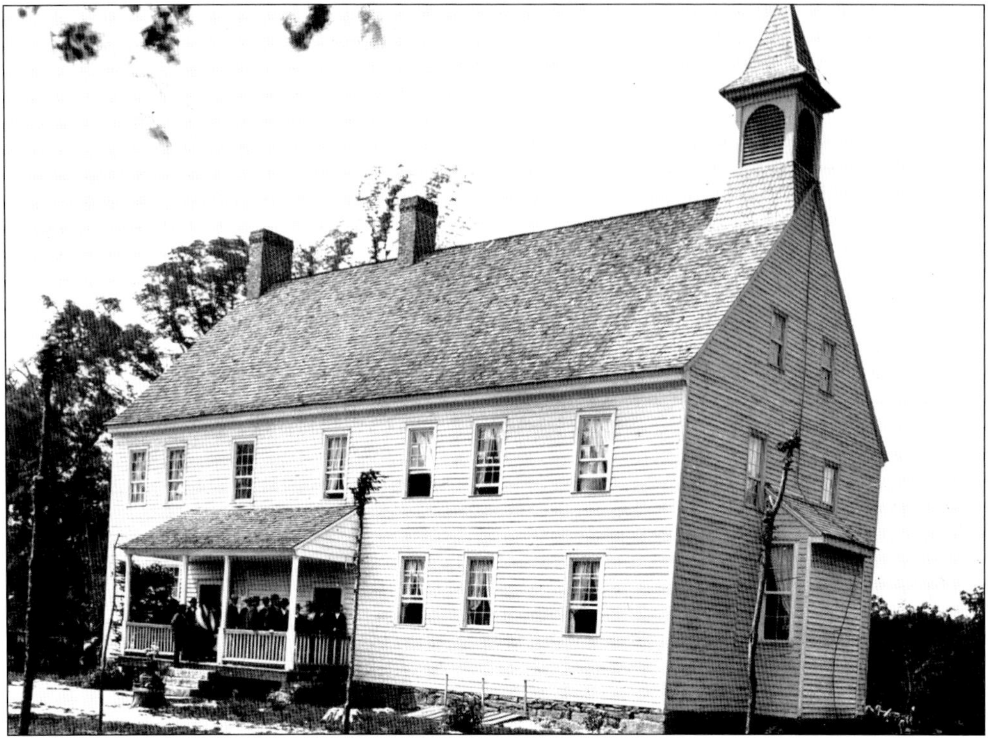

This photograph, taken c. 1882, is the earliest known photograph of Friedberg Moravian Church. This is Friedberg's third church, which was built in 1788. (Private collection; Photograph courtesy of Old Salem Museums & Gardens.)

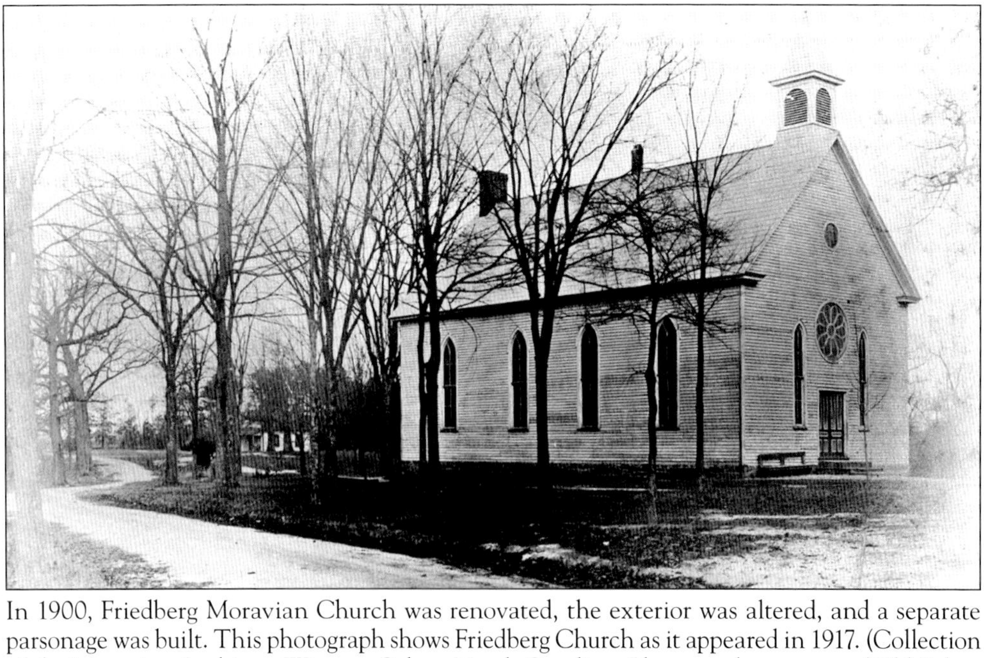

In 1900, Friedberg Moravian Church was renovated, the exterior was altered, and a separate parsonage was built. This photograph shows Friedberg Church as it appeared in 1917. (Collection of the Moravian Archives, Winston-Salem, North Carolina; Photograph courtesy of Old Salem Museums & Gardens.)

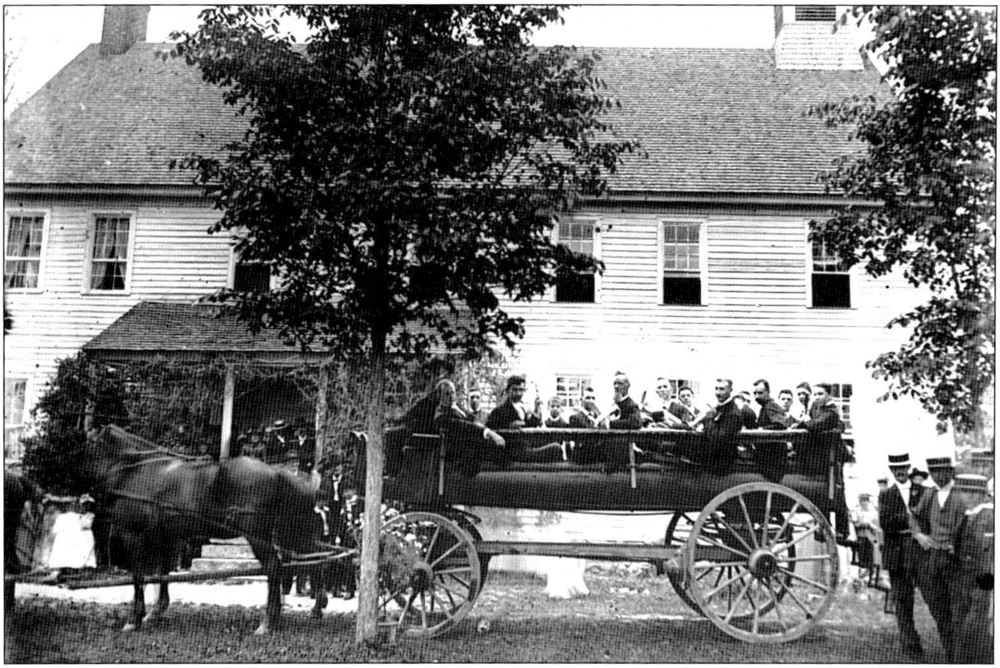

The Home Moravian Church Band visited Friedberg *c.* 1895. Samuel T. Mickey can be seen in the center of the wagon (with beard), and Bernard J. Pfohl can be seen directly behind him. (Collection of the Wachovia Historical Society; Photograph courtesy of Old Salem Museums & Gardens.)

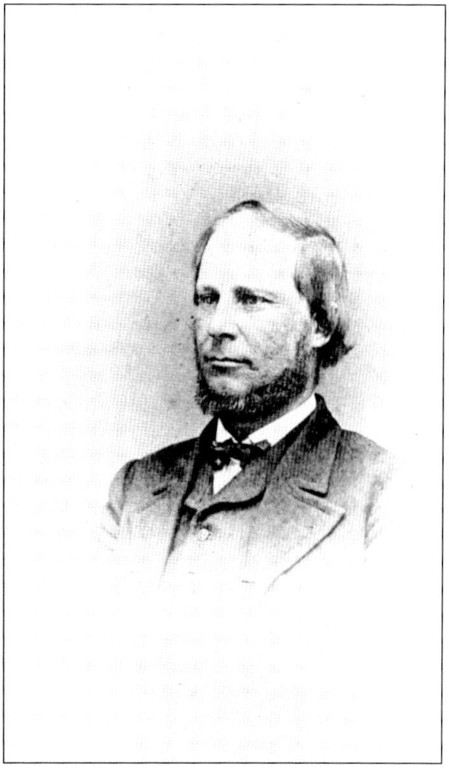

Rev. Robert Parmenio Leinbach was the pastor at Friedberg Moravian Church from 1865 to 1872. He also held other pastorates and positions within the Moravian Church. Reverend Leinbach is seen in a photograph taken by his brother Henry, *c.* 1870. (Collection of the Moravian Archives, Winston-Salem, North Carolina; Photograph courtesy of Old Salem Museums & Gardens.)

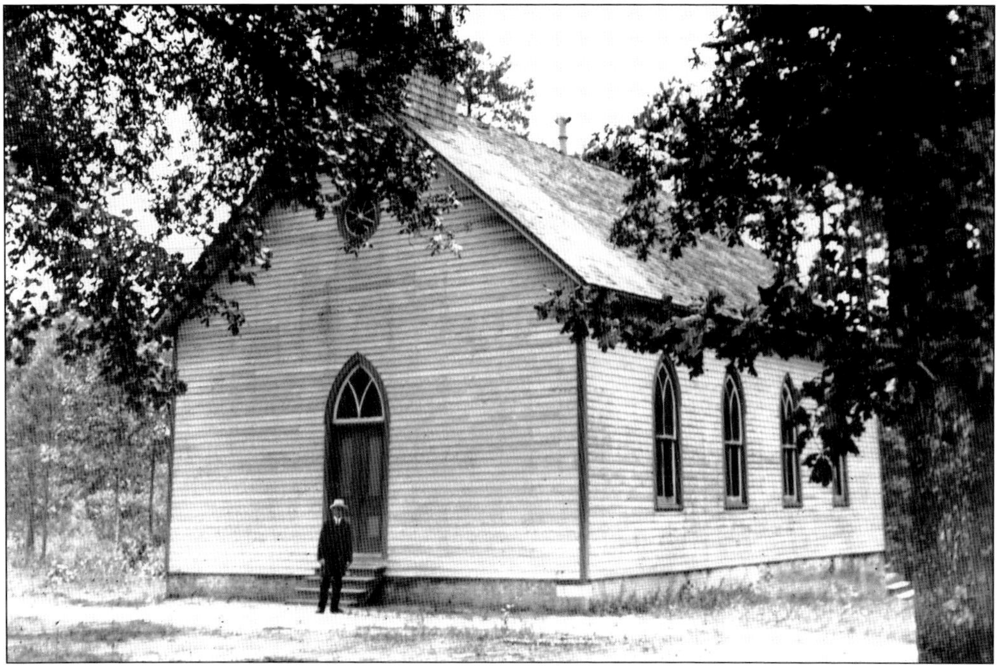

Rev. James E. Hall is seen standing in front of Hope Moravian Church in this photograph taken *c.* 1900. This was Hope's second church, built in 1896 to replace the 1775 building. Reverend Hall was the pastor at Hope from 1881 to 1921. (Collection of the Wachovia Historical Society; Photograph courtesy of Old Salem Museums & Gardens.)

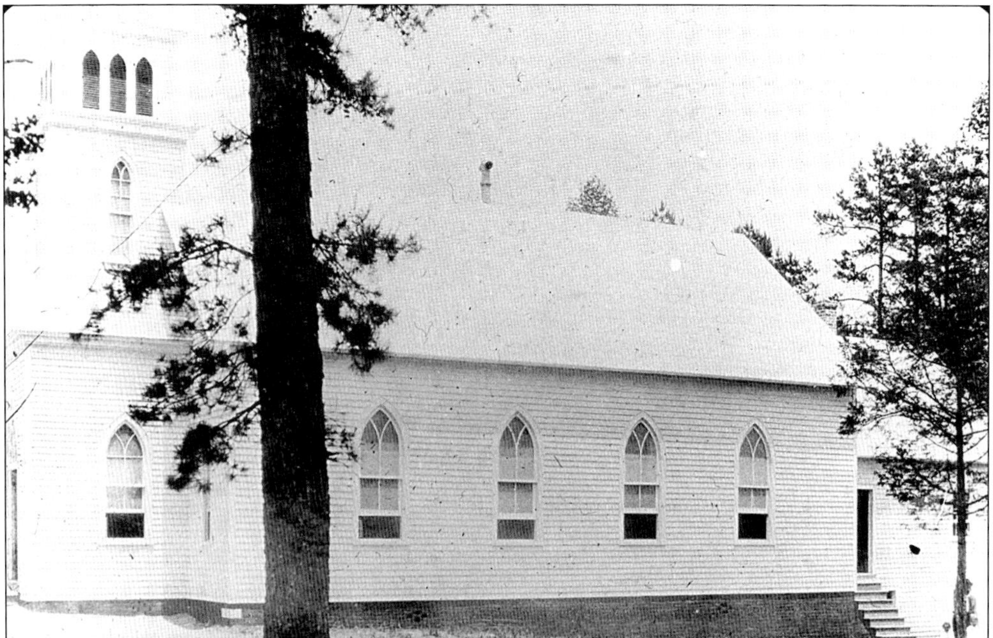

In 1923, a new vestibule and belfry were added to Hope Moravian Church. This photograph, taken that same year, shows the new additions. (Collection of the Wachovia Historical Society; Photograph courtesy of Old Salem Museums & Gardens.)

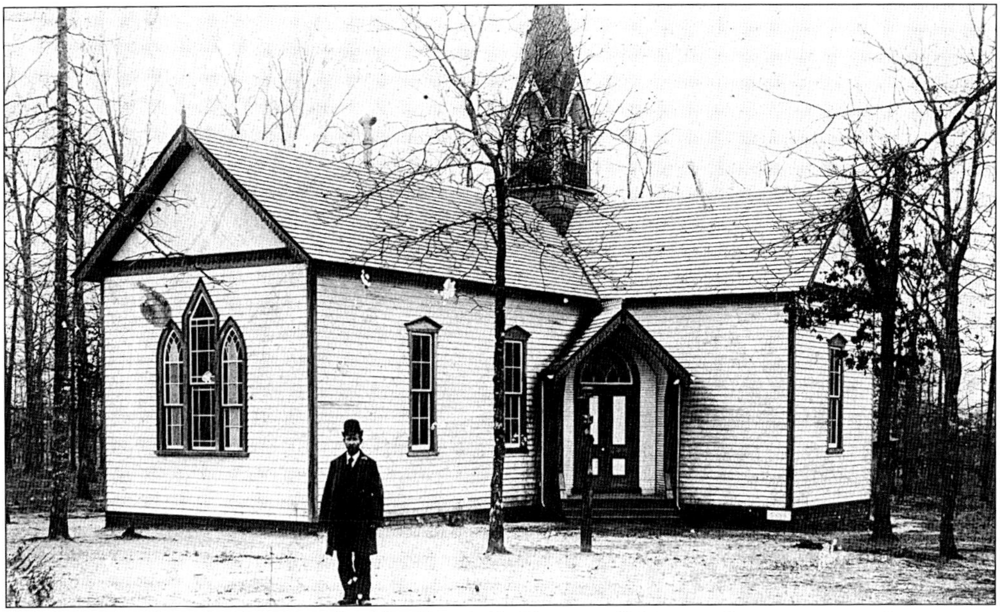

Centerville Chapel, photographed by Frank E. Hege *c.* 1890, stood on property that is now the North Carolina School of the Arts campus. It was begun through the work of young ladies from the Home Moravian Church congregation. Centerville Church was dedicated in 1886 and remained until 1912, when the congregation moved into a new building. The new building, built only a short distance away, was renamed Trinity Moravian. (Collection of Old Salem Museums & Gardens.)

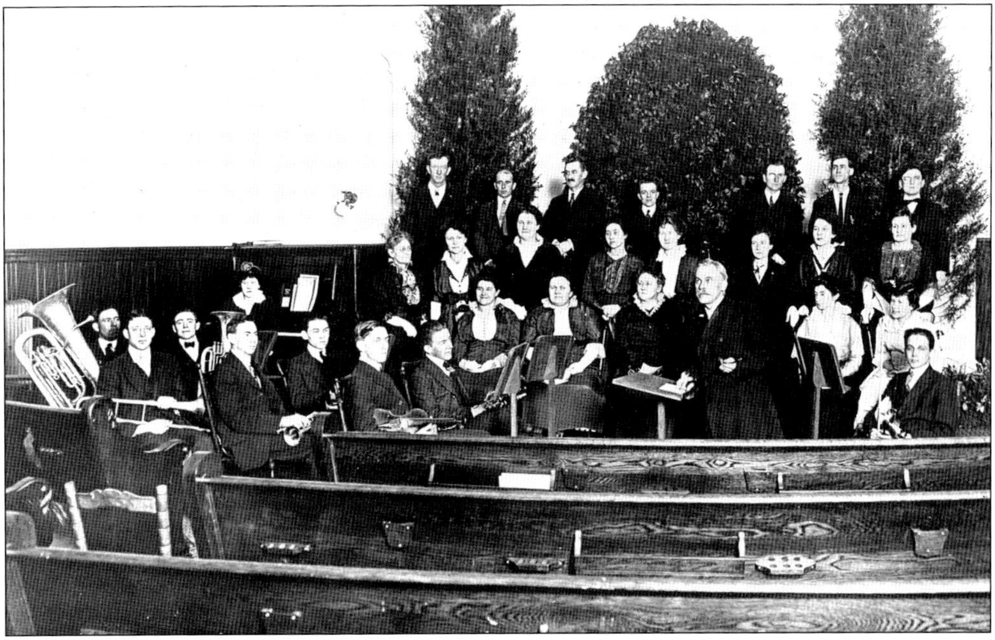

Trinity Moravian Church, located on Sprague Street in Winston-Salem, was originally organized as Centerville Moravian. Trinity became the new name of Centerville Moravian when the church was relocated in 1912. Trinity's choir and musicians can be seen during the Christmas season of 1914. (Collection of Old Salem Museums & Gardens.)

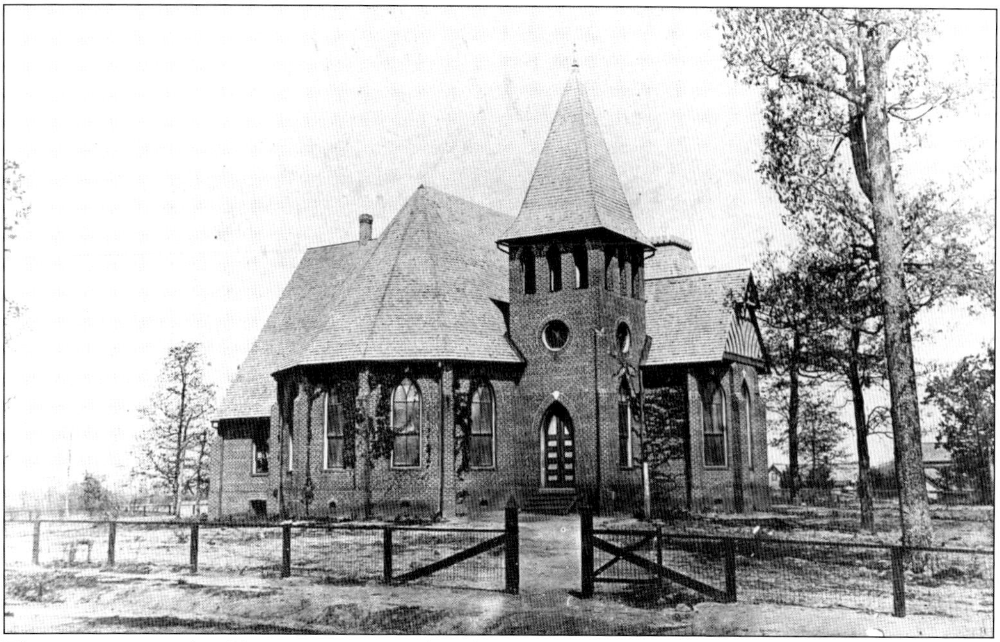

The cornerstone for Christ Moravian Church, located on Academy Street in Salem, was laid in 1895. The church, with its English Gothic architecture, is seen in this *c.* 1900 photograph. (Collection of the Moravian Archives, Winston-Salem, North Carolina; Photograph courtesy of Old Salem Museums & Gardens.)

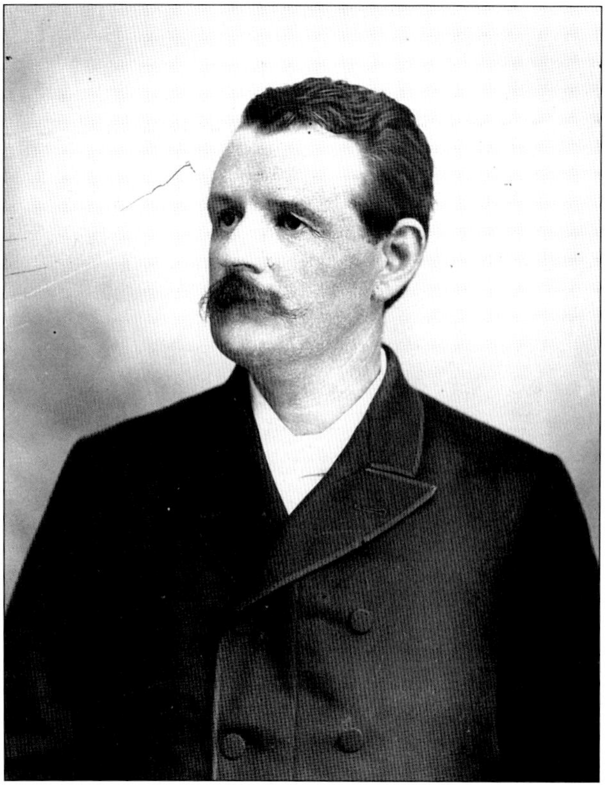

Rev. John F. McCuiston, seen in this *c.* 1900 photograph, was the pastor of Christ Moravian Church from 1908 to 1912. He also held other pastorates and positions within the Moravian Church. (Collection of the Wachovia Historical Society; Photograph courtesy of Old Salem Museums & Gardens.)

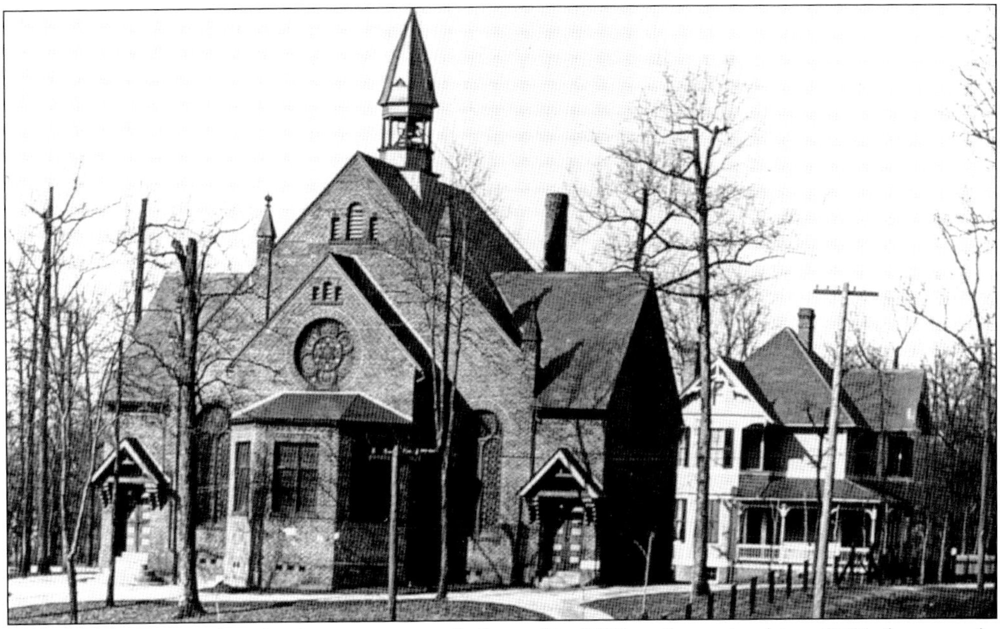

Calvary Moravian Church's first sanctuary, dedicated in 1889 and seen in this c. 1895 photograph, was located on Holly Avenue in Winston-Salem. The last services in this building were held in 1924, when the congregation began to occupy their larger building, which was also constructed on Holly Avenue. (Collection of the Wachovia Historical Society; Photograph courtesy of Old Salem Museums & Gardens.)

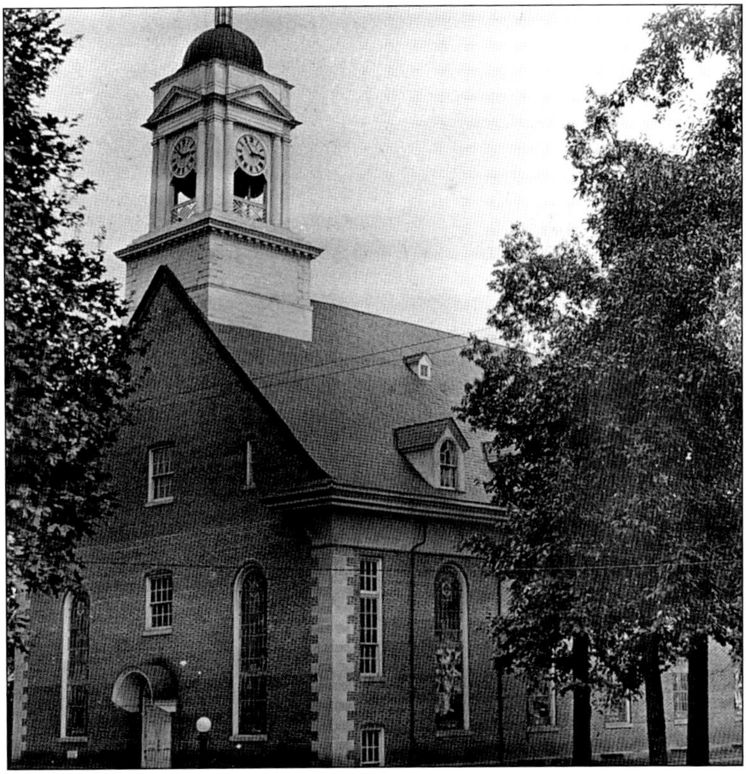

The second sanctuary of Calvary Moravian Church, located on Holly Avenue, was dedicated in 1931. The clock, located in the church steeple, was formerly the town clock of Winston and was purchased by Calvary when the old city hall building was demolished. This c. 1926 photograph shows the second church building shortly after its completion. (Collection of the Wachovia Historical Society; Photograph courtesy of Old Salem Museums & Gardens.)

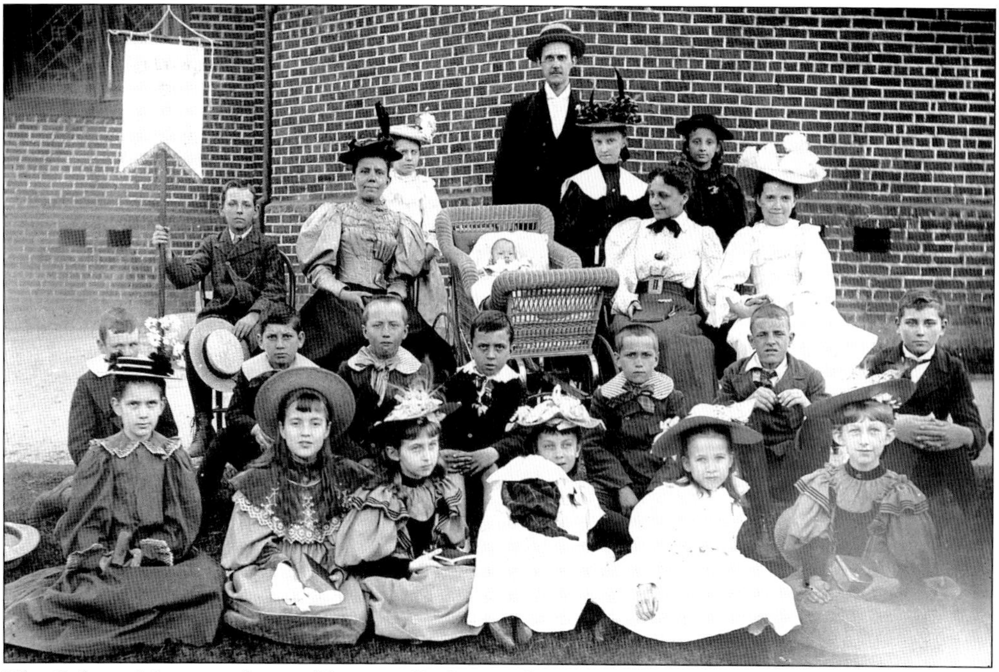

The Calvary Moravian Junior Christian Endeavor class was organized in February 1895 and posed for their portrait that same year. (Collection of the Wachovia Historical Society; Photograph courtesy of Old Salem Museums & Gardens.)

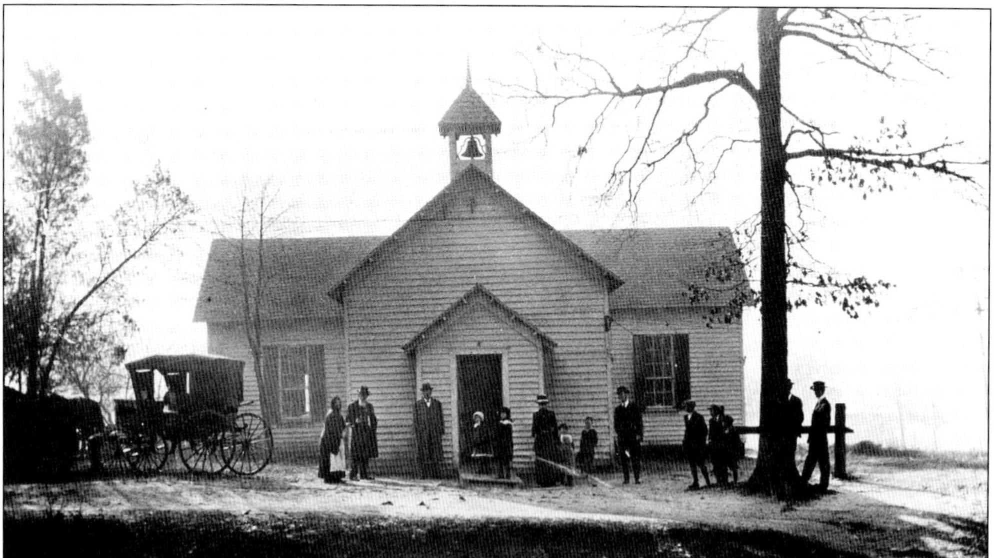

The East Salem Chapel, dedicated in 1877, was located on Belews Creek Street. In 1915, a new brick church was built on East Fourth Street and renamed Fries Memorial Moravian Church to honor the work of its devoted members Henry E. and Rosa Mickey Fries. Later, in 1943, the congregation moved to Hawthorne Road, where the new church still stands today. Henry E. Fries can be seen standing directly to the left of the door in this *c.* 1914 photograph that shows the first East Salem Chapel. (Collection of the Moravian Archives, Winston-Salem, North Carolina; Photograph courtesy of Old Salem Museums & Gardens.)

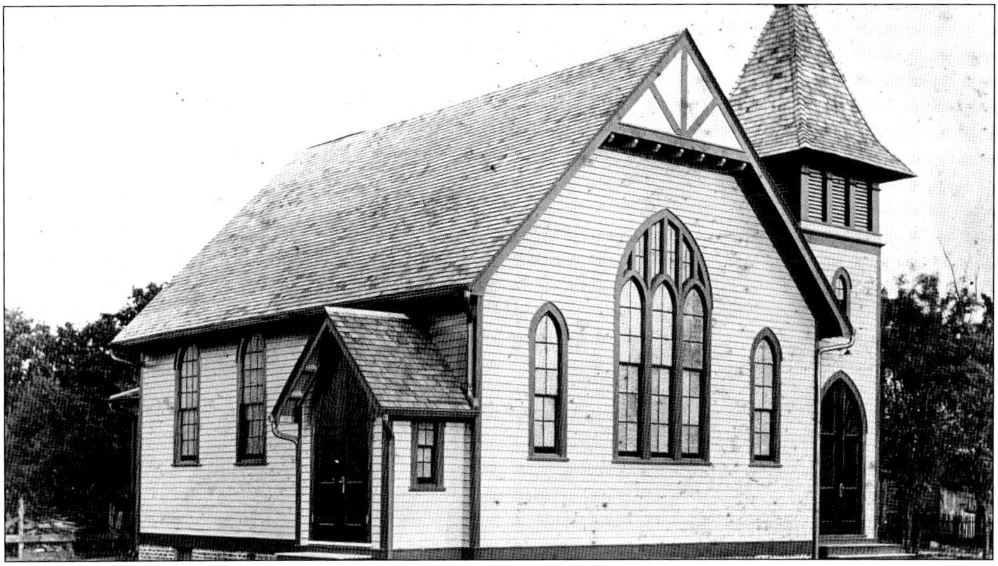

Immanuel Moravian Church was organized in 1912 on Peachtree Street in the Waughtown community of Winston-Salem. The church prospered and grew until the 1960s, when membership began to decline. In 2002, the church merged with its neighbor, New Eden Moravian Church, located on Old Lexington Road, and formed a new congregation—Immanuel–New Eden Moravian Church. The photographers Lineback and Edwards took this view of Immanuel Moravian Church in 1913. (Collection of the Moravian Archives, Winston-Salem, North Carolina; Photograph courtesy of Old Salem Museums & Gardens.)

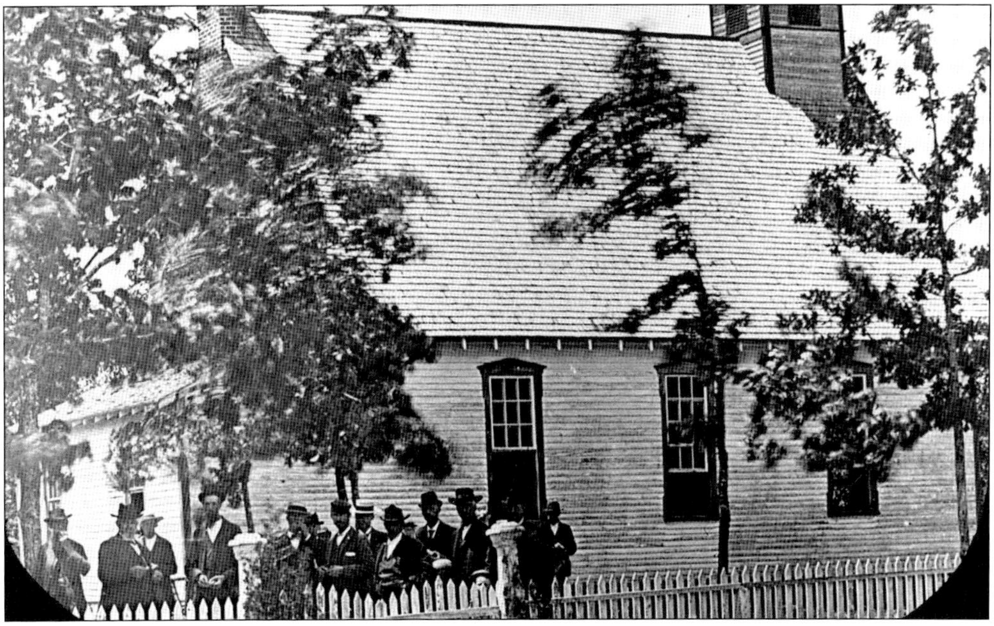

Oak Grove Moravian Church, located on Hammock Farm Road in Walkertown, was organized in 1887. The church was remodeled once in 1929 and again in 1934. In 1956, a new church was built, with the first service occurring in 1957. This photograph shows the first church building *c.* 1900. (Collection of the Wachovia Historical Society; Photograph courtesy of Old Salem Museums & Gardens.)

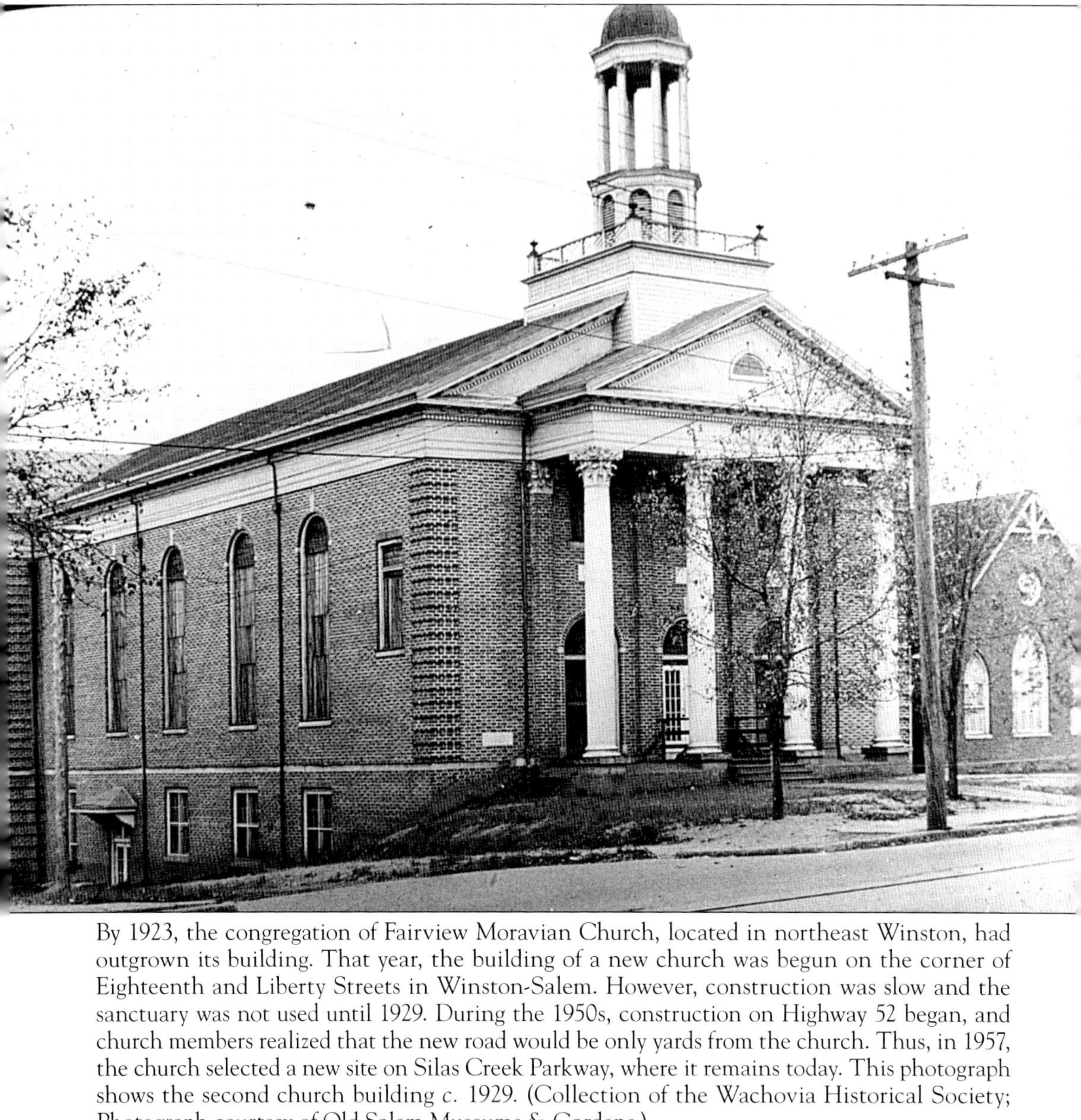

By 1923, the congregation of Fairview Moravian Church, located in northeast Winston, had outgrown its building. That year, the building of a new church was begun on the corner of Eighteenth and Liberty Streets in Winston-Salem. However, construction was slow and the sanctuary was not used until 1929. During the 1950s, construction on Highway 52 began, and church members realized that the new road would be only yards from the church. Thus, in 1957, the church selected a new site on Silas Creek Parkway, where it remains today. This photograph shows the second church building *c.* 1929. (Collection of the Wachovia Historical Society; Photograph courtesy of Old Salem Museums & Gardens.)

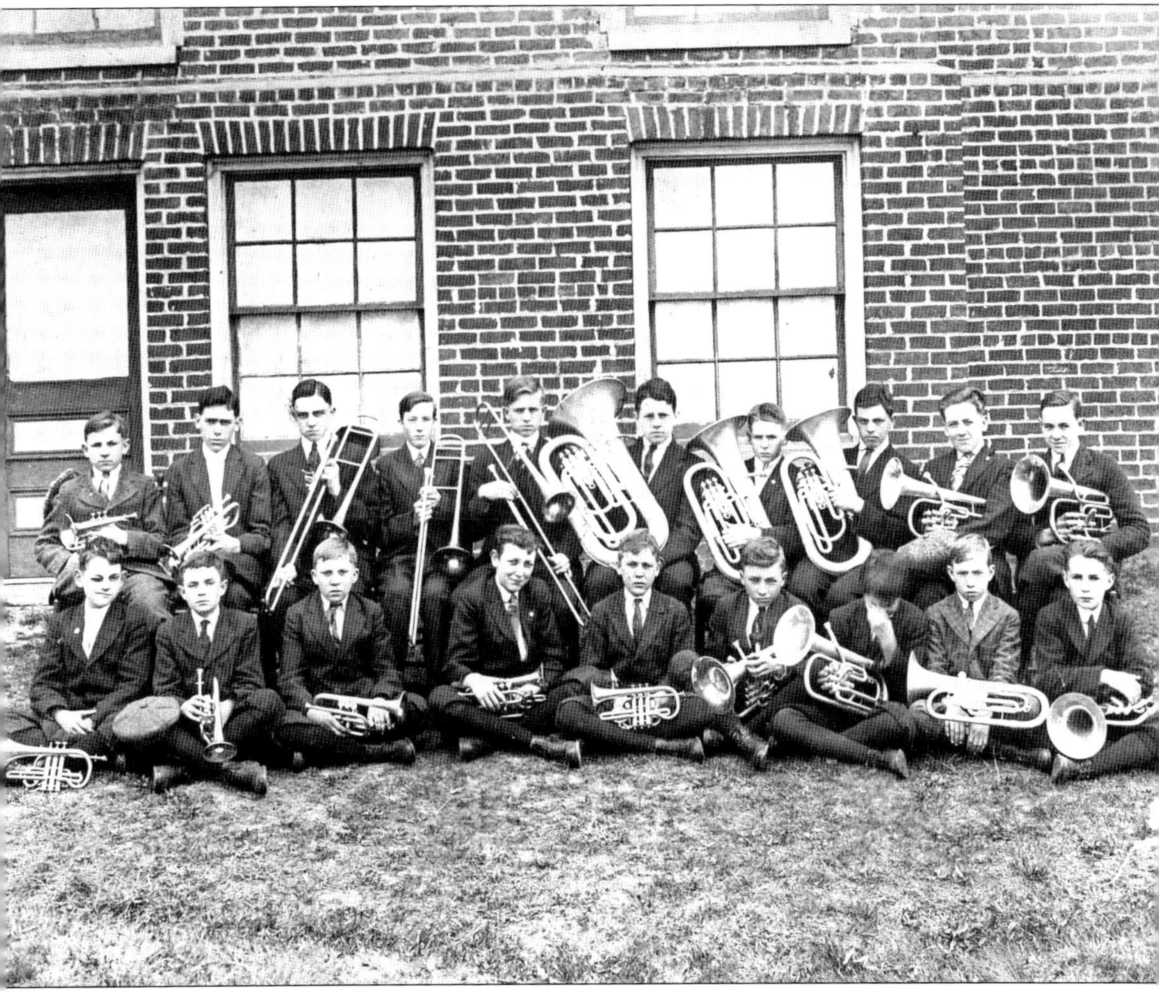

The first band of Fairview Moravian Church was organized in 1915 and can be seen in this photograph taken shortly thereafter. Band members are, from left to right, (first row) Carroll Williams, Bernie Frazier, Joe Ebert, Arthur Johnson, Louis Barnes, Ralph Knott, Hubert Watson, Malone Morgan, and John Frazier; (second row) Vernon Andrews, Dewey Pegram, Paul Ledwell, Ernest Caudle, Kyle Hopkins, Robert Lee, William Forcum, John Hopkins, Harry Phillips, and Joe Whitlow. (Collection of Old Salem Museums & Gardens.)

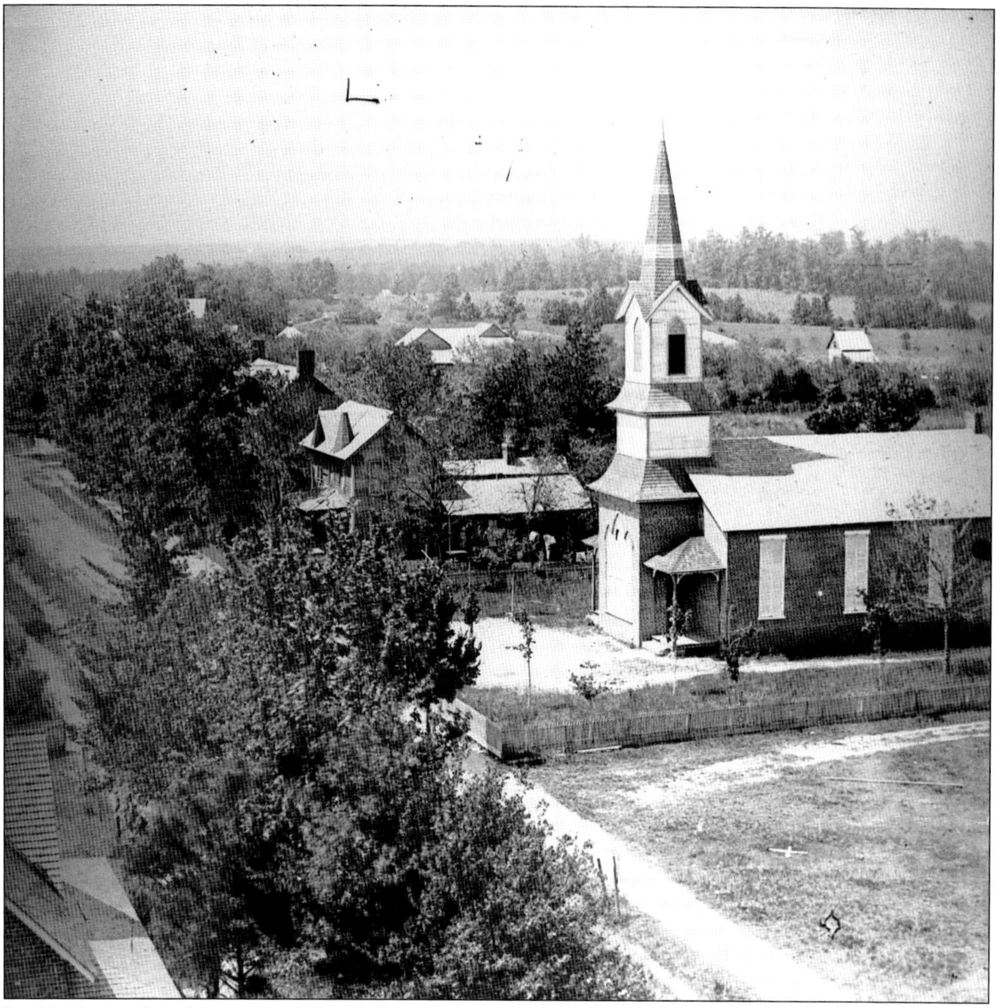

In 1866, the Southern Province of the Moravian Church purchased land from John F. Kerner in Kernersville to build a new brick church. That church, Kernersville Moravian, located on South Main Street, was consecrated in 1867. Today the church is still in operation and has been designated a historic landmark. The church is seen in this *c.* 1890 photograph, likely taken from an upper floor of Korner's Folly, the home of Jule Gilmer Korner. (Collection of the Wachovia Historical Society; Photograph courtesy of Old Salem Museums & Gardens.)

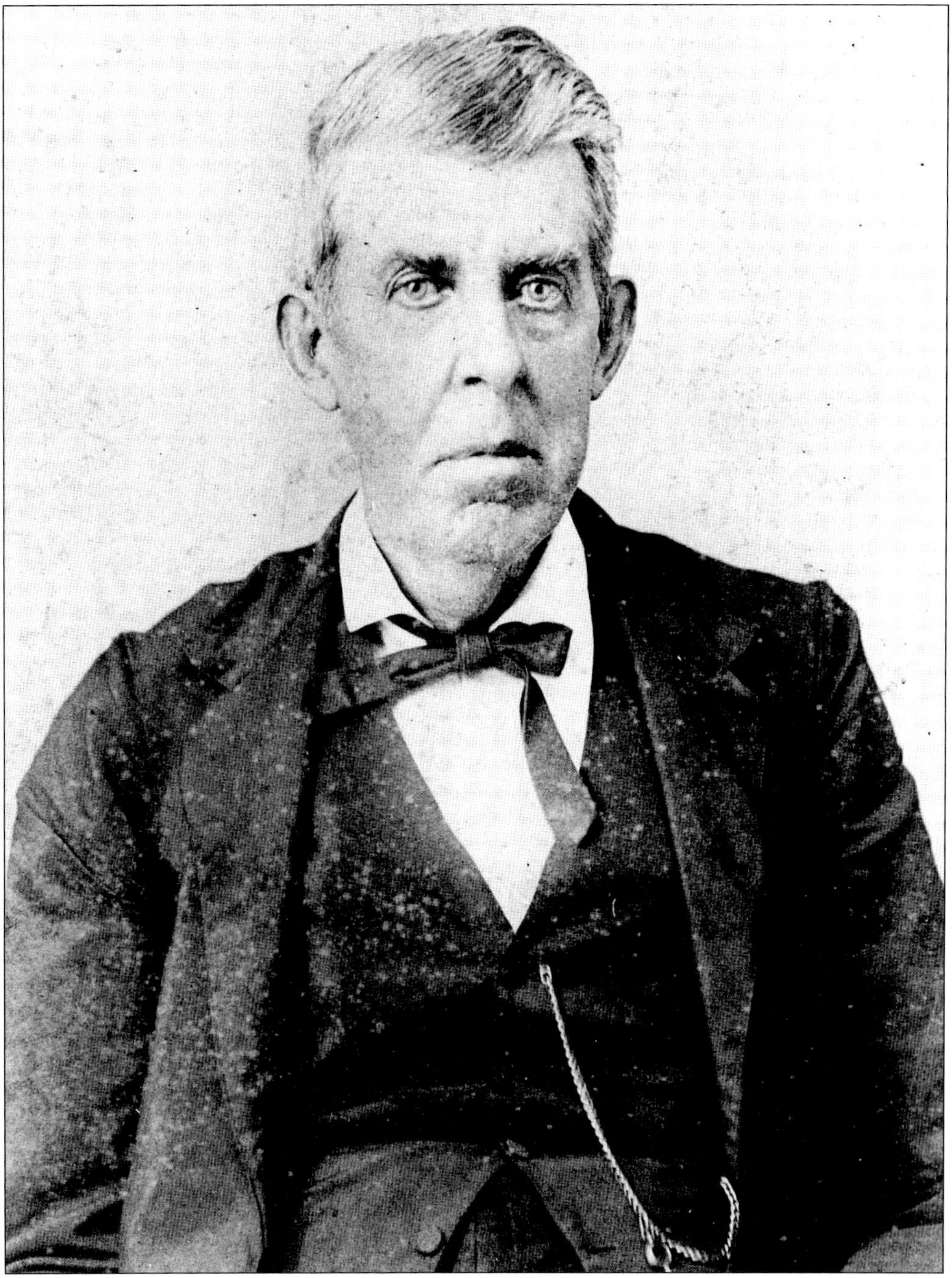

Rev. Christian Lewis Rights, seen in this *c.* 1890 photograph taken by Henry A. Lineback, was the pastor of Kernersville Moravian Church from 1873 to 1891. He also held other positions and pastorates within the Moravian Church and was president of the Provincial Elders Conference of the Southern Province from 1880 to 1890. Reverend Rights died at Tahlequah, Oklahoma, in 1891 while visiting his son and son-in-law, who were working there as missionaries. (Collection of the Moravian Archives, Winston-Salem, North Carolina; Photograph courtesy of Old Salem Museums & Gardens.)

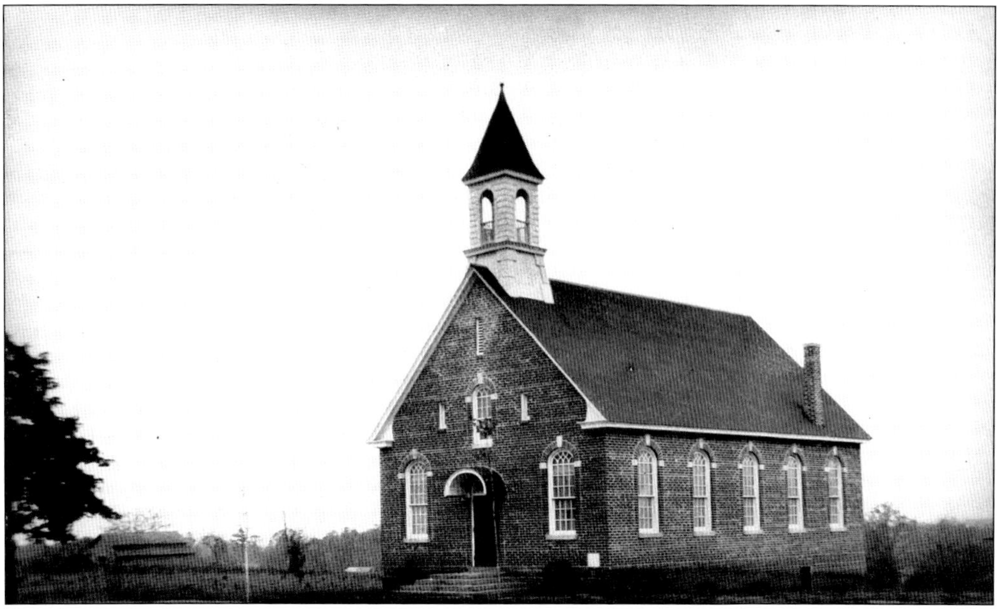

This photograph of King Moravian Church, attributed to Irvin T. Rominger, was taken shortly after its construction in 1925. A new sanctuary was built adjacent to the existing one in 1993, and both buildings still stand on Dalton Street. (Collection of Old Salem Museums & Gardens.)

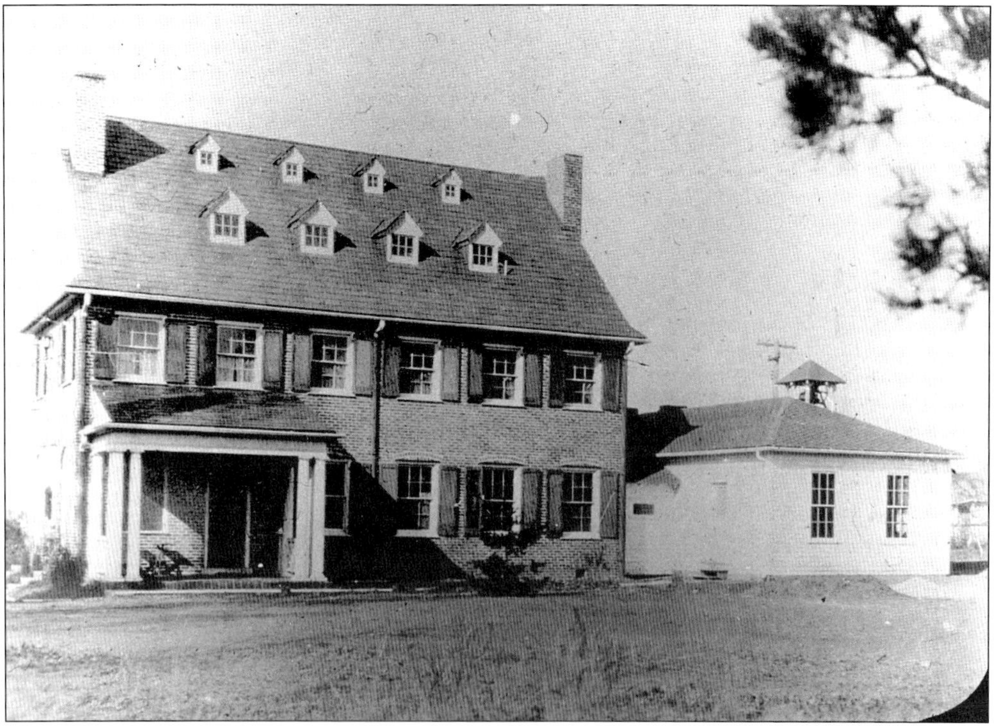

Little Church on the Lane, organized in 1920, was the first Moravian church in Charlotte. The church was designed in such a manner that if it did not succeed, the building could be converted into apartments. This photograph of the church was taken *c.* 1926. (Collection of the Wachovia Historical Society; Photograph courtesy of Old Salem Museums & Gardens.)

The first Macedonia Moravian Church building was consecrated in 1856, the second in 1878, the third in 1930, and the fourth in 1964. All four buildings were located on Highway 801 in Advance where the church still stands today. This photograph shows the third Macedonia Moravian Church, c. 1930, with Rev. James E. Hall standing in front. (Collection of Old Salem Museums & Gardens.)

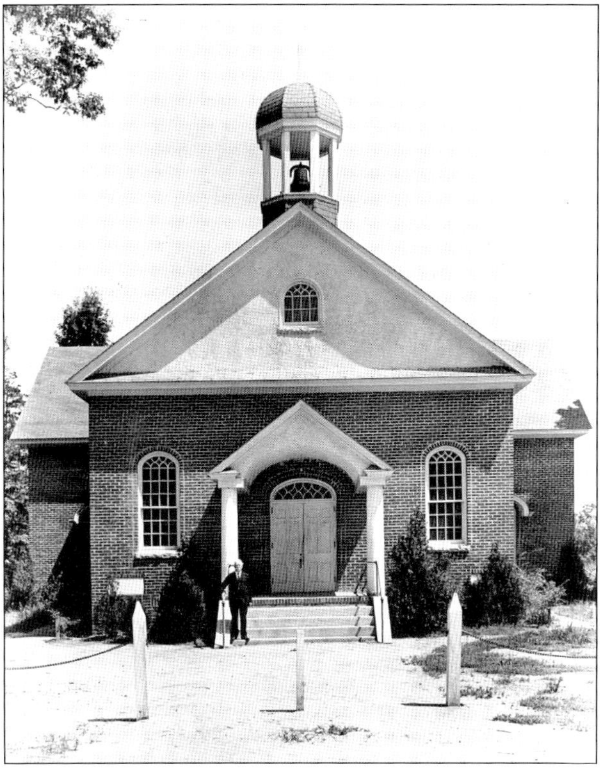

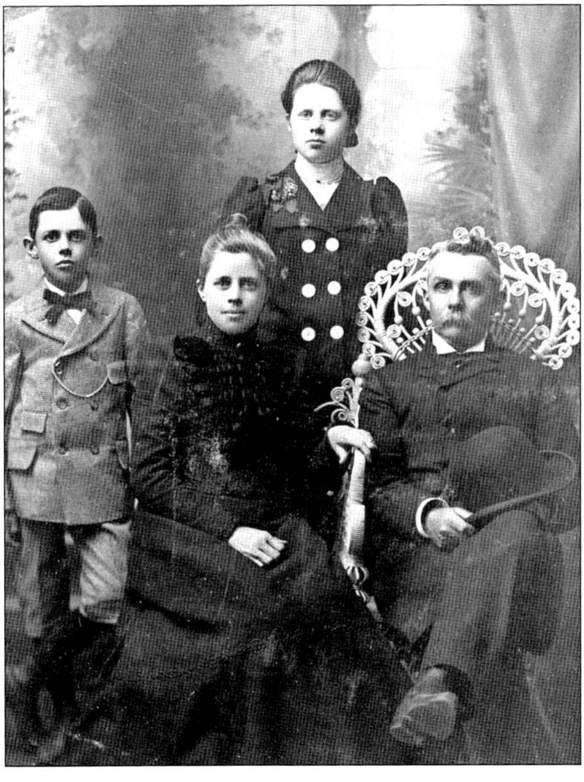

The Reverend James Ernest Hall held many pastorates and positions within the Moravian Church. One position was pastor of Macedonia Moravian Church from 1881 to 1884. Hall's family, photographed in 1898, are, from left to right, William James Hall, Martha Johnson Hall, Bertha Josephine Hall, and Rev. James Ernest Hall. (Private collection; Photograph courtesy of Old Salem Museums & Gardens.)

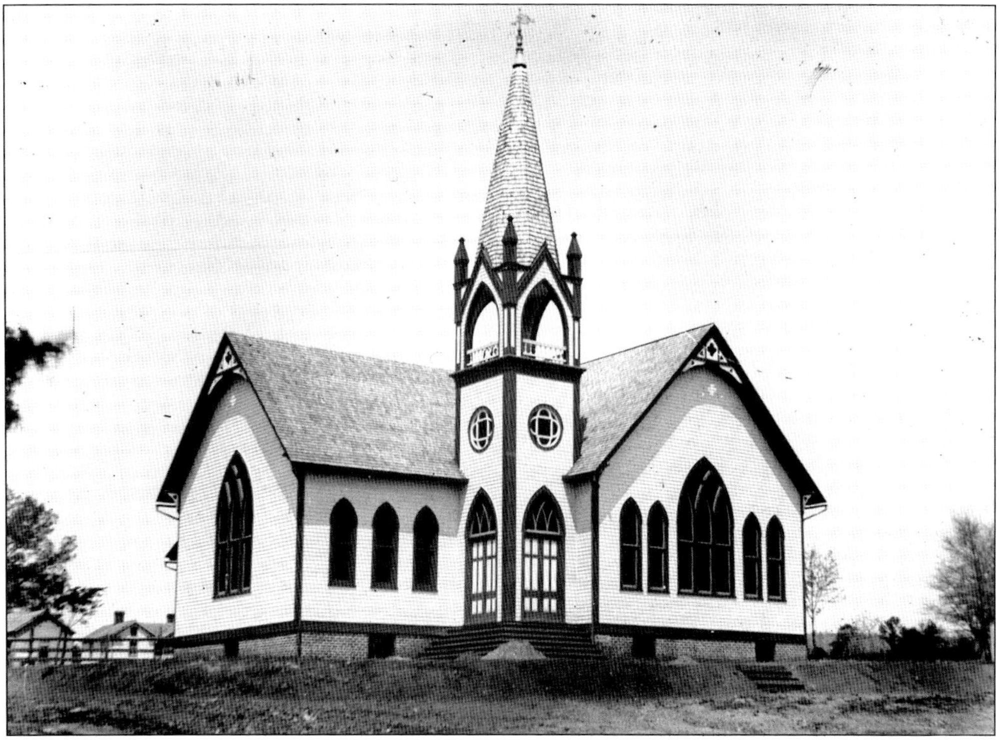

Mayodan Moravian Church, located on South Third Avenue, was organized in 1896. The church is seen in this photograph taken *c.* 1900. (Collection of the Wachovia Historical Society; Photograph courtesy of Old Salem Museums & Gardens.)

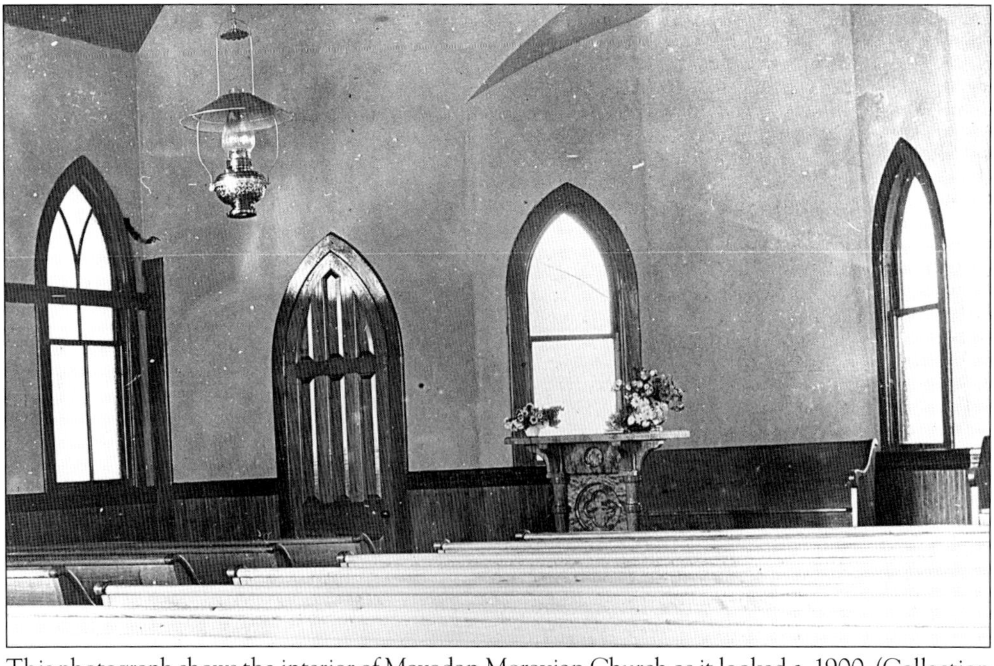

This photograph shows the interior of Mayodan Moravian Church as it looked *c.* 1900. (Collection of the Wachovia Historical Society; Photograph courtesy of Old Salem Museums & Gardens.)

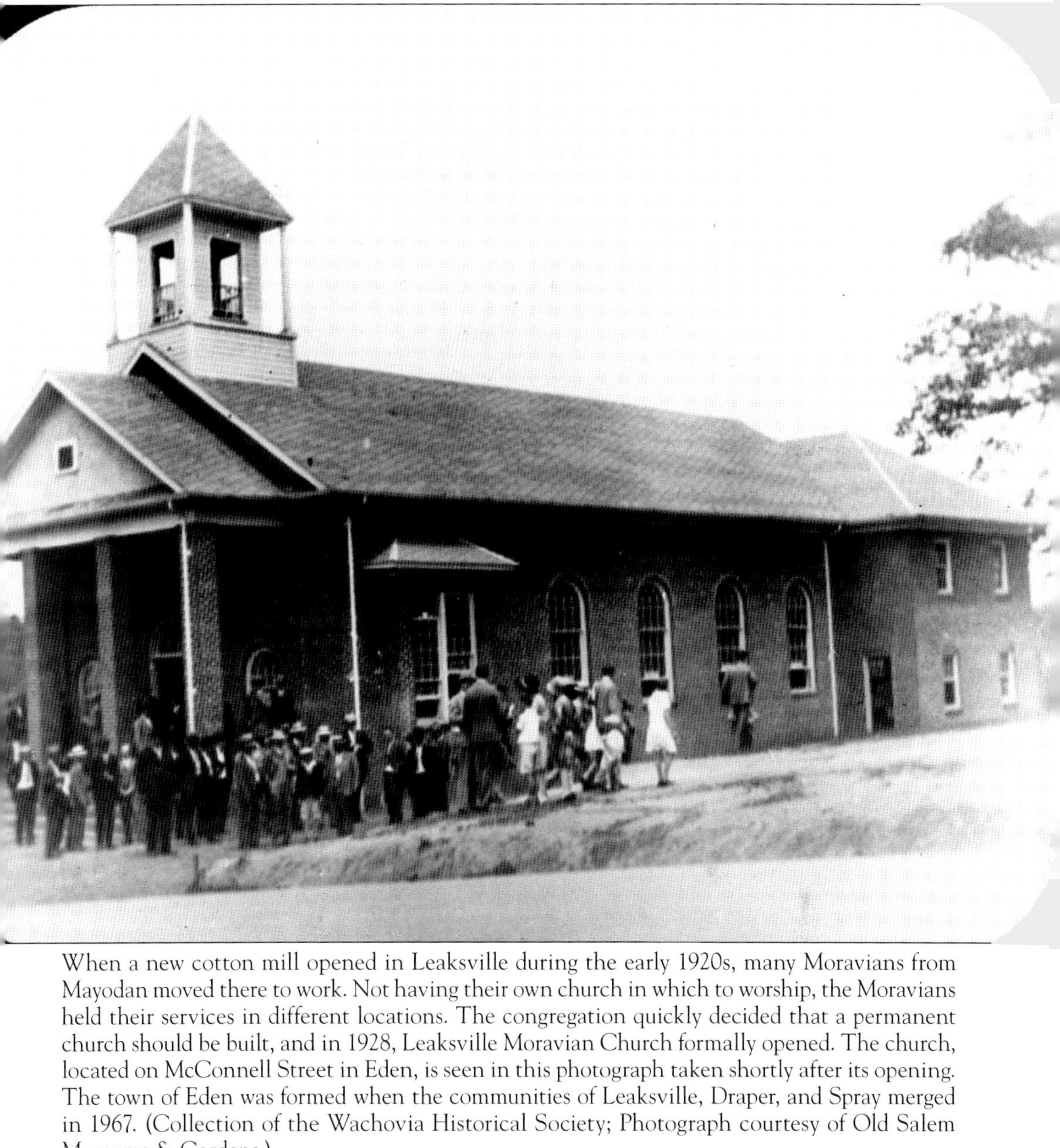

When a new cotton mill opened in Leaksville during the early 1920s, many Moravians from Mayodan moved there to work. Not having their own church in which to worship, the Moravians held their services in different locations. The congregation quickly decided that a permanent church should be built, and in 1928, Leaksville Moravian Church formally opened. The church, located on McConnell Street in Eden, is seen in this photograph taken shortly after its opening. The town of Eden was formed when the communities of Leaksville, Draper, and Spray merged in 1967. (Collection of the Wachovia Historical Society; Photograph courtesy of Old Salem Museums & Gardens.)

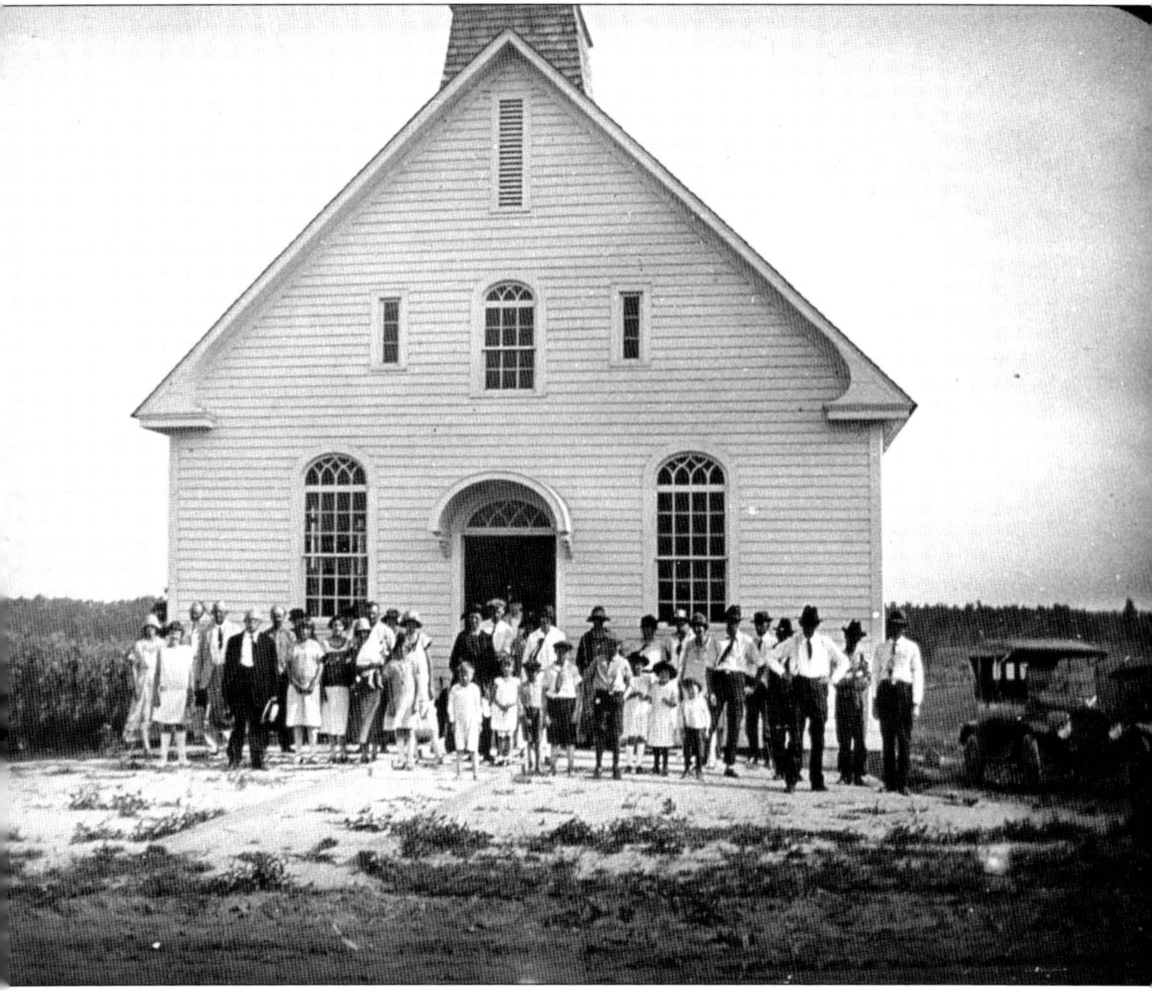

Houstonville Moravian Church, seen *c.* 1926, was located in Iredell County. The church was built in 1925, consecrated in 1926, and closed in 1944. Rev. James E. Hall can be seen, standing at left, holding his hat and wearing a dark suit. His granddaughter, Josephine Peterson, is seen standing directly to his right. (Collection of the Wachovia Historical Society; Photograph courtesy of Old Salem Museums & Gardens.)

SELECTED BIBLIOGRAPHY

Crews, C. Daniel. *My Name Shall Be There*. Winston-Salem, NC: Moravian Archives, 1995.
———. *Neither Slave nor Free*. Winston-Salem, NC: Moravian Archives, 1998.
———. *Villages of the Lord*. Winston-Salem, NC: Moravian Archives, 1995.
——— and Richard Starbuck. *With Courage for the Future*. Winston-Salem, NC: Moravian Archives, 2002.
Davis, Chester S. *Moravians in Europe and America, 1415–1865: Hidden Seed and Harvest*. Winston-Salem, NC: Wachovia Historical Society, 2000.
Fries, Adelaide L. *Customs and Practices of the Moravian Church*. Rev. ed. Winston-Salem, NC: Board of Christian Education and Evangelism, 1973.
———, et al. *Records of the Moravians in North Carolina*. Raleigh, NC: North Carolina Historical Commission, 1922–2001.
Griffin, Frances. *Less Time for Meddling*. Winston-Salem, NC: Salem Academy and College, 1979.
Niven, Penelope and Cornelia Wright. *Old Salem: The Official Guidebook*. Winston-Salem, NC: Old Salem Museums & Gardens, 2004.
People's Press, Salem, NC, 1851–1892.
Rohrer, S. Scott. *Hope's Promise*. Tuscaloosa: The University of Alabama Press, 2005.
Rondthaler, Edward. *The Memorabilia of Fifty Years, 1877 to 1927*. Raleigh, NC: Edwards & Broughton Company, 1928.
Vogler, Charles M. *Descendants of Philipp Christoph Vogler*. Camden, ME: Penobscot Press, 1994.